Colin Speakman

A Yorkshire Dales Anthology

ROBERT HALE LTD.
London

First published in Great Britain 1981

ISBN 0 7091 8925 7

Robert Hale Limited
Clerkenwell House
Clerkenwell Green
London EC1R 0HT

For Fleur; and to the memory
of Dr. Maria Penford,
a rare and generous spirit

Photoset by Art Photoset Ltd.
Printed in Great Britain by
Lowe & Brydone Ltd., Thetford, Norfolk.
Bound by Redwood Burn Ltd.

Contents

Illustrations

Acknowledgements

I must express my particular gratitude to Dr Arthur Raistrick for invaluable encouragement, advice and practical help with many aspects of this book; also to Bill Mitchell of *The Dalesman,* Lawrence Barker of Healaugh, Kit Calvert of Hawes and Alan Butterfield of Crosshills for additional generous help; to the staff at the Brotherton Library, Leeds University, and at Leeds, Northallerton, Kendal, Ilkley, Harrogate and Skipton Reference Libraries for their patience; to several of our regional booksellers and bibliophiles who have helped unearth some treasured texts; and finally to Norman Nicholson whose marvellous book *The Lake District: An Anthology* has been an inspiration.

Acknowledgements for the use of copyright material are due to the following: Methuen & Co. Limited for permission to use an extract from *The Torrington Diaries* by John Byng; Oxford University Press for Basil Bunting's *Collected Poems* © Basil Bunting 1978. Reprinted by permission; Faber and Faber for use of the extract from *Collected Shorter Poems* by W. H. Auden; William Heinemann Ltd and the author for use of the extract from *English Journey* by J. B. Priestley; Hutchinson Publishing Group Ltd for use of the extract from *Jerry and Ben* by W. R. Riley; Michael Joseph Ltd and the author for use of the extract from *If Only they could talk* by James Herriot; Mrs Pauline Dower and *The Dalesman* for use of the article by the late John Dower; Miss Marie Hartley and *The Dalesman* for use of the extract from the article *Dales Folk* by Ella Pontefract; Miss Marie Hartley and J. M. Dent & Sons for the extract from *Wensleydale* by Ella Pontefract; J. M. Dent & Sons and Miss Marie Hartley and Miss Joan Ingilby for the extract from *Life and Tradition in the Yorkshire Dales*; Mr Bill Cowley and *The Dalesman* for the extract from *Farming in Yorkshire*; Mrs Anna Adams for her poem *The Stone Men*; Dr James Riley for the extract from *Settle and the North West Yorkshire Dales* by the late Frederick Riley; William Collins, Sons & Co. for the extract from *Adam Brunskill* by Thomas Armstrong; Mr Kit Calvert and *The Dalesman* for the extract from *The Story of Wensleydale Cheese*; Mr Kit Calvert for the extract from the article *The Story of Burtersett Quarries*; Macdonald Futura and the author for use of the extract from *Food in England* by Dorothy Hartley; Mrs Margaret Batty for the extract from *Gunnerside Chapel and Gunnerside Folk*; W. R. Mitchell for the extract from *Wild Pennines*; Miss Nancy Cutcliffe-Hyne for the extract from *Ben Watson* by the late C. J. Cutcliffe-Hyne; Mrs Dorothy Scott for the extract from *Portrait of Yorkshire* by the late Harry J. Scott; Miss Jessica Lofthouse for the extract from *A Countrygoer in the Yorkshire Dales*; Cassell Ltd for the extract from *A Naturalist's Pilgrimage* by Richard Kearton; Dr Arthur Raistrick and Eyre Methuen Ltd for the extract from *Pennine Dales*; Dr Raistrick and David & Charles Ltd for the extract from *Old Yorkshire Dales*; Messrs Hamlyn for the extracts from *Moorland Tramping in West Yorkshire* by A. J. Brown; Messrs Constable for the extract from *Journey Through Britain* by John Hillaby; Mr Noel Sutcliffe for the extract from *The Striding Dales* by Halliwell Sutcliffe.

Introduction

I doubt if a paradise exists anywhere on earth. The Yorkshire Dales with a mountainous landscape and rain that often comes at the unwary sideways, might, on occasions, earn choicer epithets. It depends, to a great degree, upon how you look at landscape.

'Paradise' suggests an idealized landscape, somewhere out of space and time to which mere mortal humanity yearns. It is a product of the human imagination.

For many reasons, some of which are explored in this book, a group of poets, topographers and painters, and after them novelists, guide-book writers and photographers, have succeeded in planting in our collective imagination an image, or more correctly a series of images, that remains an immensely potent one for us.

Not that the Yorkshire Dales are unique in this respect; other regions, most notably the Scottish Highlands and the Lake District, have this power over us.

How did it happen?

The reasons are complex and many. The transformation of England, over the last two centuries, from a predominantly rural and agricultural community, to a crowded, industrial and technological society has brought changes, both social and physical, to our island which have made the remote and wilder places seem increasingly attractive. But to a great degree our emotional response to the mountain and moorland landscape is something we have learned, perhaps without knowing it, from the day of our birth, with countless exposures to stated or implied views about the countryside which have conditioned us to feel in a particular way. More than anything else, it is the poets and painters of the Romantic era of the late eighteenth and early nineteenth century whose view of the countryside has dominated our own. In a very real sense we see the Yorkshire Dales through their eyes.

I have defined the Yorkshire Dales for the purpose of this anthology, as an area somewhat larger than the present National Park, basically including that portion of the Central Pennine fell country bounded in the south by the Aire Gap, by the pass of Stainmoor and the Tees to the North, the Lune Valley to the west and the moorlands that tail off into the Vale of York and Nidderdale to the east. It is an area of high moorland and mountain, with few hills much over 2,000 feet, but including countryside as wild and bleak as anything in England. This gritstone moorland is intersected by steep-sided valleys of contrasting lushness and beauty, with scattered woodlands, waterfalls and unspoiled villages of great individuality and character. But the south of the region is dominated by the most extensive carboniferous limestone scenery in the kingdom, with crags, scars, limestone pavements, and the celebrated spectacular potholes and caves.

It is a writers' paradise in that it has, since the eighteenth century, attracted writers to it, men and women who have found particular inspiration in the landscape. But equally the writers, as much as the painters and photographers, have created that image of the Yorkshire Dales we now accept as 'natural beauty'.

So what better means than an anthology to give a taste, however inadequate, of the vast literature which the Dales have inspired? Perhaps sadly, most of this literature is the work of outsiders who have visited, or at best come to live in the Dales. There are a few exceptions, men of the calibre of Sedgwick or Farrer, but even these were scientists first and writers afterwards. As Dr Raistrick has recently suggested, literary excellence does not come easily to Dales people who are more naturally gifted farmers, masons, wallers, miners, knitters—an essentially practical people.

It has been a voyage of discovery, tracing the works of authors often named in later books, but whose original work has been forgotten. These include some of the great and famous—Wordsworth, Scott, Kingsley, Ruskin—but equally enjoyable has been the discovery of minor figures, some, like Walter White and J. H. Dixon, unjustly neglected, and others offering vivid insight not as a gifted writer offers insight through dazzling intellectual penetration, but through the humble detail of life as it was, and how people saw it.

Whilst this book has a serious theme, tracing attitudes to the countryside, it is intended to be a source book, a bedside book, a book to dip into. Any anthology is a personal choice; many cruel decisions have been taken on what to leave out, for what to exclude is often a more difficult decision than what to include. Two anthologies would not have sufficed to include everything I would have wished, and I apologize in advance if old favourites have not appeared. But if the pleasure of the reader matches that of the compiler, that heart-searching will not have been in vain.

1. Itinerants and Preachers

Until the mid-eighteenth century, the steep and rugged valleys of the Yorkshire Pennines appeared as remote from the focal points of English civilization, from London, Bath, Cambridge or even York, as the remoter parts of the expanding British Empire—America, the East Indies, Polynesia. Travel, away from the major routes, was appallingly difficult, roads, where they existed at all, rudimentary, facilities primitive. To travel in such regions for important matters of business—collecting information for government, carrying the Word of God—was an act of fortitude. To travel—the very word having its root in Norman French *travail* to labour or toil—for pleasure, was, in such circumstances, inconceivable.

Not surprisingly, the literature of the Dales from the sixteenth, seventeenth and early eighteenth centuries is correspondingly thin. The accounts of journeys that have survived, if indeed all were authentic journeys, virtually ignore the countryside. If scenery intrudes upon the writer's consciousness at all, it is merely in a negative sense. Camden complains that the limestone crags of Craven are "unpleasant to see", whilst Wesley, nearly two centuries later, refers to the "horrid" mountains of the region, without any *frisson* of delicious terror that his contemporaries felt in that adjective.

Yet these early accounts have a fascination, for their freshness, their directness, and their ability to see things quite uncluttered by the emotions that later generations were to use to colour every stream and every crag.

JOHN LELAND (1506–52), *the silent scholar who spent six years riding through England to collect material for a vast, erudite work that never came to be written, left fragmentary and episodic accounts of his travels that were not published until 1710–12, as his* Itinerary. *Although the work as a whole has been described as "unreadable", it provides one of the most comprehensive early accounts of the Yorkshire Dales in the sixteenth century.*

Wensleydale and Swaledale in the Reign of Henry VIII

Bysshops-Dale lyethe joyning to the quarters of Craven.

Ure commith thrughe Wencedale adjoining to Bisshops-Dale.

The hed of Ure in a mosse about myle above Coteren Hill is about a 14. mile above Midleham muche westward.

The upper parte of Wencedale is a forest of redd dere, longgynge to the kynge.

All the toppe of Coterne Hille, and somewhat farthar is in Richemondshire. And the utter parte of the hill, or thereabout, is a bek cawlled Hell-Gille, because it rennithe in such a deadely place. This gill commithe to Ure, and is divider of Richemont and Westmerland-Shires.

There is no very notable bridge on Ure above Wencelaw Bridge, a mile above Midleham and more.

Bainbridge is above Wencelaw Bridge, Aisker Bridge above it, where Ure ryver faulleth very depe betwixt 2 scarry rokks.

There be a great number of hopes, or small broks, that cum into eche syde of Ure out of the rokky mountayns or evar it cum to Midleham.

The bridge over Ure by Midleham is but of tymbar.

About a mile benethe Gervaux Abbay is a great old bridge of stone on Ure, caullyd Kilgram Bridge. The almoste 4 miles to Mascham Bridge of tymbar a litle bynethe Masseham, and vi miles lower Northbridge at the hether end of Ripon, it is vii arches of stone. And a qwartar of a myle, or less, lower, Huwike Bridge of 3 arches. Skelle cummithe in betwixt these 2. bridges.

Swadale lyithe by yond Wencedale, and out of the hills rokks on eche sydde cum many broks into Swale ryver.

There is a fair bridge on Swal at Gronton a 5. miles above Richemount; then Richemount bridge, and 3 miles lower Ketrike bridge of 4 arches of stone; then 5 mile to Morton . . . bridge of wood; then 5 miles to Skipton bridge of wod; then 3 miles to Topclif bridge of wood, and a 3, mils to Thornton bridg of stone, and . . . miles to Miton whereabout it goithe into Ure.

There be 4. or 5. parks about Midleham, and longing to it, whereof som be reasonably wooddyd.

There is meatly good wood about Ure Vaulx Abbay.

Bolton Village and castell is 4. miles from Midleham. The castell standithe on a roke syde; and all the substance of the lodgyngs [in] it be included in 4. prinipall towres. Yt was an 18 yeres in buildiynge, and the expencis of every yere came to 1000. marks. It was finichid or Kynge Richard the 2. dyed.

One thinge I much notyd in the haulle of Bolton, how chimneys were conveyed by tunnells made on the syds of the wauls bytwixt the lights in the haull; and by this meanes, and by no lovers, is the smoke of the harthe wonder strangely convayed.

Moste parte of the tymber that was occupied in buyldynge of this castell was sett out of the forest of Engleby in Cumberland, and Richard Lord Scrope for conveyaunce of it had layde by way dyvers drawghts of oxen to carry it from place to place till it cam to Bolton.

There is a very fayre cloke at Bolton *cum motu solis et Lunae*, and other conclusions.

There is a park waullyd withe stone at Bolton.

There is a hille withe a lead mine 2. miles beyond Bolton.

Vensela is a litle poor market towne *in ripa superiore* Uri. It standith not far from the Wesparke end of Midleham.

Grenton is a litle market towne *ripa citer* Sualae, a vi miles west above Richemont. The houses of these two tounes be partly slatid, partly thakkid.

The market is of corne and linyn cloth for men of Suadale, the wich be much usid in digging leade owre.

On each side of Suadale be greate hilles where they digge.

Little corne growith in Suadale.

Syr James Metcalf hath a very goodly howse caullid Nappe in Wensedale. Wensedale and the soile about is very hilly, and berith litle corne, but norisith many bestes. Wensedale, as sum say, taketh name of Wensela market. For Wensele standith on the hither side of Ure, and straite on the farther side beginnith Wensedale.

(Vennones men of Wensedale.)

Nappa is abowt a vii miles west from Vensela Market, but communely it is caullid No Castel.

Bisshops Dale lying by Ure *in ripa citer*. and conteining a sorte of greate felles with dere liyth south west within a quarter of a mile of Nappe. So that this dale lieth upward weste betwixt the upper partes of Uredale and Sualedale.

Bisshops Dales longith to the king, and yn the hilles about hit be redde deer. In faire winters the deere kepe there, in sharp winters they forsake the extreme colde and barennes of them.

Abbayes and Priories on Suale

Marik a priory of blake nunnes of the foundation of the Askes. It stondith *ripa ulter,* v mile above Richemont. Grenton is a mile above Marik.

Syr Rafe Bowmer hath a place at Marik towne stonding on a hille side half a mile from the priori stonding in a bottom.

Ellerton *ab alnis dictum* a priory of white clothid nunnes (Monachae Cistertienses) stonding in avalle *in ripa citer.*, a mile beneth Marik Priory.

Apon Ure

Gervalx (*Urivallis*) Abbay of white monkes *ripa citeriori* a ii miles beneth Midleham.

Lord Marmion was the first founder, whose landes cam to the Fitzhughes, and so to the Parres.

Apon Cover

Coverham a howse of white chanons *in ripa ulter.* scante ii miles from Midleham by west.

There was good singing in Coverham.

Apon Skel

Fountaines Abbey of white monkes yn Richemontshire.

Arkengarth dale liith most up north, and bereth sum bygge and otys, litle or no woodde, and is devidid from Sualdale by a bekk callid after the dale.

Sualedale little corne and much gresse, no wodd, but linge and sum nutte trees. The woodde that they brenne their lead is brought owte of the parte of the shire, and owt of Dirhamshir.

Uredale very little corne except bygg or otes, but plentiful of grasse in communes.

Coverdale is worse than Sualedale or Uresdale for corne, and hath no woodde but about Coverham Abbay.

Bisshops Dale liyth right west at the hedde of Coverdale more up into Westmerland, having no corn, but deere. In these dales and the great hilles about them is very little or no woodde.

There is a praty car or pole in Bisshops Dale.

The hole cuntery of Richemontshire be este from the hylles and dales ys plentiful of whete, rye and meately good medows and woods.

The best wooddes liyth be est of Suale and Ure rivers.

In the dales of Richemontshire they burne linge, petes and turffes.

In places where they cutte downe linge good grasse spingith for the catel for a yere or ii ontil the ling overgrowth hit.

There is plenty of good stone (to) be squarid (in) very many places in Richemontshire.

There be no cole pittes in Richemont; yet the (eastarly) parts of Richemontshire burne much se coles brought owt of Dyrhamshire.

John Leland, *Itinerary,* 1546

WILLIAM CAMDEN (1551–1623) *is famed as Queen Elizabeth's historian, and author of the massive* Britannia, *a remarkable account of his travels through England in 1582—six years before the Spanish Armada. The work was originally in Latin, but translated into suitable rolling Jacobean prose by Philemon Holland in 1610.*

Airedale

This river *Are* springing out of the hill Pennigent, which among the Westerne hils mounteth aloft above the rest, doth forthwith so sport himself with winding in an out, and doubtfull whether he should returne backe to his spring-head, or runne on still to the sea, that myselfe in going directly forward on my way was faine to pass over it seven times in an houres riding. It is so calme, and milde, and carryeth so gentle ans slow a streame, that it seemeth not to runne at all but to stand still, whence I suppose it tooke the name. For, as I have said before, *Are* in the British tongue betokeneth *Milde*, *Still* and *Slowe*; whereupon that slow River in France *Araris* hath his name. The Country lying about the head of this River, is called in our tongue *Craven*, perchance of the British word *Crage*, that is, *a Stone*. For, the whole *Tract* there, is rough all over and unpleasant to see to, with craggy stones, hanging rocks and rugged waies; in the middest whereof, as it were in a lurking hole, not farre from *Are* standeth Skipton; and lyeth hidden and enclosed among steep Hilles, in the like manner as *Latium* in Italie, which *Varro* supposeth to have been called, because it lyeth close under the *Apennine* and the *Alps*. The Towne (for the manner of their building among these Hilles) is faire enough, and hath a very proper and strong Castle, which *Robert de Rumely* built, by whose posterity it came by inheritance to the Earles of *Aumerle*. And when their inheritance for default of heires fell by escheat into the King's hands, *Robert de Clifford*, whose heires are now Earles of Cumberland, by way of exchange obtained of King Edward the Second both this Castle, and also faire lands round about it every way, delivering into the King's hand in lieu of the same, the possessions that he had in the Marches of Wales.

William Camden, *Britannia,* 1590
translated from the Latin by Philemon Holland, 1610

Wharfedale

This *Wharf* or *Wharfe*, in the English Saxon's language *Guerth*, commeth downe out of Craven, and for a while runneth in a parallell distance even with *Are*. If a man should think the name to be wrested from the word *Guer,* which in British signifieth *swift and violent*, verily, the nature of that River concurreth with his opinion; For he runneth with a swift and speedy streame, making a great noise as he goeth, as if he were forward, stubborn and angry; and is made more full and teasty with a number of stones lying in his chanell, which he rollth and tumbleth before him in such sort that it is a wonder to see the manner of it, but especially when he swelleth high in Winter. And verily it is a troublesome River and dangerous even in Summer time also, which I my selfe had experience of, not without some perill of mine owne, when I first travailed over this Country. For, it hath such slippery stones in it that an horse can have no sure footing on them, or else the violence of the water carryeth them away from under his feete. In all his long course which from the Spring head into the *Ouse* is almost fifty miles, he passeth onely by little Townes of no especiall account: running down by *Kilnesey Cragge*, the highest and steepest rocke that ever I saw in a midland Country by *Burnsall*, where Sir *William Craven* Knight and Alderman of London there borne, is now building a Stone bridge: who also hard by, of a pious minde and beneficiall to this Country hath of late founded a Grammar Schoole; also by *Barden-Towre* a little turret belonging to the Earle of *Cumberland*, where there is round about a good store of game and hunting of fat Deere: by *Bolton*, where sometimes stood a little Abbay: by *Bethmesley* the seat of the notable Family of *Claphams*, out of which came John Clapham a worthy warrior, in the civill broiles between *Lancaster* and *Yorke*. From thence commeth he to Ilekeley, which considering the site in respect tof *Yorke* out of *Ptolomee*, and of the affinity of the name together, I would judge to be OLICANA. Surely that is an old Towne (beside the Columnes engraven with Roman worke lying in the Churchyard and elsewhere) and was in Severus time reedified by the meanes of *Virius Lupus*, Lieutenant Generall and Propraetor then of Britaine, this inscription lately digged up hard by the Church doth plainly show:

IM. SEVERUS AUG. ET ANTONINUS CAES. DESTINATUS RESTITUERUNT CURANTE VIRIO LUPO LEGEORUM PR. P.R.*

That the second Cohort of *Lingones* abode heer, and Altar

*Emperors Severus, Augustus and Antoninus. Caesar elect. Restores under the care of Virius Lupus, their Legate. Pro Praetor.

beareth witnesse which I saw there, upholding now the staires of an house, and having this Inscription set upon it by the Captaine of the second Cohort of the Lingones, to VERBEIA, haply the Nymph or Goddesse of Wharfe, the River running there by, which River they called VERBEIA as I suppose out of so neere affinity of the names.

VERBIAE SACRUM CLODIUS FRONTO D PRAEF. COH. II LINGON*

William Camden, *Britannia*, 1590

Hell Gill

Where this country bordereth upon Lancashire, among the mountains, it is in most places so waste, solitary, unpleasant and unsightly, so mute and still, also that the borderers dwelling thereby have called certain rivulets creeping this way *Hell Becks*. But especially that about the head of the river Ure, which having a bridge over it of one entire stone, falleth down such a depth that it striketh a certain horror to as many as look down. And in this tract there be safe harbour for goat and deer, as well red as fallow, which for their huge bigness, with their ragged and branching horns, are most sightly.

William Camden, *Britannia*

The Nymph of the Ebb and Flowing Well

In all my spacious tract let them (so wise) survey
My Ribble's rising banks, their worst, and let them say;
At Giggleswick, where I a fountain can you show,
That eight times in a day is said to ebb and flow!
Who sometimes was a nymph, and in the mountains high
Of Craven, whose blue heads, for caps, put on the sky,
Amongst the oreads there, and sylvans, made abode
(It was ere human foot upon those hills had trod),
Of all the mountain-kind and since she was most fair;
It was a satyr's chance to see her silver hair
Flow loosely at her back, as up a cliff she clame,
Her beauties noting well, her features, and her frame,
And after her she goes; which when she did espy,
Before him, like the wind the nimble nymph did fly.
They hurry down the rocks, o'er hill and dale they drive,

*To Verbeia Sacred Clodius Fronto Ded. Prefect of the Cohort, Second Lingones.

To take her he doth strain, t'outstrip him she doth strive,
Like one his kind that knew, and greatly fear'd his rape,
And to the Topic gods by praying to escape,
They turn'd her to a spring, which, as she then did pant,
When, wearied with her course, her breath grew wondrous scant,
Even as the fearful nymph than thick and short did blow,
Now made by them a spring, so doth she ebb and flow.

Michael Drayton, *Polyolbion* (Song XXVIII), 1622

Drunken Barnaby's Wanderings

Thence to *Wensley*, valley-seated,
For antiquity respected;
Sheep and shepherd, as one brother,
Kindly drink to one another;
Till pot-handy, light as feather,
Sheep and shepherd sleep together.

Thence to *Middleham*, where I viewed
Th'castle, which so stately shewd:
Down the stairs, 'tis truth I tell ye,
To a knot of brave boys fell I:
All red noses, no dye deeper,
Yet none but a peace-keeper.

Thence to *Aysgarth*, from a mountain
Fruitful valleys, pleasant fountain;
Woolly flocks, cliffs steep and snowy
Fields, ferns, sedgy rushes saw I;
Which high mount is call'd the *Temple*
For all prospects an example.

Thence to *Worton*; being lighted
I was solemnly invited
By a captain's wife most yearly
Though, I think, she never knew me:
I came, call'd, call'd, toy'd, trifled, kissed:
Captain cornu-cop' I wished.

Thence *Askbrig*, market noted
But no handsomeness about it
Neither magistrate nor mayor

Ever were elected there:
Here poor people live by knitting,
To their trading, breeding, sitting.

Thence to *Hardraw*, where's hard hunger
Barren *Cliffs* and *Clints* of wonder;
Never here *Adonis* lived
Unless in *Cole*'s harbour hived;
Inns are nasty, dusty, fusty,
With both smoke and rubbish musty.

Richard Braithwaite, *Barnaby's Journal*, 1648–50

The Yorkshire Dales occupy a special position in the history of Quakerism, because it was in the Northern Dales that this great world-wide Christian movement began. GEORGE FOX, (1624–90) *was the founder of the Friends; his account of the events leading up to his historic sermon on Firbank Fell, near Sedbergh, has the compulsion of momentous events told in vigorous prose.*

The Sermon on Firbank Fell

As so I passed away being among the fell Countreys, and lay out all night, and a stranger and so that the next day I passed upp to a Market town, upon a Market day, and spoke to the people and bid them repent (and take heed of the deceitfull merchandize) and woshippe God in the spirit and truth and so I passed away up winadayle, and declared the truth though all the towns as I went, and people took mee for a madd man and distracted and some followed and questioned with mee and was astonished and then followed me a Schoolemaster and get mee into a house and thought I had been a young man that was gone distracted that was gone away from my parents or thought to have kept mee, but they being astonished at my answers and the truth I spake to them they could not tell what to say, and would have me to have staied all night, but I was not to stay butt passed away (and wandered in the night).

And at last I came to an alehouse where there was some fellows drinking and I walked up and down in the lane and after a time they beganne to drink to mee and then I spake to them the truth and warning them of the mighty day of the lord was comeing and bid them take heed to that which shewed them sin and evill in their hearts upon which one rose against mee with a clubb, and so they held one another, and then they were quiet, I walking out as to have gone to have then all night outdoors; and hee that would have strucke mee followed mee and so I was moved to come into ye house again and so staid with them all night, and the next morning I was moved to tell the man of the house that I was the sonne of God and was come to declare truth to them, and so hee had me down among some professors who after I had declared truth to them and they received it, and they directed mee to other professors.

And then I came to one Bousfields (in Gasdaile) who received where there were many convinced, and from thence I was directed to Gervase Benson where there was a meeting of professing people; and I lay at Richard Robinson and speaking to him he was convinced, and the next day being the first day of the week I went down to the meeting, where they were generally carried out that day, and generally received Truth, and came to the teacher with the Christ Jesus.

Presently after there was a great fair to be at Sedbury, near Gervase Benson, where many young people came to be hyred and I went through the fair and spake, and then went to the steeple house yard (and got upp by a tree) and spake to the people largely, many Professors and priests being there; and to bring them off, of their worshipps, to worship God, in the spirit, and had no opposition, but only one Captain which said that the steeple house was the Church, which I told him it was a place of limestone and wood (for the Church was God as in This. 1 and 1) and so after had some few words hee passed away, and the truth came over all, and I was satisfied concerning it; and when I was passing away, one priest said to the people I was distracted, his mouth being stopped by the powers of God for opposeing, that was his only Cover to the People, and so I passed away and had some other meetings upp and down in that Country, when divers were Convinced and received the Truth.

And then I came to ffirbank Chappel, where there was a great meetting of the sober people, of the Country and severall speakers, whence moderate people desired mee not to speak unto the speakers because they are something contrary to the world, and there were many sorts of people there, and so not to speak to them in the steeplehouse; and indeed there was nothing upon me to speak to them; and so afterward when the meeting was done in the forenoon, I went up upon the hill in the afternoone; and the people came to mee for the steeple house would not hold them in the morning and some would me want to go into the steeple house as being a strange thing for a man to speak out of the steeplehouse; and so after a while I beganne to speak to the People and all quiet, and the greatest part of a thousand people were convinced that day.

George Fox, *Journal*, 1652

Richmond and the River Swale at the Time of King William and Queen Mary

This Leades me the ffarthest way to Richmond it being but 8 miles the ready Road from Darlington, but this way is 10 miles and very tedious miles. Three miles off Darlington I passed over Crofton Bridge which crosses ye river Teese which Divides Durham ffrom Yorkshire, and so Entered the North Riding of Yorkshire in which is that they Call Richmondshire a shire of 30 miles. The way was good but Long, I went through Lanes and woods an Enclosed Country; I passed by a house of Sr Mark Melbourn on a hill, a Brick building and severall towers on the top, good gardens and severall rows of trees up to the house, it standing on a hill, ye trees Runns along ye Ridge of ye same—Looks very finely.

Richmondshire has in it 5 waking takes as they Call then, answerable to that they Call hundred in other Countys; Each waking takes has market towns in them and are under a Baliffe Each, which are nominated by the Earle of Holderness who is the Sole Lord of the whole—its 30 miles in Extent. Richmond town one cannot see till just upon it, being Encompass'd w'th great high hills: I descended a very steep hill to it from whence saw the whole town which itself stands on a hill tho' not so high as these by it. Its buildings are all stone, ye streetes are like rocks themselves, there is a very Large space for the Markets w'ch are Divided for the ffish market, the fflesh market, and Corn; there is a Large market Crosse, a square space walled in with severall steps up, and its flatt on the top of a good height. There is by it a Large Church and the ruins of a Castle, the pieces of the walls on a hill. I walked round by the walls, the River running beneath a great descent to it, its full of stones and Rocks and soe very Easye to Make or keep up their wires or falls of water, which in some places is naturall ye water falls over Rocks with great force which is Convenient for Catching Salmon by spere when they Leap over those Bayes. All rivers are Low and Dryer in summer, soe I saw them at the greatest disadvantage being in some places almost drye and the Rockes and stones appear bare, but by those high and large stone bridges I pass'd which lay across the Rivers showed the Great Depth and breadth they used to be in ye Winter tymes. There was two good houses in ye town, one was Mr Dareys the Earl of Holderness' brother, the other was Mr

Yorkes, both stood then were chosen Parliament men. They had good gardens walled in, all stone, as in the whole town, though I must say it Looks Like a sad shatter'd town and fallen much to Decay and Like a Disregarded place.

Celia Fiennes, *Through England on a Side Saddle,* 1690s

Sir Solomon Swale

The town of Richmond (Cambden calls it a city) is wall'd, and had a strong castle; but as those things are now slighted, so really the account of them is of small consequence, and needless; old fortifications being, if fortification was wanted, of very little significance; the river Swale runs under the wall of this castle, and has some unevenness at its bottom, by reason of rocks which intercept it passage, so that it falls like a cataract, but not with so great a noise.

The Swale is a noted river, though not extraordinary large, for giving name to the lands which it runs through for some length, which are called Swale Dale, and to an antient family of that name, one of whom has the vanity, as I have heard, to boast, that his family was so antient as not to receive that name from, but to give name to the river it self. One of the worthless successors of this line, who had brought himself to the dignity of what they call in London a Fleeter, used to write himself, in his abundant vanity, Sir Solomon Swale, of Swale Hall, in Swale Dale, in the county of Swale, in the North Riding of York.

The addition of *dale*, first given here to the low lands about the head of the Swale, is grown up into a custom or usage from all the rivers which rise in those western hills north of this, quite to and into Scotland; for example,

Teesdale for the River Tees.
Wierdale for the Wier which runs through Durham.
Tine Dale for the Tine, which runs to Newcastle.
Tweedale for the Tweed, which passeth by Berwick.
Clydsdale, Nydsdale, and many others.

Daniel Defoe, *Tour through the Whole Island of Great Britain* (Letter VIII), 1724

Preaching in Lovely Wensleydale

We crossed over the enormous mountain into lovely Wensleydale, the largest by far of all the Dales as well as the most beautiful. Some years since, many had been awakened here, and joined together by Mr. Ingham and his preachers. But since the bitter discussion between their preachers, the poor sheep have all been scattered. A considerable number of them have been gleaned up and joined together by our preachers. I came into the midst of them at Redmire. As I rode through the town the people stood staring on every side, as if we had been a couple of monsters. I preached in the street, and they soon ran together, young and old, from every quarter. I reminded the elder of their having seen me thirty years before, when I preached in Wensley church; and enforced are we to "Believe in the Lord Jesus Christ, and thou shalt be saved." When I rode back through the town, it wore a new face. The people were profoundly civil; they were bowing and curtseying on every side. Such a change in two hours I have seldom seen.

Hence we hasted to Richmond, when I preached in a kind of square. All the Yorkshire Militia were there; and so were their officers, who kept them in awe, so that they behaved with decency. At six I preached at the end of our house in Barnard Castle. I was frail and feverish when I began; but the staying an hour in a cold bath (for the wind was very high and sharp) quite refreshed me, so that all my faintness was gone, and I was perfectly well when I concluded.

John Wesley, *Journal*, Tuesday 14th June, 1774

The Work of God in Rugged Places

We reached Grassington about tea. The multitude of people contrived me to preach abroad. It was fine for all the time I was preaching, but afterwards rained much. At Pateley Bridge the vicar afforded me the use of his church. Though it was more than twice as large as our preaching-house, it was not near large enough to contain the congregation. How vast is the increase of the work of God! Particularly in the most rugged and uncultivated places! How does He "send the springs of grace" also into the valleys, "that run among the hills".

John Wesley, *Journal*, 1st May, 1780

2. The first tourists arrive

The word 'tourist' is of relatively recent origin, coming into use in the early nineteenth century, suggesting literally a 'tour' or circular journey undertaken purely for pleasure. It assumes two important things—people with sufficient wealth and leisure to make a tour, and an adequate means of conveyance to bring the tourist safely and easily to and from the chosen area.

By the later eighteenth century these requirements were, to a degree, fulfilled. A network of excellent turnpike roads now connected the capital with the North of England, and stage-coaches operated regularly along these roads, served by new road-houses and inns.

Not that travel was easy. As William Bray warned his readers in his *Sketch of a Tour into Derbyshire and Yorkshire* in 1777:

> The traveller who sets out on a long journey with the expectation of meeting with the same accommodation on the road that he has in his own house, will soon find himself mistaken . . .

Bray does not dwell on the discomforts and even miseries of the remoter country inns in the Dales for whom tourists were a rarity. Few turnpike roads were ever built through the Dales compared with other parts of England, and these generally late in the turnpike era. Even those that were, were often only open for carriage traffic between May and October. Outside these months, deep and impenetrable quagmires were certain hazards to be met with, when indeed the long Pennine winters did not block the valleys with snowdrifts. Most early travellers to the Dales came, in fact, on horseback, but even for a strong horse and rider the minor roads, mere stony tracks over the moorland passes, were something of an ordeal.

Why did they come?

Two reasons, initially. The idea of a young nobleman's Grand Tour, that would take in the fashionable cities of the Continent, Paris, Rome, Athens, the cultural sights which included the major antiquities and choicest scenery, captured the eighteenth-century imagination.

It was not long before the taste for travel turned to the remoter parts of the British Isles. Johnson and Boswell made their celebrated tour to the Hebrides in 1773; Thomas Pennant went twice to Scotland in 1769 and 1772; his second tour included an extensive visit to the Lake District and the Yorkshire Dales. An unsigned article in *The Gentleman's Magazine* in March 1761 had described some of the strange phenomena to be seen in the vicinity of Ingleborough Mountain. From then on it became the custom for many travellers bound for the Lakes or Scotland to include the 'curiosities' of the Dales in their itinerary.

Not that the Dales were without their local apologists. Thomas Hurtley, the Malham schoolmaster could complain, in 1786 that:

> Indeed till these few years a Travelled Englishman either knew not we had any Natural Curiosities to admire, or deemed it unfashionable to acknowledge there was anything in Britain worth the attention of a man of taste or ordinary Information . . .
>
> . . . juvenile foppery may even affect to sneer at our description of SKIDDAW when he is talking of MOUNTSERRAT, or laugh at the mention of the NORTHERN LAKES when compared with those of CONSTANCE or GENEVA.

—but men of "real sense" now recognized that it was

> no longer either vulgar or derogatory to the character and pursuits of the polite world to visit, to admire, to decorate or to portray the native elegance or majestic scenery of our own Clime.

And indeed it was his native Yorkshire to which he drew his countrymen's attention:

> a country which seems in his (perhaps partial) estimation to have been hitherto unaccountably neglected.

The second reason was the French Revolution and the rise of Napoleon. During the prolonged French Wars, continental travel was extremely difficult. But it did wonders for the nascent English tourist trade. One enterprising publisher, in 1798, collected together a number of the most popular accounts of touring in Britain in five calf-bound 'pocket form' volumes. Entitled *The British Tourists; or Travellers Pocket Companion through England and Wales, Scotland and Ireland comprehending the most Celebrated Tours in the British Isles* it was edited by one William Mavor, LL.D., who set the scene most eloquently:

> Roused, at last, from the lethargy of indifference about what was within their reach, and inspired with more patriotic motives than formerly, of the pleasure and utility of home travels, we have, of late years, seen some of our most enlightened countrymen, as eager to explore the remotest parts of Britain as they formerly were to cross the Channel, and to pass the Alps.

Among the "remotest parts of Britain" awaiting our "enlightened countrymen" were, of course, the Yorkshire Dales.

Houses Built in the Fields

From Hardraw I went westward, and saw a fall of ten feet at a rivlet called Cotter with several small cascades above it. We ascended a hill of the same name, which is very high, our guide guessed from the top down to the Ure 600 yards, but I did not think it so much. We went along the side of this hill, and came to Hellgills, called in the maps Helbeck Lunes; it is a rivlet which rises a little further to the north, and has worn down the rock about twenty feet deep and about four feet in width. It is curious to see the waters run at so great a depth in such a narrow channel, and to step over it. To the east of it is another very small stream, which divides the county of York from the county of Westmoreland, and falls, if I mistake not, into the Hellgills. Hellgill is the rise of the Eden, which falls in at Caerlisle. About half a mile lower there is deep water in it, from which they say the Ure rises, the water going under the ground about a quarter of a mile, and coming out in a field called Lin Park, and they say they have put chaff into the one and it has come out of the other.

About two miles to the north rises the river Swale, a little beyond a natural rock call'd Hugh Seat, and ten or twelve from Apelby. There are no deer in these mountains. The prospect from the height of Cotter is the most awful and grand I ever beheld. The mountains all round, some with their lofty heads at a distance, as Ingleborough and Penigent and the valley beneath, which, tho' it is much narrower to the west of Ascrig, yet it is still a fine vale of good pasturage, and, what is uncommon, there are houses built in most of the fields, which is an unusual prospect, and at a distance make the appearance of scatter'd villages. About Hardrow they find freestone flags, which rise very large, and in them are figures of worms, snakes, and the like, but whether only accidental figures, as such reptiles inclosed, I cannot take upon me to say, but I rather think the former.

On the 24th, leaving this fine dale, we went to the south-west, over the vale in which Widhill Beck runs, having Weather Fell to the right; and ascending up Tenant Hill to the south-east, we had a fine view of the green vale and lofty mountains all round. On this hill we came to some shafts where they had dug for lead. The stones they dug up are of an ash-colour'd marble, and full of trochi and entrochi, and so I observed the rocks were as we went along the mountain. We soon came to Camhill, and near to some cabbins called camhouses, to the north of which are two springs near each other, which soon joyn, and fall into the valley, and then it is called Cam Beck; this they call the rise of the Ribble. In the valley below, a litle to the north of it, is a wet moor, out of which there arises a spring, which is the head of the river Wharfe. A rivlet comes in a short space on each side, and several other afterwards, so that it soon becomes a large river. I observed one of the springs of the Ribble, if I mistake not the southern one, that it incrusts the pebbles with a loose stony matter, which rises up in little columns about half an inch high, and is doubtless caus'd by the stony, coarse particles the water brings along with it, finer particles frequently either petrifying or incrusting with a stone coat.

Richard Pococke, *Journal*, May 31st, 1751

A Melancholy Sight

From *Brough*, the road, if I may give it that name, to *Askrigg*, lies over one continuous range of mountains, here called moors. The cultivated vallies are too inconsiderable to deserve a mention. Most of these fifteen miles, however dreadful the road, are tracts of very improveable land; if a good turnpike road was made from *Askrigg* to *Brough*, the first great step to cultivation would be over; for it is almost impossible to improve a country with spirit, the roads of which are impassable. It is extremely melancholy to view such tracts of land that are indisputably capable of yielding many beneficial crops, remaining totally waste, while in many parts of the kingdom farms are so scarce and difficult to procure, that one is no sooner vacant, than twenty applications are immediately made for it.

Arthur Young, *A Six Months Tour Through the North of England*, 1771

The State of the Roads

We now proceeded from Malham to Settle, seven miles. The road (when it can be called such) leads us over a wild, hilly country, and extensive tracts of moors. Ascending a steep hill from Malham, we come upon a rocky common, and presently lose almost every vestige of a path. Here are several pits from which calamine (a kind of fossil bituminous earth) is dug, close to the road. We continue to traverse a high, elevated country, till at length we descend rapidly to Settle, in the vale of the Ribble.

Excepting the moors, we see little besides large grazing farms, with stone walls dividing the fields. It is wholly a limestone soil, the rocks of which are peeping up above the surface very frequently, and in some places being up on the sides of the hills in awful precipices. The road is nowhere good, and some of it almost impassible, notwithstanding the abundance of excellent materials everywhere at hand: but its being not much frequented is probably the reason that so little labour and care are bestowed upon it. On the moor the traveller has no other guide than some distant mountain to direct his steps, of which he is deprived in misty weather, which is frequent in this country. When we crossed this mountainous pass, a thick mist surrounded us in darkness, and would certainly have caused us to deviate from the right path, had not the tracks of a cart, which had passed that morning from Settle to the fair at Malham, acted as a guide, and conducted us safely. This road between Settle and Malham is by no means to be recommended to strangers except in clear weather; and even then with every necessary direction and precaution; that by way of Long Preston, though tolerably good, is a circuitous route of about fifteen miles.

John Housman, *A Descriptive Tour and Guide to the Lakes Caves and Mountains and other Natural Curiosities in Cumberland, Westmorland, Lancashire and part of the West Riding of Yorkshire,* 1800
third edition, 1808

This celebrated account by a clergyman—'PASTOR' *in the* Gentleman's Magazine *in 1761 is rightly cited as the moment when tourism in the Dales really began. It created wide interest and many other accounts of the strange phenomena of the Ingleborough area were soon to follow.*

A Remarkable Mountain

It is a mountain, singularly eminent, whether you regard its height, or the immense base upon which it stands. It is near 20 miles in circumference, and has *Clapham*, a church town to the South; *Ingleton* to the west; *Chapel le Dale* to the north; and *Selside*, a small hamlet to the east; from each of which place the rise, in some parts is even and gradual; in others rugged and perpendicular. In this mountain rise considerable streams, which at length fall into the *Irish Sea*. The land round the bottom is fine, fruitful pasture, interposed with many acres of limestone rocks. As you ascend the mountain, the land is more barren, and under the surface is peat-moss, in many places two or three yards deep, which the country people cut up and dry for burning, instead of coal. As the mountain rises, it becomes more rugged and perpendicular, at length so steep that it cannot be ascended without great difficulty, and in some places not at all. In many parts there are fine quarries of slate, which the neighbouring inhabitants use to cover their houses; there are also many loose stones, but no limestones; yet, near the base, no stones but limestones are else found. The loose stones near the summit the people call *greet-stone*.

The foot of the mountain abounds with springs on every side, and on the west side there is a very remarkable spring near the summit. The top is very level, but so dry and barren that it offers little grass, the rock being barely covered with earth. It is said to be about a mile in circumference, and several persons now living say that they have seen races upon it. Upon that part of the top facing *Lancaster* and the *Irish Sea*, there are still to be seen the dimensions of an house, and the remains of what the country people call a *beacon, viz.* a place erected with stones, three or four yards high, ascended with stone stairs; which served in old times, as old people tell us, to alarm the country, upon the approach of an enemy, a person being always kept there upon watch, in time of war, who was to give notice in the night, by fire, to other watchmen placed upon other mountains within view, of which there are many, particularly Whernside, Woefell, Camfell, Pennygent, and Pennhill. There are likewise discoverable a great many mountains in *Westmoreland* and *Cumberland* besides the town of *Lancaster*, from which it is distant about 20 miles. The westward sides are most steep and rocky; there is, on one part to the south, where you may ascend on horseback; but whether the work of nature, or of art, I cannot say.

A part of the said mountain jutts out to the northeast near a mile, but somewhat below the summit; this is called *Park-fell*; another part jutts out in the same manner, towards the east, and is called *Simon-fell*; there is likewise another part towards the south, called *Little Ingleborough*; the summits of all of which are lower than the mountain itself. Near the base, there are holes or chasms, called swallows, supposed to be the remains of *Noah*'s deluge; they are among the limestone rocks, and are open to an incredible depth.

The springs towards the east all come together, and fall into one of these swallows, or holes, called *Allun Pott*; and after passing under the earth about a mile they burst out again, and flow into the river *Ribble*, whose head, or spring, is but a little further up the valley. The depth of this swallow, or hole, could never be ascertained; it is about 20 poles in circumference, not perfectly circular, but rather oval. In wet foggy weather, it sends out a smoak, or mist, which may be seen a considerable distance. Not far from this hole, nearly north, is another hole, which may be easily descended. In some places the roof is 4 or 5 yards high, and its width the same; in other places, not above a yard; and was it not for the run of the water, it is not to be known how far you might walk, by the help of a candle, or other light. There is likewise another hole, or chasm, a little west from the other two, which cannot be descended without difficulty. You are no soon entered than you have a subterranean passage, sometimes wide and spacious, sometimes so narrow you are obliged to make use of both hands, as well as foot, to crawl a considerable way; and as I was informed, some persons have gone several hundred yards, and might have gone much further, durst they have ventured.

'Pastor', *The Gentleman's Magazine,* March 1761

A Visit to Settle

Cloud berries are found plentifully on the moors between *Malham* and *Settle*. They take their name from their lofty situation. I have seen the berries in the Highlands of Scotland served as a desert. The *Swedes* and *Norwegians* preserve great quantities in autumn to make tarts and other confections, and esteem them as excellent antiscorbatics. The *Laplanders* bruise them and eat them in the milk of rein deer, and preserve them quite fresh till spring by burying them in the snow.

I descended an exceedingly tedious and steep road, having on the right a range of rocky hills with broken precipitous fronts. At the front of a monstrous limestone rock called *Castleberg,* that threatens destruction, lies *Settle*, a small town in a little vale, exactly resembling a shabby French town with a *place* in the middle. Numbers of coiners and filers lived about the place at this time entirely out of work; by reason of the recent salutary law respecting the weight of gold.

I dined here at the neatest and most comfortable little inn I ever was at, rendered more agreeable by the civility and attention of the landlady. This is a market town, and has a small trade in knit-worsted stockings, which are made here from two to five shillings a pair. The great hill of *Penygent* is seen from hence, and is about six miles distant.

Thomas Pennant, *A Tour from Downing to Alston Moor,* 1773

COLONEL JOHN BYNG (1743–1813) *a former Lieutenant-Colonel in the Guards Regiment who saw extensive service overseas, became a Civil Servant with the Inland Revenue before inheriting the title of the fifth Lord Torrington just a few months before his death. He undertook a number of remarkable journeys through England in the late eighteenth century, between 1781 and 1794.*

The journals he kept were not published until many years after his death, and provide a unique record of life in provincial England.

His account of the journey through the Yorkshire Dales in June 1792 from Teesdale to Swaledale, Askrigg, Hawes, Gearstones, Ingleton, Settle, Skipton and Malham is remarkable for the accuracy of its observation, its trenchant humour and the vitality of its author's style.

The Discomforts of a Drovers' Inn

The ascent of the Mountain Cams is one of the longest, steepest, and most stoney in Great Britain; for they say it is 9 miles to the summit; the 1st 4 are very steep. If the roads are bad, the country barren, and the winters long, yet the inhabitants are compensated by the plenty of coal, the trout fishing, and the grouse shooting; which is a season ardently wish'd for; and brings a short harvest to the small inns. Upon the hillside we were encounter'd by some sharp stones. . . .

I was much fatigued by the tediousness of the road—whereupon we at last met two farming men, with whom we conversed about the grouse, and their abundance. Crossing a ford, Mr Blakey led me to a public house—call'd Grierstones, the seat of misery, in a desert; and tho' filled with company, yet the Scotch fair upon the heath added to the horror of the curious scenery; the ground in front crowded by Scotch cattle and the drovers; and the house cramm'd by the buyers and sellers, most of whom were in plaids, fillibegs, etc. The stable did not afford hay. My friend, who knew the house, forced his way thro' the lower floor, and interned himself in the only wainscotted bedroom up stairs, where we at length we procured some boil'd slices of stale pork, and some fry'd eggs; with some wretched beer and brandy—to which my hunger was not equal; and from which my delicacy revolted. When our room was invaded by companions he call'd out "This is a private chamber."

The only custom of this hotel, or rather hovel, is derived from grouse shooters, or from two Scotch Fairs; when at the conclusion of the days of squabble, the two Nations agree in mutual drunkenness, the Scotch are allways wrap'd up in their plaids—as a defence against heat, cold or wet; but they are preventions of speed or activity; so wherever any cattle stray'd they instantly threw down the plaid, that they might overtake them. All Yorkshire around, tho' black, and frightful, seem of small account in the comparison of Ingleborough—at whose base we now travel. Mr Blakey's dog who was my only diversion on the road, seems thoroughly master of his business and worth 4 times the sum (3 guineas) that Mr B. gave for him. I believe he could sell him for 5 guineas. The reckoning being paid, very genteely, by me, I proposed to Mr. Blakey to ride forward to accelerate our intention.

There fell many storms of rain; and these come upon you in a mist, from the mountains, without giving the least warning. Our poor horses were glad to be delivered from their stye; and I then pursued Mr. Blakey's steps to a vale, call'd Chapel-in-dale; where, from the first house, he call'd to me. This was the habitation of a jolly shoemaker, a fine bold-looking fellow; and his wife, to whom he had not long been married, was an excellent contrast of sweet expression and feminine softness: he is the guide to the neighbouring caves, the noblest of which, Wethercote, is adjoining to his house, and presented us with ale in a *Silver* cup!! Perhaps there is no corner of this island that can afford wilder scenery; but Jobson thinks it is paradise: (and the winters roar but bind him to his native valley more.)

There is a horrid chas'm, just below his house, call'd Gingle-pot; down which we peep'd, and threw stones. But how shall I describe the wonders of Wethercote-Cave (Cove pronounced)?

From the top of this perpendicular cave are to be seen the falls of water that lose themselves at the bottom; and to which we approach'd by a most laborious descent; here two cascades are to be seen thro', upon a small passage leading into a horizontal cave: much wetting is to be encountered, and some danger apprehended. These cascades fall with an horrid din, filling the mind with a gloom of horror.

Honest Jobson now assured us that "He must guide us to Yordas Cave—which was near at hand, and highly worth seeing"; but from the cold and frequent wettings, my curiosity was quell'd: however, Jobson insisted, and Mr B. appeared anxious to see it.

So off we set; passing the small chapel, and some neighbouring houses, where Jobson bought a pound of candles, to carry with him to be lighted at the cave, from the burning turf he took in his hands. Our guide was a merry, hearty, fellow, and with much fun defended his County from our abuse, while we were crossing the terrible, stoney, mountain call's Gragareth—tho' he call'd it a short step, and strided away, (often renewing his fire with fresh peat,) where from bog, and stone, our horses could not keep pace with him, yet it appear's to me a distance of three miles.

Crossing a nasty, stoney brook, we arrived at Yordas Cave; where leaving our horses at the entrance, and lighting our candles we enter'd the cavern: it is well worthy of inspection, not too tedious, and beautifully closed by a cascade. Jobson stuck up candles by the way, which gave a most fanciful effect.

John Byng, *A Tour to the North*, 1792
(from *The Torrington Diaries*)

The Challenge of a Mountain

Though a stranger, and without a guide, I soon determined to try my strength in treading on the sides and summit of this noble mountain. I left my horse at a cottage, and in my ascent was surprised to find, that while many of the fertile plains of England were withering under the long-continued drought, the lower slopes of Ingleborough were luxuriant with verdure, and even afforded spoils for the scythe. In my ascent I disturbed many a homely couple of moor-game, who, in return, loudly scolded me for the intrusion, and hurried indignantly out of my sight; their rage was like the scolding of hens, but far louder.

I now came to my difficulties, and, as a child learning to walk, and afraid of falling, creeps on his hands and knees, then, to gratify my ambition, I crawled among the rocks fallen from the summit of the mountain. I durst not look behind me, lest my head should become giddy, so with alternate glimpses to what was above me, I looked right down to the earth; consequently my prospect extended but a few yards.

When I had nearly arrived at the top, I fell into a path, which, if I had entered at the beginning, my ascent would have been comparatively easy. I now stood on a plain, and I walked without apprehension. Two respectable persons that I joined, told me I had come up the worst way. Ingleborough may be said to take precedence of all the Yorkshire mountains: it stands prominent before the rest, and forms on its summit a spacious plain (said to be a mile in circumference), whereon might almost stand the adult population of the county. I should not have any objection to see it so assembled; but not to hold races, as I have been informed was sometimes the case. What would please me better, would be to see the population of Yorkshire so assembled around their late representative Wilberforce, and him on horseback addressing the multitude.

. . . Sunshine and shade furnished the beauties of contrast. The sun shining on a full sea from Lancaster to Millthorp and Ulverston appeared to spread as a plain, or rather to form a swell of glittering silver. The towers of Lancaster Castle, and its adjoining steeple, rose venerably in the distance. Clustering villages and white cottages, amid green fields and yellow harvests, spoke of peace and comfort to the admiring beholder.

In the Yorkshire part of the landscape was a peculiar trait. Far below where I stood at another season of the year, would have appeared considerable districts of snow; indeed they now, when the sun shone, seemed to glitter like fields of ice, and they literally appeared to be divided like fields in the landscape. The fact is, a species of white rock spreads over many scores of acres in this neighbourhood, and rises so little above the earth, and is so uniform on its surface, that a stranger might be so deceived as to pronounce it snow, ice, or fields spread with lime. I now looked over a limestone country a great distance, and the thought occured to me, that if all that ingredient in the composition of the earth now beneath my survey were to be burned into lime, it would furnish that article for the whole world for many ages.

Thomas Wilkinson, *Tours to the British Mountains,* 1824

PROFESSOR BOYD DAWKINS'*s classic account of caves and caving belongs to a later epoch than other accounts of discovering the Dales. But his account of the first descent of Alum Pot is not another tourist tale; it captures the mixture of bravado and improvisation which made the early descents of the great potholes of Craven exploration on the heroic scale.*

The First Descent of Alum Pot

The Helln Pot, into which the stream flowing through the Long Churn Cave falls, is a fissure a hundred feet long by thirty feet wide, that engulfs the waters of a little stream on the surface, which are dissipated in spray long before they reach the bottom. From the top you look down on a series of ledges, green with ferns and mosses, and, about a hundred feet from the surface, an enormous fragment of rock forms a natural bridge across the chasm from one ledge to another. A little above this is the debouchement of the stream flowing through Long Churn Cave through which Mr. Birkbeck and Mr. Metcalfe made the first perilous descent in 1847.

The party, consisting of ten persons, ventured into this awful chasm with no other apparatus than ropes, planks, a turn-tree, and a fire-escape belt. On emerging from the Long Churn Cave they stood on a ledge of rock about twelve feet wide, and which gave them free access to the "bridge". This was a rock about twelve feet wide, which rested obliquely on the ledges. Having crossed over this, they crept behind the waterfall which descended from the top, and fixed their pulley, five being let down while the rest of the party remained behind to hoist them up again. In this way they reached the bottom of the pot, which had never been trod by the feet of man. Thence they followed the stream downwards as far as the first great waterfall, down which Mr. Metcalfe was venturous enough to let himself with a rope, and to push onwards until daylight failed. He was within a very little of arriving at the end of the cave into which the stream flows, but was obliged to turn back into the daylight without having accomplished his purpose. The whole party eventually, after considerable danger and trouble, returned safely from the bold adventure.

J. Boyd Dawkins, *Cave Hunting,* 1874

3. In Search of the Sublime

The term 'Romantic' means many things to different people. I use it in its historic sense, as a related series of ideas which have had a profound, and lasting effect on our appreciation of the countryside.

It began innocuously enough as a taste for the curious and the strange, the real or artificially constructed 'Gothick' ruin in the landscaped gardens of a gentleman's country seat. It developed into a full-blown revolt against the sterility of neo-classical conventions in art, music, literature and architecture, a revolt which was as much based in new beliefs about the nature of human character and society as the superficialities of fashion.

One early manifestation was the cult of the 'picturesque'—an attempt to see in landscape the tranquil beauty of the paintings of Claude Lorraine, or the drama of Salvator Rosa. It absorbed a fascination with things medieval—Bishop Percy's *Reliques of Ancient English Poetry* was published in 1765 and created a new interest in the border ballads. By way of English literature, it developed into that splendid form, the 'Gothic' novel as seen in the works of Horace Walpole, Mrs Radcliffe and 'Monk' Lewis with their elaborate stage-trappings of castles, moonlight, graveyards, wolves, bats and vampires, a tradition that still endures in the popular imagination. But the early Gothic novels were rich in description of landscape, the landscape of terror, a landscape of cliffs, crags, caverns, ravines.

Edmund Burke's famous *Philosophical Inquiry into our Ideas of the Sublime and Beautiful* of 1756 formulated a comprehensive definition of what he termed the "sublime" in nature. This included anything which inspired awe or terror, "the gloomy forest, and in the howling wilderness". The young aesthetes, the poets, the painters, well versed in their Virgil, their Dante, their Milton, responded enthusiastically to Burke. The Yorkshire Pennines—with crags, caves, ravines, and waterfalls in abundance—were perfect for an experience of the sublime.

Pioneer travellers were followed by aesthetes, with notebook or easel, eager to record experiences. Their journeys were often pilgrimages to those almost sacred places recorded by earlier travellers as sources of sublime feeling. Aysgarth Falls, Bolton Priory and Gordale Scar—whose stupendous crags had an almost hypnotic fascination for the early Romantics—were among features most eagerly visited. But most of all it was the caves that captured the spirit of the Gothic horror.

It has been remarked how close the Yorkshire Dales came to being known as 'The Cave District' because of their unique labyrinths of underground caverns, the vast, spectacular 'pots' down which intrepid travellers could peer and, equipped with candle and rope, occasionally descend. Few things thrilled the Romantic imagination more than these "caverns measureless to Man" with all their implications of terror, horror and the unknown.

Amongst the gifted artists drawn to the area at this time were Edward Dayes, Thomas Girtin, John Cotman, James Ward, whose masterpiece is a huge canvas of Gordale painted in 1812, now in the Tate Gallery, and Joseph Mallory Turner, arguably England's greatest painter who stayed at Farnley Hall, near Otley, on many occasions, and whose work included many splendid Dales water-colours. His illustrations for Whitaker's *Richmondshire* are highly prized.

If the descriptions of the Dales produced by some of the writers seem a little too highly coloured, they were exhibiting one of those characteristic symptoms of Romanticism from which we ourselves still suffer—imposing upon the external realities of the environment a subjective and emotionally charged response, giving the rocks, the stones, the water, the trees a significance that went far beyond mere objective reality. The cult of 'Nature' was born.

The Beauties of Wensleydale

Wensleydale, a beautiful fertile vale, narrow, bounded by high hills, inclosed with hedges, and cultivated far up, in many parts cloathed with woods, surmounted by long ranges of scars, white rocks, smooth and precipitous in front, and perfectly even at their tops. The rapid crystal Ure devides the whole, fertilising the rich meadows with its stream. . . .

Reach *Aysgarth* or Aysgarth Force, remarkable for the fine arch over the Ure built in 1539. The scenery above and below is most uncommonly picturesque. The banks on both sides are lofty, rocky, and darkened with trees. Above the bridge two regular precipices cross the river, down which the water falls in beautiful cascades, which are seen to great advantage from below. The gloom of the pendant trees, the towering steeple of the church above, and the rage of the waters beneath the ivy-bowered arch, form together a most romantic view . . .

. . . The eye is finely directed to this beautiful cataract by the scars that board the river, being lofty, precipitous and quite of a smooth front, and their summits fringed with hollies and other trees. . . .

. . . and of Wharfedale

. . . Continue our journey along a pleasant vale. Rode beneath Kilnsey Crag, a stupendous rock, ninety-three yards high, more than perpendicular for it overhangs at the top in a manner dreadful to the traveller. The road bad, made of broken limestones uncovered. This vale ends in a vast theatre of wood, and gives one the idea of an American scene. Ahead and get into hilly and less pleasing country. Overtake many droves of cattle and horses, which had been at grass the whole summer in the remotest part of Craven, where they were kept for nine shillings to forty per head, according to their size.

Thomas Pennant, *Second Tour in Scotland,* 1772
(1776 edition)

The Horror of Gordale Scar

As I advanced the crags seem'd to close in but discovered a narrow entrance turning to the left between them. I followed my guide a few paces and lo the hills open'd again into no large space and then all further away is bar'd by a stream, that at the height of 50 feet gushes from a hole in the rock and spreading in large sheets over its broken front dashes from steep to steep and then rattles away in a torrent in the valley. The rock on the left rises perpendicular with stubbed yew trees and the shrubs, starting from its base to a height of at least 300 feet. But these are not the thing! It is that to the right and under which you stand to see these fall, that forms the principal horror of the place. From its very base it begins to slope forwards over you in one black and solid mass without any crevice in its surface and overshadows half the area below with its dreadful canopy where I stand. . . .

. . . the gloomy and uncomfortable day well suited the savage aspect of the place and made it still more formidable. I stay'd there (not without shuddering) a quarter of an hour and thought my trouble richly paid, for the impression will last for life.

Thomas Gray, *Journal to Lord Wharton,* 11th October, 1769

A Horrid Place

The first curiosity we were conducted to was *Hurtlepot,* about eighty yards above the chapel. It is a round deep hole, between thirty and forty yards in diameter surrounded with rocks almost on all sides, between thirty and forty feet perpendicular above a deep black water, in a subterranean cavity at its bottom. All round the top of this horrid place are trees, which grew secure from the axe: their branches almost meet in the centre, and spread a gloom over a chasm dreadful enough of itself without being heightened with any additional appendages: It was indeed one of the most dismal prospects I had yet been presented with. The descent of *Aeneas* into the infernal regions came fresh into my imagination. . . .

After viewing for some time with horror and astonishment its dreadful aspect from the top, we were emboldened to the margin of this Avernian lake. What its depth is we could not learn: but from the length of time the sinking stones we threw in continued to send up bubbles from the black abyss, we concluded it to be very profound. How far it extended under the huge pendent rocks we could get no information, a subterranean embarkation having never yet been fitted out for discoveries. In great flood we were told this pot runs over; some traces of it then remained on the grass. While we stood at the bottom, the awful silence was broken four or five times in a minute by drops of water falling into the lake from the rocks above, in different solemn keys. The sun shining on the surface of the water, illuminated the bottom of the superincumbent rocks, only a few feet above; which, being viewed by reflection in the lake, caused a curious deception, scarce any where to be met with: They appeared at the like distance below its surface in form of a rugged bottom. But alas! How fatal would be the consequence if any adventurer should attempt to wade across the abyss on this fallacious principle. This deep is not without its inhabitants; large black trout are frequently caught in the night by the neighbouring people.

John Hutton, *A Tour to the Caves,* 1781

Gordale's Promiscuous Ruin

My first excursion was to the *tarn* (or little lake) skirted on one side by a peat bog, and rough limestone rocks on the other; it abounds in fine trout, but has little else remarkable, except being the head of the river Air, which issuing from it, sinks into the ground very near the lake, and appears again under the fine rock which faces the village. In the time of great rains, this subterranean passage is too narrow; the brook then makes its way over the top of the rock, falling in a most majestic cascade full 60 yards in one sheet.

This beautiful rock is like the age-tinted wall of a prodigious castle; the stone is very white, and from the ledges hang various shrubs and vegetables, which with the tints given it by the bog water. & c. gives it a variety that I never before saw so pleasing in plain rock.

Gordale-scar was the object of this excursion. My guide brought me to a fine sheet cascade in a glen about half a mile below the scar, the rocks of beautiful variegation and romantic shubbery. We there proceeded up the brook, the pebbles of which I found incrusted with a soft petrified coating, calcarious, slimy, and of a light brown colour.

I saw the various strata of the limestone mountains approach daylight in extensive and striking bands, running nearly horizontal, and a rent in them (from whence the brook issued) of perpendicular immense rocks.

On turning the corner of one of these, and seeing the rent in the complete—good heavens! what was my astonishment! The *Alps*, the *Pyrenees, Killarney, Loch Lomond*, or any other wonder of the kind I had ever seen, do not afford such a chasm. Consider yourself in a winding street, with houses above 100 yards high on each side of you;—then figure to yourself a cascade rushing from an upper window, and tumbling over carts, waggons, fallen houses, & c. in promiscuous ruin, and perhaps a cockney idea may be formed of this tremendous cliff. But if you would conceive it properly, depend upon neither pen nor pencil, for 'tis impossible for either to give you an adequate idea of it.—I can say no more than I believe the rocks to be above 100 yards high, that in several places they project above 100 yards over the base, and approach the opposite rock so near that one would almost imagine it possible to lay a plank from one to the other. At the upper end of this rent (which may be about 300 yards horizontally long) there gushes a most threatening cascade through a rude arch of monstrous rocks, and tumbling through many fantastic masses of its own forming, comes to a rock of entire petrifaction, down which it has a variety of picturesque breaks, before it enters a channel that conveys it pretty uniformly away.

I take these whimsical shapes to be the children of the spray, formed in droughty weather, when the water has time to evaporate, and leave the stony matter uninterrupted in its cohesion. These petrifactions are very porous; crumbly when dry, and pulpy when wet, and shaped a good deal like crooked knotty wood.

Adam Walker, 20th September, 1779

Addendum to the fourth edition of West's *Guide to the Lakes,* 1789

EDWARD DAYES (1763–1804) *was a gifted water-colourist and engraver, draughtsman of the Duke of York and an important influence on many of the younger painters of the period, particularly his own brilliant pupil Thomas Girtin and on the young Turner. His* Picturesque Tour of Yorkshire and Derbyshire *was destined to include a number of engravings, only some of which were completed, to illustrate the sublime descriptions of the text. He never lived to complete the project, dying, tragically, by his own hand in 1804. The book was published by his friends to raise money for his widow.*

The Soul of Salvator Rosa at Gordale

Here a stupendous mass of rocks forms a ravine, through the bosom of which flows a considerable stream. This opening contracts till you are led into a corner, where every object conspires to produce one of the grandest spectacles in nature. The rocks dart their bold and rugged fronts to the heavens, and impending fearfully over the head of the spectator, seem to threaten his immediate destruction. Here rock is piled on rock in the most terrific majesty; and what greatly improves the grandeur of the scene, is an impetuous Cataract, that rushes down their dark centre, almost tearing it up, as it were, with its irresistible force, the very foundations of the earth. Good heavens, what a scene! how sublime! Imagine blocks of limestone rising to the immense height of two hundred yards, and in some places projecting twenty over their bases; add to this the roaring of the Cataract, and the sullen murmurs of the wind that howls around; and something like an idea of the savage aspect of the place may be conceived.

Here the timid will find an end put to their journey: myself and the guide, with some difficulty, ascended the crags up to the fall, keeping the water to the right hand, and arriving at a large opening, where massy fragments of rocks are scattered about in the most wild and fantastic manner. Above, through a large hole, at the height of twenty or thirty yards, poured down the collected force of the whole stream, which forms the cascade below. This is, perhaps, the finest part of the whole place, and should by no means be neglected, however difficult the ascent to it may be. Return hence was impossible; we therefore scrambled to the top of the rocks, a height of not less than three hundred yards from the stream below: here, on looking back into the yawning gulph we had passed, the words of Shakespeare came forcibly into my mind:

"Stand still—how fearful
And dizzy 'tis to cast one's eye so low
I'll look no more,
Lest my brain turn, and the deficient sight
Topple down headlong."

The opening in the rocks, which gives passage to the stream, is said to have been carved by the force of a great body of water, which collected in a sudden storm, some time about the year 1730. The lover of drawing will be much delighted with this place: immensity and horror are its inseparable companions, uniting together to form subjects of the most awful cast. The very soul of Salvator Rosa would hover with delight over these regions of confusion.

Edward Dayes, *A Picturesque Tour in Yorkshire and Derbyshire,* 1805

An Ascent of Gordale Waterfall

After keeping to the footpath close to the stream, for a short time I lost sight of him, for he had abruptly turned round a projecting point of rock.—I followed—and, in a moment,—stood before "Gordale Scar", a scene it is utterly impossible for me to properly describe; but the feeling that overpowered me was an implied safety of situation with a consciousness of great fear. I never recollect the awe of Nature's arm being so strongly put upon me, and I write this with the recollection of having encountered many perils and gales of wind in many seas. It appears to have been a solid mass of rock, rent asunder by a convulsion of nature, affording a passage to the pent up torrent which rushes through the yawning fissure, and revelling in its liberty, dashes downwards, forming a grand and terrific cataract.

By the projection from either side of its base, the two rocks, though considerably distant at the bottom, admit a narrow line of light from above, whilst the cleft in the rocks' sides, or wherever a lodgement of earth appears, the deep and glossy green of the yew refreshes the eye in its wandering over the pale grey of the vast rock. My guide waded across the water at the shallowest part, and considerably above his knees, with all the unconcern imaginable. I asked him if he intended me to follow the same feat:—he only answered by pointing to the top of the rock in the extreme left of the torrent, and as nearly perpendicular as possible, "we must go up there." I never thought the word "must" sounded so imperious, particularly from so juvenile a voice. I, however, obeyed him, and certainly did it in a very slovenly manner: he had been accustomed to jumping from stone to stone, perhaps from very infancy, and the precision of his eye rarely if ever betrayed him: as I had not danced in the same school I soon found that the knee was a limit to the water's encroachment, and that the sooner I was at it, the more satisfactory the proceeding would be. As my guide did not laugh, I was sure that all was natural, and that where I had been others had been before. I write this before a comfortable fire, and can now look upon my "crossings" merrily, though at the period of pursuing them my face was more conical than comical: the wind was exceedingly high, three days of rain had swollen the waters, and the torrent was rushing impetuously down, whilst I had to secure my footing upon the top of the least shelving of rock at the fall's base. I followed my fearless companion, who commenced climbing with the speed of a young goat. For some time—for travelling here is rather slow—our track was within a few inches of the fall; and wherever I paused to take breath, my remaining breath was almost taken from me by the awfulness of my situation. At last we reached the summit of the mountain, when, looking down into the chasm beneath, horror and immensity were defined with thrilling truth; but nothing short of the reality could give you the slightest notion of this spot. A journey of fifty miles would be most amply repaid by a visit to Gordale Scar alone, exclusive of the attractions of the Cove, Jannet's Cove, and Malham Tarn.

Frederic Montagu, *Gleanings in Craven,* 1838

ROBERT STORY *(d. 1860) schoolmaster and parish clerk of Gargrave, was a minor poet who enjoyed a slender reputation in his own day. Influenced by Scott, Byron and the whole complex paraphernalia of the Gothic tradition, Story's best work has a considerable period charm.*

Banditti at Gordale

(The beautiful Lady Margaret Percy, of the famous Northumberland family, is visiting the Yorkshire Dales "to see the beauties of the district" and to enjoy the "pleasures of the Chase". In the company of a mysterious guide—dressed in the habit of a monk—she is separated from her noble companions and taken to view the terrors of Gordale in a thunderstorm.)

Through vista wide and rugged, showed
A sight—the man that ne'er gloried
Such to behold, needs ne'er aspire
To Painter's brush, or Poet's lyre!
—Still towered in front, and on each hand
The rocks in masses high and grand,
Formless, or cast in every form
The granite taken from time and storm,
And where they tower'd most great and high,
An opening gleamed that showed the sky,
And poured, as from a bursting cloud,
A constant rapid, fierce, and loud;
Which, dashed from ledge to ledge, at last
With foam and brawl the strangers passed.
So deep was now the cavern's might
That the broad fall of water's white
Resembled, dashing through the gloom
A gush of moonshine from the womb
Of some huge cloud!
But soon a flash
More bright then comes from water's dash,
An instant clothed, with fiery gleam,
The startled cave and rushing stream,
And, swiftly followed on the flame,
A crash of thunder o'er them came,
So fierce and loud that in its roar,
The torrent's sound was heard no more,
And seemed as every separate rock
Returned an echo to the shock!

"Lady away!" with voice that far
Was heard amid the tempest's jaw,
Exclaimed the Guide, with outstretched arm,
And pale and breathless with alarm,

Aysgarth Falls and Bridge—engraved by Sparrow, 1774

Greta Bridge by John Sell Cotman—painted whilst Cotman was staying with the Morritt family, at Rokeby, in 1805. (Reproduced by permission of the Trustees of the British Museum)

Gordale Scar by James Ward, 1812. (The Tate Gallery, London)

Weathercote Cave by J. M. W. Turner, 1818; engraved by S. Middiman for Whitaker's *Richmondshire*, 1821

The Lady Margaret almost sunk
On the firm bosom of the Monk
Who bore her from that cavern wild
As father would sustain a child. . . .

Beneath a small green knoll they stood,
Washed by a brooklet's falling flood,
And by many a wild shrub clomb
And decked by many a flower whose home
—Away from the crowded town—is still
In the sweet glen and heathy hill
A spot retired, but widely known;
To every wandering tourist shewn,
Whom love of nature calls from far
To view the wondrous Cove and Scar.
The peasant skilled in fairy lore
Will tell of revels here of yore
—Ere yet the Gospel's holy light.

Dispelled the shades of Pagan night—
Brings those that love the wold and wave;
And hence he names it Gennet's Cave.
For Cave there is of ample room*
In that green hillock's rocky womb;
Its entrance bare, polluted now,
But then so veiled by furze and bough,
The boldest guess would scarcely dare
To say that such existed there.
—The Outlaw, stopping, tore aside
The woodbine-twigs in blossomed pride
From the Cave's aperture; and bade
The lady enter undismayed.
One glance she gave the fleeting sky,
A second secured the Outlaw's eye
Of proper ill as ought to speak,
Calm was his glance, and calm his cheek;
And Margaret entered, glad to gain
A shelter from the fire and rain.

*I have used a little poetic licence in the description of this Cave. Whatever it may formerly have been, it certainly is not now of sufficient magnitude for the events of which I have made it the same.

On table rough of mountain stone
A single lamp of iron shone,
Discovering, as it flashed aloof,
Each point and angle of the roof;
And lighting many a visage grim
And stalwart arm, and sinewy limb!
For, seated round on branches wild,
A savage group with can and pot
Held deep carouse in Gennet's grot
—St. Mary! does no sign of fear
In Margaret's countenance appear?
No—she whose hurt had quelled of late
When every flash seemed winged with fate,
Turned on her treacherous Guide an eye
Proud and majestic, calm and high
As if to pierce his soul, and dare
One lawless thought to waken there!
As if, in mock and virtue strong,
Her glance could blast who offered wrong!

Robert Story, "The Hunting of Craven", from *Craven Blossoms,* 1826

Yordas

Having travelled about four miles from Ingleton, we find ourselves at Yordas Cave, one of the principal objects of this excursion. It is situated near the east end of the vale, under the mountain Gregroof, and to which we turn a little out of the road, on the left, over a carpet of bent grass interspersed with fragments of grey rock.—The cave does not appear till we get through some sheepfolds, and are within a few yards of its entrance, which is rather alarming; for we no sooner descend gently through a rude arched opening, four yards by seven, than we see stones of enormous weight pendant from the roof, apparently loose, and ready to fall down upon our heads. From these surprising objects our attention is directed to the solemn and gloomy mansions which we now enter, when the noise of a waterfall is heard in the distance. The roof rises to a height concealed in darkness, and large drops, distilling therefrom, fall among the stones at the bottom with a solemn sound: this, added to the flowing of an invisible stream heard just before us, and the slipperiness of the loose stones under our feet, rouses our apprehension for personal safety, and we stop short.

Our guide now places himself upon the fragment of a rock, and strikes up his light, consisting of six or eight candles, pit into as many holes of a stick, with which, by the help of a long pole fixed therein, he can illuminate a considerable space. His tobacco-pipe, being prepared and lighted, is held in his mouth, with his flambeau in one hand and a staff in the other, the cock of his hat being placed before, he gives us the signal of a march by, "Now come along".—Though under the conduct of such an experienced leader, and assured that the danger is merely imaginary, we journey on with cautious steps.

The cave opens into an apartment so spacious and extensive, that, with all the blaze of our elevated candles, we could scarcely see either its roof or its walls. On turning to the right, we immediately lose sight of day; the noise of the cataract increases, and we soon find ourselves on the brink of a subterranean rivulet.—No cave of romance, no den of lions, giants or serpents, nor any haunts of ghosts or fairies, were ever described more frightfully gloomy and dismal than this now before us.

After passing the brook, and cautiously proceeding 30 or 40 yards further, we are under the necessity of climbing over a rugged heap of huge rocks, which had, some time or other, fallen from the roof or side of the cave; but now are incrusted over with a smooth calcareous substance. Being at length more habituated to darkness, our light had a better effect; the high smooth roof and walls were seen distinctly, as well as the curious petrifactions hanging therefrom. On the right we observed among several other curiously incrusted figures, a projecting, which our guide called the Bishop's Throne, from its great resemblance to that appendage of a cathedral; on the other side a seemingly emblematic monument springs from the wall, about three yards above the floor, with various uncouth representations, of which that of a lion's head is the most conspicuous. Another confused mass of incrusted matter bears some resemblance to a large organ.—We now enter a narrow pass of five or six yards, where the roof is supported by seven pillars; there is room only for one person in breadth; but the height is very considerable. The internal brook pushes along this crevice, which renders it the most difficult part of our subterranean excursion, and which, after great rains, effectually excludes a passage.

The slipperiness of the stones had nearly occasioned an unpleasant event during our visit to this cave; our guide, with his collection of luminaries, tumbled into the brook, and had nearly left us in darkness; but when he fell, we were particularly afraid lest he should drop into some deep chasm of the rock, which might have proved fatal. However he arose without receiving much injury; and resuming our journey, we soon reached the cascade which we had heard for some time at a distance. It issues from an opening in the rock, and falls about four or five yards into a circular apartment some visitants have named the Chapter-house.

The broad sheet of water, the spray arising from the fall, and the beautiful petrifications, all illuminated with the light of the candles, produce effects in this natural edifice which the puny efforts of art may attempt to imitate, but in vain.

Near the Chapter-house, there is an opening, through which a person may creep, and arrive at other large apartments; but we did not attempt the experiment. The colonnade affords a number of curious recesses: its pillars are broad, extremely thin, rudely indented, and perforated in several places. On our return we could discern the nature and dimensions of this spacious cavern more distinctly. It walls are a sort of black marble, the roof pretty smooth, and beautifully veined with red and white; the floor is strewed with stones and pieces of rock. The whole length of this singular cavern is between 50 and 60 yards; its breadth 13 yards; and height 27 feet. On entering this cave its area enlarges every way, and we reach the opposite wall, after walking about 23 yards; the principal part, just described, lies to the right; but it extends also on the other hand, and unfolds some wonderful closets, called Yordas Bedchamber, Yordas Oven, &c. Here also the brook buries itself still deeper, and proceeds under the ground to Keldhead, before mentioned. This brook rises in the mountains above Yordas, and falls in among the rocks just before it reaches that cave.

We leave the dark excavations with redoubled sentiments of gratitude towards the Almighty, for the blessings he affords us in the light of the sun, which, after being buried for some time in these murky regions, we now enjoy with still greater pleasure.

John Housman, *A Descriptive Tour and Guide To the Lakes, Caves Mountains and other Natural Curiosities in Cumberland, Westmorland, Lancashire and part of the West Riding of Yorkshire,* 1800

Weathercote Cave—Sublime and Terrible

. . . we proceeded about a hundred and twenty yards higher when we came to *Weathercote-cave* or *cove* the most surprising natural curiosity of the kind in the island of *Great Britain*. It is a stupendous subterranean cataract in a huge cave, the top of which is on the same level with the adjoining lands. On our approach to its brink, our ears and eyes were equally astonished with the sublime and terrible. The margin was surrounded with trees and shrubs, the foliage of which was of various shapes and colours, which had an excellent effect, both in guarding and ornamenting the steep and rugged precipices on every side. Where the eye could penetrate through the leaves and branches, there was room for the imagination to conceive this cavern more dreadful and horrible, if possible, than it was in reality. The cave is of a lozenge form, and divided into two by a rugged and grotesque arch of limestone rock: The whole length from south to north is about sixty yards, and the breadth about half its length. At the south end is the entrance down into the little cave; in the right of which is a subterranean passage under the rocks, and a petrifying well: A stranger cannot but take notice of a natural seat and table in a corner of this grotesque room, well suited for a poet or philosopher: Here he may be secluded from the bustle of the world, though not from the noise; the uniform roaring however of the cascades will exclude from the ear every other sound, and his retirement will conceal him from every object that might divert the eye. Having descended with caution from rock to rock, we passed under the arch and came into the great cave, where we stood some time in silent astonishment to view this amazing cascade. The perpendicular height of the north corner of this cave, was found by an exact measurement to be thirty six yards; near eleven yards from the top issues a torrent of water out of an hole in the rock, about the dimensions of the large door in a church, sufficient to turn several mills, with a curvature which shews, that it has had a steep descent before it appears in open day; and falls twenty five yards at a single stroke on the rocks at the bottom, with a noise that amazes the most intrepid ear. The water sinks as it falls amongst the rocks and pebbles at the bottom, running by a subterranean passage about a mile, where it appears by the side of the turnpike road, visiting on its way other caverns of *Ginglepot* and *Hurtlepot.* The cave is filled with the spray that arises from the water dashing against the bottom, and the sun happening to shine very brightly, we had a small vivid rainbow within a few yards of us, for colour, size and situation, perhaps nowhere else to be equalled. An huge rock that had sometimes been rolled down by the impetuosity of the stream, and was suspended between us and the top of the cascade, like the coffin of *Mahomet* at *Medina*, had an excellent effect in the scene, Though the stream had polished the surfaces of the pebbles on which it fell at the bottom by rolling them against each other; yet its whole force was not able to drive from its native place the long black moss that firmly adhered to the large immoveable rocks. We were tempted to descend into a dark chamber at the very bottom of the cave, covered over with a ceiling of rock above thirty yards thick, and from thence behind the cascade, at the expense of having our cloaths a little wet and dirtied, when the noise became tremendous, and the idea for personal safety awful and alarming. We were informed that in a great drought the divergency of the stream is so small that we might with safety go quite round the cascade. At the bottom we were shewn a crevice where we might descend to the subterranean channel, which would lead us to *Ginglepot*, and perhaps much further; we were also shewn above, a shallow passage between the strata of rocks, along which we might crawl to the orifice out of which the cascade issued, where it was high enough to walk erect, and where we might have the honour of making the first expedition for discoveries; no creature having yet proceeded in that passage out of sight of daylight: But as we were apprehensive the pleasures would not be compensated by the dangers and difficulties in our progress, we did not attempt to explore these new regions.

John Hutton, *A Tour to the Caves,* 1781

The Stygian Gulphs of Ribblesdale

Horton is about six miles from Settle, and the last village on the upper road to Askrigg. From Horton I immediately entered on the moors, where all is dreary, wild and solitary. Having proceeded about a mile, I was surprised by a most horrid roaring to the right, which I discovered to arise from a considerable stream ingulphen by a chasm, as black as the entrance into the informal regions.* It is reported, but the tale is rather improbable, that a short time ago a person was let down into this gulph by a rope, to the depth of one hundred; but his courage failing him, he roared out lustily, and his companions drew him up again. I threw several large stones into this Stygian gulph but could not hear when they reached the bottom.

Scarcely had the surprise excited by the above spectacle subsided, when the road again brought me on to the edge of a precipice, where the River Ribble is dashed from rock to rock in wild variety.† Here Silence never dwells, but horrid Uproar holds his everlasting reign! This place does not prevent a single fall only, but a succession of them, where cataract tumbles over cataract; the power of the water having a passage under a solemn mass of rock, the bulk of which is

*I think this place is called Hunt Pot.
†Probably called Lingill.

incredible, and from it issues with a hideous din, that deafens the sense. In some places the water by undermining the crags, has precipitated huge fragments in the gulph below. With such a scene under the eye, alone on an open moor, the heavens foreboding a storm, and not a single habitation to be seen as far the utmost stretch of human ken, what language could be adequate to describe its effects on the mind, or the feelings it excited! A considerable quantity of rain having fallen, it contributed greatly to increase the grandeur of the whole. Those who are fond of the wild, will find enough to satisfy them: but it would be advisable to engage the attendance of some person from Horton who, by possessing a knowledge of the paths, might be able to shew them its wonder from below. My being alone, prevented me from descending into these scenes of chaotic confusion.

The road in many places runs along the edge of steep declivities, down which there is great danger of being precipitated, particularly in stormy weather. It is reported that a lady and gentleman in a post-chaise, venturing this way, were blown over, and narrowly escaped falling to the bottom. Scarcely a tree is to be seen, and all the mighty expanse consists but of one tiresome sweep intersecting another.

Edward Dayes, *A Picturesque Tour in Yorkshire and Derbyshire,* 1805

The Awfulness of Dib Scar

After plunging again into the thicket, and pursuing the different windings which opened a passage through the wood, we were at length brought into a deep and solitary glen, beset on each side with steep and craggy precipices, whose perilous ascent made me quake as I thought of the danger I had been in had I come alone in quest of this object of nature's gloomiest contrivance. As we advanced up the avenue, the stroke of the woodman's hatchet, whom we had left on the height, which the loneliness of the place made audible, was a relief from the indescribable tremor which pervaded the senses of my guide and me, as we walked along in moody silence, making the place re-echo with the sound of our feet, which occasionally struck against some broken fragments of stones, which strewed the pathway before us. The hoarse croaking of the raven, which seemed terrified at the approach of a human footstep, and the sudden fluttering of their wings as the feathered tenantry began to forsake their lonely residence, were a signal for us to expect a speedy sight of the bluff battlement which rose on the extremities of the two environing crags. On reaching the scar we were struck with the dismalness of its appearance: its whole contour is but an expression of hoary grandeur and fallen pomp, which nothing but its hereditary strength and unbending haughtiness could have supported through so many ages. We, as it were, however, felt the power of its native dignity, and were awed in the presence of so august a monument of true and natural greatness. It forms like a huge battery on either side, and in front it resembles an old castle, built after the fashion of ancient times, with a porthole at the top, to pour unseen and immediate destruction upon an enemy, should he dare to make an encroachment on its warlike territory. The roof from off this part has been scathed, as if in some desperate struggle to maintain its hard contested right, and the batteries on either side have been partly demolished by the slow but sure engines of consuming time, but still retain their natural prowess and unshrinking attitude of self-preservation, and an earthquake alone could remove them from their firm and entire foundations. The altitude of the rock, as nearly as I can guess (only judging from memory) may be about two hundred feet. The strata are irregularly placed, and beneath is a spacious canopy, perhaps seven yards high, from the base sloping upwards, under which are rows of shelves inartificially arranged, on which the weary *pilgrim* in this desolate spot may sit, and fancy himself shut up in total seclusion, so calm and peaceable is this retired haunt, so seldom visited by men.

Rev. James Leslie Armstrong, *Scenes in Craven*, in a Series of Letters containing interesting sketches of characters and notices of some of the Principal natural curiosities of the most picturesque and romantic district in Yorkshire, 1835

4. A Prospect of Perfection

It was the Industrial Revolution, more than anything else, that shaped our attitude to the countryside. The notion of the unspoiled hills and dales of the Pennines as a reservoir of beauty, goodness and simplicity, notwithstanding the fact that the Industrial Revolution was in evidence in the Dales themselves, grew throughout the nineteenth century, to become a dominant feeling.

Of course it can be argued such a view was false. The Dales did have industry, did suffer from economic decline, the people were no better and no worse than anywhere else in England. But the growth of industrial Lancashire and West Riding, with their hideous slums, infant mortality, suffering and unrest, became an increasingly savage contrast to the more slowly changing communities in the Dales.

So the mythology began, the myth of the Dales as a source of goodness and beauty. Like all mythologies, artists and writers gave it credence, and in the case of the Yorkshire Dales some major figures of the nineteenth century were to seek in the Dales symbols of their own spiritual salvation which have continued to have a potency for us.

Penhill Beacon—and Aysgarth Falls

See beacon'd Penhill, view its stately rise,
Whose scaling altitude invades the skies;
Go, climb its brow, its airy tracks explore,
Where breezes wanton from the western shore;
Freely survey fair Cleveland's distant strand,
And golden Durham's terminating land.
The eye descending now o'er Penhill's base,
We decent Witton's pleasing prospects trace.
Here fleecy troops adorn the sloping green,
There grouping herds diversify the scene;

Now waves voluptuously the pregnant blade
With Bolton's swelling woods of deeper shade;
While the gay buck, as if his hours vain,
Asserts the empire of his active plain;
In rank supreme among the brutal race,
When smoaks his haunch as he inspires the chase
Last in the view, wild surging mountains lie,
That blend their distant summits with the sky.

But now, O Aysgarth, let my rugged verse
The wonders of thy cataracts rehearse.
Long ere the toiling sheets to view appear
They found a prelude to the pausing ear.
Now in rough accents by the pendent wood
Rolls in stern majesty the foaming flood;
Revolving eddies now with raging sway,
To Aysgarth's ample arch incline their way.
Playful and slow the curling circles move
As when soft breezes fan the saving grove;
Till prone again, with tumult's wildest roar,
Recoil the billows, reels the giddy shore;
Dash'd from its rocky bed, the winnow'd spray
Remounts the regions of the cloudy way,
While warring columns fiercer combats join,
And make the rich, rude, thundering scene divine.

Thomas Maude, *Wensleydale—or rural contemplation,* 1780
fourth edition, 1816

The Wordsworths in Wensleydale I

On leaving Askrigg we turned aside to see another waterfall, 'twas a beautiful morning with driving snow-showers that disappeared by fits, and unveiled the east which was all one delicious pale orange colour. After walking through two fields we came to a mill which we pass'd and in a moment a sweet little valley opened before us, with an area of grassy ground, and a stream dashing over various lamina of black rocks close under a bank covered with firs. The bank and stream on our left, another woody bank on our right, and the flat meadow in front from which, as at Buttermere, the stream had retired as it were to hide itself under the shade. As we walked up this delightful valley we were tempted to look back perpetually on the brook which reflected the orange light of the morning among the gloomy rocks with a brightness varying according to the agitation of the current. The steeple of Askrigg was between us and the east, at the bottom of the valley; it was not a quarter of a mile distant, but oh! how far we were from it. The two banks seemed to join before us with a facing of rock common to them both, when we reached this point the valley opened out again, two rocky banks on each side, which, hung with ivy and moss and fringed luxuriantly with brushwood, ran parallel to each other and then approaching with a gentle curve, at their point of union, presented a lofty waterfall, the termination of the valley. Twas a keen frosty morning, showers of snow threatening us but the sun bright and active; we had a task of twenty one miles to perform in a short winter's day, all this put our minds in such a state of excitation that we were no unworthy spectators of this delightful scene. On a nearer approach the water seemed to fall down a tall arch or rather nitch which had shaped itself by insensible moulderings in the wall of an old castle. We left this spot with reluctance but highly exhilarated. When we had walked about a mile and a half we overtook two men with a string of ponies and some empty carts. I recommended to D. to avail herself of this opportunity of husbanding her strength, we rode with them more than two miles, twas bitter cold, the wind driving the snow behind us in the best stile of a mountain storm. We soon reached an Inn at a place called Hardraw, and descending from our vehicles, after warming ourselves by the cottage fire we walked up the brook side to take a view of a *third* waterfall. We had not gone above a few hundred yards between two winding rocky banks before we came full upon it. It appeared to throw itself in a narrow line from a lofty wall of rock; the water which shot manifestly some distance from the rock seeming from the extreme height of the fall to be dispersed before it reached the bason, into a thin shower of snow that was toss'd about like snow blown from the roof of a house. We were disappointed in the cascade though the introductory and accompanying banks were a noble mixture of grandeur and beauty. We walked up to the fall and what would I not give if I could convey to you the images and feelings which were then communicated to me. After cautiously sounding our way over stones of all colours and sizes encased in the clearest ice formed by the spray of the waterfall, we found the rock which before had seemed a perpendicular wall extending itself over us like the ceiling of a huge cave; from the summit of which the water shot directly over our heads into a bason and among fragments of rock wrinkled over with masses of ice, white as snow, or rather as D. says like congealed froth. The water fell at least two yards from us and we stood directly behind it, the excavation not so deep in the rock as to impress any feeling of darkness, but lofty and magnificent, and in connection with the adjoining banks excluding as much of the sky as could well be spared from a scene so exquisitely beautiful. The spot where we stood was as dry as the chamber in which I am now sitting, and the incumbent rock of which the groundwork was limestone veined and dappled with colours which melted into each other in every possible variety. On the summit of the cave were three festoons or rather wrinkles in the rock which ran parallel to each other like the folds of a curtain when it was drawn up; each of them was hung with icicles of various length, and nearly in the middle of the festoons in the deepest valley made by their waving line the stream shot from between the rows of icicles in irregular fits of strength and with a body of water that momently varied. Sometimes it threw itself into the bason in one continued curve, sometimes it was interrupted almost midway in its fall, and, being blown towards us, part of the water fell at no great distance from our feet like the heaviest thunder shower. In such a situation you have at every moment a feeling of the presence of the sky. Above the highest point of the waterfall large fleecy clouds drove over our heads and the sky appeared of a blue more than usually brilliant. The rocks on each side, which, joining with the sides of the cave, formed the vista of the brook were chequered with three diminutive waterfalls or rather veins of water each of which was a miniature of all that summer and winter can produce of delicate beauty. The rock in the centre of these falls where the water was most abundant, deep black, with adjoining parts yellow, white, purple, violet and dove colour'd, or covered with water-plants of the most vivid green, and hung with streams and fountains of ice that in some places seemed to conceal the verdure of the plants and the variegated colours of the rocks and in some places to render their hues more splendid. I cannot express to you the enchanted effect produced by this Arabian scene of colour as the wind blew aside the great waterfall behind which we stood and hid and revealed each of these faery cataracts in irregular succession or displayed them with various gradations of distinctness, as the intervening spray was thickened or dispersed. In the luxury of our imaginations we could not help feeding on the pleasure which in the heat of a July noon this cavern would spread through a frame exquisitely sensible. That huge rock of ivy on the right! the bank winding round on the left with all its living foliage, and the breeze stealing up the valley and bedewing the cavern with the faintest imaginable spray. And then the murmur of water, the quiet, the seclusions, and a long summer day to dream in! Have I not tired you? With difficulty we tore ourselves away, and on returning to the cottage we found we had been absent an hour. Twas a short one to us, we were in high spirits, and off we drove, and will you believe me when I tell you we walked the next ten miles, by the watch over a high mountain road, thanks to the wind that drove behind us and a good road, in two hours and a quarter, a marvellous feat of which D. will long tell. Well! we rested in a tempting inn, close by Garsdàle chapel, a lowly house of prayer in a charming little valley, here we stopp'd a quarter of an hour and then off to Sedbergh 7 miles farther in an hour and thirty five minutes, the wind was still at our backs and the road delightful.

William Wordsworth, *Letter* to Samuel Taylor Coleridge, 24th & 27th December, 1799

HART LEAP WELL *is situated by the roadside alongside the old Askrigg–Richmond road, a short distance to the west of Catterick Camp, capped in incongruous concrete and on the edge of a military training area. Wordsworth's poem, from his early* Lyrical Ballads *period, uses the legend of the hunted deer, on the site of whose death-leap an ornamental well-head was constructed, as a fable of man's callousness against the innocence of Nature—a theme which runs through much Romantic literature.*

Hart Leap Well

As I from Hawes to Richmond did repair,
It chanced that I saw standing in a dell
Three aspens at three corners of a square;
And one, not four yards distant, near a well.

What this imported I could ill divine:
And, pulling now the rein my horse to stop,
I saw three pillars standing in a line,—
The last stone-pillar on a dark hill-top.

The trees were grey, with neither arms nor head;
Half wasted the square mound of tawny green;
So that you just might say, as then I said,
"Here in old time the hand of man hath been."

I looked upon the hill both far and near,

More doleful place did never eye survey;
It seemed as if the spring-time came not here,
And Nature here were willing to decay.

I stood in various thoughts and fancies lost,
When one, who was in shepherd's garb attired,
Came up to the hollow:—him did I accost,
And what this place might be I then enquired.

The Shepherd stopped, and that same story told
Which in my former rhyme I have rehearsed.
"A jolly place," said he, "in times of old!
But something ails it now: the spot is curst.

"You see these lifeless stumps of aspen wood—
Some say they are beeches, others elms—
These were the bower; and here a mansion stood,
The finest palace of a hundred realms!

"The arbour does its own condition tell;
You see the stones, the fountains, and the stream;
But as to the great Lodge! you might as well
Hunt half a day for a forgotten dream.

"There's neither dog nor heifer, horse nor sheep
Will wet his lips within that cup of stone;
And oftentimes, when all are fast asleep,
This water doth send forth a dolorous groan.

"Some say that here a murder has been done,
And blood cries out for blood: but, for my part,
I've guessed, when I've been sitting in the sun,
That it was all for that unhappy Hart."

William Wordsworth, from *Hart Leap Well,* 1799

The Wordsworths in Wensleydale II

When we passed through the village of Wensly my heart was melted away with dear recollections, the Bridge, the little water-spout, the steep hill, the Church. They are among the most vivid of my own inner visions, for they were the first objects that I saw after we were left to ourselves, and had turned our whole hearts to Grasmere as a home in which we were to rest. The Vale looked most beautiful each way. To the left the bright silver stream inlaid the flat and very green meadows, winding like a serpent. To the Right we did not see it so far, it was lost among trees and little hills. I could not help observing as we went along how much more *varied* the prospects of Wensly Dale are in summer time than I could have thought possible in the winter. This seemed to be in great measure owing to the trees being in leaf, and forming groves, and screens, and thence little openings upon recesses and concealed retreats which in winter only made part of the one great vale. The *beauty* of the summer time here as much excels that of the winter as the variety, owing to the excessive greeness of the fields, and the trees in leaf half concealing, and where they do not conceal, softening the hard bareness of the limey white roofs. One of our horses seemd to grow a little restive as we went through the first village, a long village on the side of a hill. It grew worse and worse, and at last we durst not go on any longer. We walked a while, and then the Post-Boy was obliged to take the horse out and go back for another. We seated ourselves again snugly in the Post-Chaise. The wind struggled about us and rattled the window and gave a gentle motion to our chaise, but we were warm and at our ease within. Our station was at the Top of a hill, opposite Bolton Castle, the Eure flowing beneath. William has since wrote a sonnet on this our imprisonment—Hard was the Durance Queen compared with ours. Poor Mary! Wm. fell asleep, lying upon my breast and I upon Mary. I lay motionless a long time, but I was at last obliged to move. I became very sick and continued so for some time after the Boy brought the horse to us. Mary had been a little sick but it soon went off. We had a sweet ride till we came to a public house on the side of a hill where we alighted and walked down to see the waterfalls. The sun was not yet set, and the woods and fields were spread over with the yellow light of Evening, which made their greeness a thousand times more green. There was too much water in the River for the beauty of the falls, and even the banks were less interesting than in winter. Nature had entirely got the better in her struggles against the giants who first cast the mould of these works; for indeed it is a place that did not in winter remind one of God, but one could not help feeling as if there had been the agency of some "Mortal Instrument" which Nature had been struggling against without making a perfect conquest. There was something so wild and new in this feeling, knowing as we did in the inner man that God alone had laid his hand upon it that I could not help regretting the want of it, besides it is a pleasure to a real lover of Nature to give winter all the glory he can, for summer *will* make its own way, and speak its own praises.

Dorothy Wordsworth, *Grasmere Journal,* October 1802

JOHN NICHOLSON *(1790–1843) of Bingley, the 'Airedale Poet', like Robert Story, is another local poet who only just failed to make a national reputation. A self-taught man, his verse is inevitably imitative, aiming at Byron but often achieving bathos. At his best he can sustain the grand manner, and his verse has vigour and gusto.*

Wharfedale's Noble Ruin

O Bolton, what a change! but still thou art
Noble in ruin, great in every part!
When we behold thee, signs of grandeur, gone,
Live on thy walls, and shine on every stone;
Thy shades are lovely through each varied day,
Thy rocks, thy woods, thy streams, where beauties play,
Lovely, when rosy in the east, the sun
Shows the high hills the cheerful day's begun.
Throughout the day, in all the hours which shine,
Peace, beauty, and rich scenery are thine;
But, when evening shades, like curtains, are
Thrown o'er the wheels of day's resplendent car;
When the broad moon, as tho' she rose to see
The hoary columns of antiquity;
Then, solemn grandeur greets the changing queen,
And Wharfe's reflection helps to light the scene.
At every well-selected point of view
Fresh scenes appear, as beautiful as new;
There the broad river shining with the sun,
And there the streams in eddying circles run:
Deep roars the Strid in snow-white robe of spray,
At rest below the wearied waters stay.
Thus have I seen the rock-verged deep at rest,
The foam, like marble, varying on its breast;
The ivy bower, secure from summer's heat,
For contemplation, what a blest retreat!
Where the gray ruin, and each varied hill,
Exceed in beauty fine descriptive skill.
There may the rural poet sit and write,
The learned astronomer survey the night;

The West Front of the Priory Church at Bolton; an engraving by Taylor for Whitaker's *Craven* (2nd edition), 1812

The Falls at Aysgarth by J. M. W. Turner, 1818; engraved by S. Middiman for Whitaker's *Richmondshire*, 1821

The White Doe of Rylstone—an engraving by Birket Foster for a Victorian edition of Wordsworth's poem, 1867

The love-sick lover here may sit and dream,
Lulled to his slumber by the murmuring stream:
But streams and woods, and waterfalls and flowers,
Lovers' retreats, rich lawns, and shady bowers,
Have all been sung in lovers' verse so fine,
No room is left to hold another line.

John Nicholson, *The Lyre of Ebor*, 1827

Chapel le Dale Churchyard

The little church, called Chapel-le-Dale, stands about a bow-shot from the family house. There they had all been carried to the font; there they had each led his bride to the altar; and there they had, each in his turn, been borne upon the shoulders of their friends and neighbours. Earth to earth they had been consigned for so many generations, that half of the soil of the church-yard consisted of their remains. A hermit who might wish his grave to be as quiet as his cell, could imagine no fitter resting place. On three sides was an irregular low stone wall, rather to mark the limits of the sacred ground, than to enclose it; on the fourth it was bounded by the brook whose waters proceed, by a subterranean channel, from Weathercote Cave. Two or three alders and rowan trees hung over the brook, and shed their leaves and seeds into the stream. Some bushy hazels grew at intervals along the lines of the wall; and a few ash trees as the winds had sown them. To the east and west some fields adjoin it in that state of half-cultivation which gives a human character to solitude: to the south, on the other side of the brook, the common, with its limestone rocks appearing everywhere above ground, extended to the foot of Ingleborough. A craggy hill, feathered with birch, sheltered it from the north.

The turf was as soft and fine as that of the adjoining hills; it was seldom broken so scanty was the population to which it was appropriated; scarcely a thistle or a nettle deformed it, and the few tombstones which had been placed there, were now themselves half-buried. The sheep came over the wall when they listed, and sometimes took shelter in the porch from the storm. Their voices and the cry of the kite wheeling above were the only sounds that were heard there, except when the single bell which hung in its niche over the entrance tinkled for service on the Sabbath day, or with a slower tongue gave notice that one of the children of the soil was returning to the earth from which he sprung.

Robert Southey, *The Doctor*, 1847

JOHN RUSKIN *made his first trip to the Dales whilst working on his massive* Modern Painters *(published in 1862) when he literally traced Turner's footsteps to visit the sites of his paintings. He became increasingly attached to the area, frequently visiting Bolton Abbey and staying with Walter Morrison at Malham Tarn.*

A Truly Wonderful Country

Hawes, Sunday March 6th, 1859
I had a most interesting drive yesterday, and Aysgarth force is out and out the finest thing I've seen in water in these islands; or perhaps the Falls of Clyde may be better, but nothing else certainly can come near this fair body of water, and one gets close to it as to the falls of the Rhine, the rocks going out in perfectly flat tables above it. The country round large in scale and beautifully rustic—wild walls everywhere — moss, crag, and mist, wilder than in the Highlands. This is a fine little inn—white home-made bread, fresh trout etc. — and really something like mountains visible out of the back window. . . .

Settle, March 7th, evening
The drive today has been the most interesting by far I ever had in England; a truly wonderful country—like the top of Cenis for desolation. Ingleborough a really fine mass of hill, the streams in the limestone behaving in the most extraordinary manner, perpetually falling into holes and coming out again half a mile afterwards. Pen y Ghent a fine hill too; and a wind blowing over the whole that seemed as if it would blow Ingleborough into Lancaster Bay. I got out at the top of the moors as the horses were feeding, just to feel what the wind was, and walked backwards and forwards for half an hour, and felt the better for it. I should think I have air enough to last me six months, at least.

The afternoon got splendidly clear as I got down off the moors, and the mosses in the stone walls were just one perpetual blaze of green fire; such curious villages too—all stone-built of course, and on stone; nothing else to build upon—fitted into the little hollows by the streams—nice respectable three-windowed houses—that kind of thing with tidy gardens and doors with brass knockers and all sorts of respectabilities, standing on ledges of the roughest rocks just jutting over the rushing streams, when one expects nothing but a Highland bothy—stepping stones instead of bridges up to the doors.

John Ruskin, *Journal*

At Malham Cove

In Malham Cove the stones of the brook were softer with moss than any silken pillow; the crowded oxalis-leaves yielded to the pressure of the hand, and were not felt; the cloven leaves of the herb-robert and robed clusters of its companion overflowed every rent in the rude crags with living balm; there was scarcely a place left by the tenderness of happy things where one might not lay down one's forehead on their warm softness and sleep.

John Ruskin, *Proserpina*

CHARLES KINGSLEY (1819–75), *novelist and social reformer, has achieved lasting fame with* The Water Babies. *A friend of Walter Morrison of Malham Tarn House, where he often stayed, Kingsley used the scenery of Malhamdale and Littondale (the Vendale of the novel) as the idyllic rural setting in which Tom, the pathetic child chimney-sweep can escape the cruelty and oppression of industrialism.*

Vendale

A mile off, and a thousand feet down. So Tom found it; though it seemed as if he could have chucked a pebble on to the back of the woman in the red petticoat who was weeding in the garden, or even across the dale to the rocks beyond.

For the bottom of the valley was just one field broad, and on the other side ran the stream; and above it, grey crag, grey down, grey stair, grey moor, walled up to heaven.

A quiet, silent, rich, happy place; a narrow crack cut deep into the earth; so deep, and so out of the way, that the bad bogies can hardly find it out. The name of the place is Vendale; and if you want to see it for yourself, you must go up into the High Craven, and search from Bolland Forest north of Ingleborough, to the Nine Standards and Cross Fell; and if you have not found it, you must turn south, and search the Lake Mountains, down to Scaw Fell and the sea; and then if you have not found it, you must go northwards again by merry Carlisle, and search the Cheviots all across, from Annan Water to Berwick Law; and then, whether you have found Vendale or not you will have found such a country, and such a people, as ought to make you proud of being a British boy.

So Tom went to go down; and first he went down three hundred feet of steep heather, mixed up with loose brown gritstone, as rough as a file; which was not pleasant to his poor little heels, as he came bump, stump, jump, down the steep. And still he thought he could throw a stone into the garden.

Then he went down three hundred feet of limestone terraces, one below the other, as straight as if a carpenter had ruled them with his ruler and then cut out with his chisel. There was no heath there but—

First, a little grass slope, covered with the prettiest flowers, rockrose and saxifrage, and thyme and basil, and all sorts of sweet herbs.

Then bump down a two-foot step of limestone.

Then another bit of grass and flowers.

Then bump down a one foot step.

Then another bit of grass and flowers for fifty yards, as steep as the house-roof, where he had to slide down on his dear little tail.

Then another step of stone, ten feet high; and there he had to stop himself and crawl along the edge to find a crack; for if he had rolled over, he would have rolled right into the old woman's garden and frightened her out of her wits.

Then, when he had found a dark narrow crack, full of green-stalked fern, such as hangs in the basket in the drawing room, and he had crawled through it, with knees and elbows, as he would down a chimney, there was another grass slope, and another step, and so on, till—oh dear me! I wish it was all over; and so did he. And yet he thought he could throw a stone into the old woman's garden.

At last he came to a bank of beautiful shrubs; whitebeam with its great silver-backed leaves, and mountain-ash, and oak; and below them cliff and crag, cliff and crag; while through the shrubs he could see the stream sparkling, and hear it murmur on the white pebbles. He did not know it was three hundred feet below.

Charles Kingsley, *The Water Babies,* 1863

The Beauties of Craven

Then, pardon me, if now I raise
A stave or two to sound the praise
Of Craven's hills an' caves;
Of fertile daals an flowin' brooks,
Of watter-faus an' shady brooks
Whar t'fir an' t'hazel waves.

Of frownin' cliffs an' lofty crags,

Which raise aloft their points an' jags
Romantic'ly an' grand;
Of rounded piles of limestone white,
Like batter'd towers of ancient might
Built by some giant's hand.

Were ye to come across our way,
On some fine, sunny, summer day,
When ye hev time to spar,
'Twad pleease me weel wi' ye to rove
To see sich spots as Malham Cove
An' far-famed Gordale Scar.

Thaar cliff uprear their shaggy waus,
An' down below a streamlet flows,
Wi' rough an' blusterin' din;
While masses of projectin' rock
Owerhing as if the slightest shock
Wad send 'em thunderin' in.

Amang sich varied scenes as these
Of hills, an' meadows, rocks an' trees,
I live fra trouble free:
The crowded city's grand display,
An' arts an' fashions proudly gay
Possess naa charm for me.

Tom Twistleton, from "Letter to Joe Steel" in
Poems in the Craven Dialect, 1907

5. The Curious and the Beautiful

It was perhaps inevitable, after the sense of wonder and intensity of feeling of the early tourists and aesthetes, that the growing demand for guide-books should produce a tendency towards repetition, staleness of phrase, and cliché, finally hardening into the hackneyed phraseology of the late Victorian and Edwardian guide-books, before the ultimate degradation of telegrammatic prose and a system of 'stars' to denote the principal attractions of a neighbourhood.

This was not so, however, with the first real guide-books that were published in the earlier part of the nineteenth century, books designed to help the traveller with essential information, but retaining a good prose style and a sense of vitality and freshness. It was, of course, a matter of directing the traveller to so-called 'beauty spots', generally viewpoints or 'prospects', often the self-same ones discovered by earlier poets or painters. Anything natural or man-made sufficiently out of the ordinary to be deemed a 'curiosity' also achieves a mention. Most of these features have now been institutionalized into tourist attractions, although a few are almost totally forgotten as tastes change.

It is, nonetheless, fascinating to realize just how influential earlier propagandists of the Dales have been in bringing the tourist industry into being. Disciples of the Romantic poets and painters themselves, they have shaped our attitudes, and our behaviour.

Three Sublime Peaks

But the most sublime features of this romantic district are the mountains of Ingleborough, Pennigant, and Wharnside. The perpendicular height of Ingleborough is, according to Mr. Jeffrey, exactly one mile above the level of the sea, but by other measurements and calculations it is much less. The base of this mountain is an immense mass of limestone; but towards the summit the rock is for the most part a sandy grit. The eastern and southern sides are extremely steep, the latter bending in the form of a crescent, with a deep morass at the bottom. On this side a boggy moor, and above half a mile in breadth, must be crossed in approaching the mountain from the village of Austwick, by the way of Cromack Farm, the nearest road from Settle. The north side of Ingleborough is less steep than the eastern and southern sides; but the western side is the most sloping, and the easiest ascent from eastern and southern sides. (The writer thinks it not amiss to mention this circumstance, and would advise every tourist that visits Ingleborough, or other mountains of this district, to provide himself with a guide; for want of this precaution he found himself bewildered amidst the rocks and morasses, and found the approach to Ingleborough on the southern side, from the village of Austwick, very laborious, chiefly through ignorance of the road.)

The sides, where not perpendicular, are springy: the ground indeed, to the very summit, emits water at every pore; for this mountain being the first check that the western clouds meet with in their passage from Ireland, is almost continually enveloped in mists, or washed with rains, which occasion an extraordinary degree of humidity. From this cause, however, the soil is covered with verdure, and flocks of sheep graze on the highest parts of the mountain. The top of Ingleborough is level and horizontal, extending in nearly an easterly and westerly direction, about half a mile in length, but of much less breadth. Here was formerly placed a beacon for giving the alarm to the country in case of sudden danger, particularly during the incursions of the Scots. From this stupendous elevation the prospects are romantic, sublime and extensive. To the east, the picturesque country of Craven presents a confused assemblage of hills, gradually diminishing in height, till they vanish in the horizon. Pennigant at the distance of four miles, appears almost within a leap. Towards the south, the rocks near Settle and Pendle hill, towering aloft seem close at hand. The northern and north-western prospect exhibits a mass of mountains; Wharnside is within distance of six miles; Snowden, Cross-fell etc. are clearly visible. Towards the west, the flat country of Lancashire lies as in a map. And the prospect extends far into the Irish sea, the nearest shores of which are almost 24 miles from Ingleborough. This mountain is said to be the first land that sailors descry in the voyage from Dublin to Lancaster. About the base are many deep holes or pits, called swallows.

Pennigant, about seven miles north from Settle, and four miles south east from Ingleborough, is a steep and towering mountain, of which the perpendicular height, according to Mr Jeffrey's measurement, is 1740 yards above the level of the sea. At its base are two frightful orifices, called Hulpit and Huntpot holes: the former looks like the ruins of a large castle, with the roof fallen in and the walls standing; the latter resembles a deep funnel. Through each of these runs a subterraneous brook, passing underground for about a mile, and then emerging, one at Dowgill-Scar, and the other at Bransil Head.

Whernside, the highest mountain in either England or Wales, is situated about six miles to the northwest of Ingleborough in the midst of a vast amphitheatre of hills. Its perpendicular height is, according to Mr Jeffrey, 5340 feet, or one mile and 20 yards above the level of the sea. Near the summit are several pools or small lakes here called tarns, two of which are at least 180 yards in length, and but little less in breadth. The prospects from the top of this mountain are very extensive, and towards the east remarkably fine, commanding the whole of the beautiful vale of Wensleydale and its neighbouring scenery; but, like those of Ingleborough, they are often obscured by the mists and clouds which so frequently envelope these elevated regions.

John Bigland, *The Beauties of England and Wales*
Volume XVI, 1812

A Prospect of the Sea

The walk up the West Field is one of the most agreeable that can be conceived; here woods, water and hills are united to variegate the scene, and the refreshing breeze with its salubrious breath seems to restore exhausted natures. On ascending Whitcliffe Scar we see the convolutions this globe must have received at the Great Deluge, when the earth was torn from its centre, and rocks, water, and woods, separated from their old habitations, and removed to a distance. Bold craggy rocks project on every side to the very verge of the precipice, afford plenty of subjects for the Draughtsman. From this place there is a fine view of Marske Hall, formerly belonging to the Conyers, where improvements have been made worthy of observation of the agriculturist. . . .

On the opposite side of the River, the village of Hudswell has a forlorn appearance, from the enclosing of the Moor and Waste Lands, and from the planting of the hedges and trees about it, good crops of corn will be produced, where nothing but ling and whin used to grow.

Crossing the top of the hill over the training-ground, to the North, we come to a high Mount call'd Beacon Hill from a beacon being placed upon it to alarm the country in times of public danger. Here nothing is necessary but a clear atmosphere, free from cloud or mist, when every object the eye can reach may be distinctly perceived. From this elevated spot the prospect is wonderfully extensive; to the south the lofty hills of Wensleydale may be seen, and Pennel, the highest in Richmondshire; to the North, the County of Durham, where Raby Castle, the seat of Lord Darlington appears the most conspicuous. Eastwards, in a Summer's afternoon view, and a bright sun after rain, the tower of Hartlepool Church is very distinct, and the long range of the sea to Redcar: when if you catch the lucky moment of a fleet of Colliers sailing past, the white sails of the ships surprise the beholder. . . .

Bowman's, *History of Richmond,* 1814

Penyghent

The cart track across the moor winds along a circuitous route to the summit of PENYGHENT, but the usual place of ascent on this side is up what is called Greenrake, a broad grassy track between two projecting rocks. The early morning, the noon, and the evening have each their peculiar advantages for the ascent of such mountains as Penyghent and Ingleborough. Soon after sunrise, when the clouds are dispersing and beginning to assume a higher altitude, their slow and solemn motion, the haze in the valleys, the illumined summits of the hills, like pleasant islands in those lakes of mist, the grand pictorial effects of light and shade, and the purity and freshness of the air, may well tempt the tourist to select such an hour. In the evening too, the pageantry of a sunset may have its peculiar charms, but as the chief object in ascending a mountain is to obtain an extensive view of the surrounding country, the noon, unless there has been a succession of dry and hot days, will be found the most eligible time for such a purpose.

On most of the lofty hills the officers of the Ordnance Survey have erected a pile of stones, and consequently the one on Penyghent will afford the most complete point of view. To the north the prospect is limited by a succession of high and desolate fells; on the east are Scoska Moor and Fountains Fell, which latter still retains the name of the monastery to which it anciently belonged, all the pastures from thence to Kilnsey having been once ranged by the flocks and herds of Fountains Abbey; the southern view extends some miles beyond the eastern arm of Pendle, and includes an extensive range, the principal features of which have been already enumerated; and to the west and north are Lunesdale and Morecambe Bay, Ingleborough, and arm of Whernside, and the distant mountains of the Lake District.

Near the summit are some horizontal shafts from which coal is procured for lime burning, and near the cart track below these, a scanty spring (which is sometimes a desideratum here) may be found.

William Howson, *An Illustrated Guide to the Curiosities of Craven,* 1850

WALTER WHITE (1811–93) *of Berkshire was a thoroughly professional journalist, essayist and traveller. After the break-up of his marriage in the 1840s, he spent several years travelling in Britain and Europe, producing a number of popular travel books, including the immensely popular* A Month in Yorkshire *which continued to be reprinted right until the end of the nineteenth century.*

A Glittering Fairy Palace

Here in Clapdale, a dale which penetrates the slopes of Ingleborough is the famous Ingleborough Cave, the deepest and the most remarkable of all the ones hitherto discovered in the honeycombed flanks of that remarkable hill. Interested to see this, I left unvisited the other caves which have yet been mentioned as lying to the right and left of the road as you come from *Gearstones*.

The fee for a single person to see the cave is half-a-crown; for a party of eight in turn a shilling each. The guide, who is an old soldier, and a good specimen of his class, civil and intelligent, called at his house as we passed to get candles, and presently we were clear of the village, and walked uphill along a narrow lane. Below us on the right lay cultivated grounds and well-kept plantations, through which, as the old man told me, visitors were once allowed to walk on their way to the cave—a pleasing and much less toilsome way than the lane, but the remains of picnics left on the grass, broken bottles, greasy paper and wisps of hay, became such a serious abuse, that Mr Farrer, the proprietor, withdrew his permission. "It's a wonder to me," said the guide, "that people shouldn't know how to behave themselves."

In about half an hour we came to a hollow between two grassy acclivations, out of which runs a rapid beck, and here on the left, in a limestone cliff prettily screened by trees, is the entrance to the cave, a low, wide arch, that narrows as it reaches into the gloom. We walked in a few yards; the guide lit two candles, placed one in my hand and unlocked the iron gate which, very properly, keeps out the perpetrators of wanton mischief. A few paces takes us beyond the last gleam of daylight, and we come to a narrow passage, of which the sides and roof are covered with a brown incrustation resembling gigantic clusters of petrified moss. Curious mushroom-like growth hung from the roof, and throwing his light on them, the guide says we are passing through the Inverted Forest. So it continues, the roof still low, for eighty yards, comprising the Old Cave, which has been known for ages; and we come to a narrow passage hewn through a thick screen of stalagmite. It was opened twenty years ago by Mr Farrer's gardener, who hacked at the barrier until it was breached, and a new cavern of marvellous formation was discovered beyond. An involuntary exclamation broke from me as I entered and beheld what might have been taken for a glittering fairy palace. On each side, sloping gently upwards till they met the roof, great bulging masses of stalagmite of snowy whiteness lay outspread, mound after mound glittering as with millions of diamonds. For the convenience of explorers, the passage between them has been widened and levelled as far as possible, whilst the beck that we saw outside fills a channel after unusual rains. You walk along this passage now on sand now on pebbles, now on bare rock. All the great white masses are damp, their surfaces are rough with countless crystallised convolutions and minute ripples, between which trickle here and there tiny threads of water. It is to the moisture that the unsullied whiteness is due, and the glistening effect; for wherever stalactite or stalagmite becomes dry, the colour changes to brown, as we saw in the Old Cave. A strange illusion came over me as I passed slowly across the undulating ranges, and for a moment they seemed to represent the great rounded snow fields that whiten the sides of the Alps.

The cave widens: we are in Pillar Hall; stalactites of all dimensions hang from the roof, singly and in groups. Thousands are mere nipples, or an inch or two in length; many are two or three feet; and the whole place echoes with the drip and tinkle of water. Stalagmites dot the floor, and while some have grown upwards the stalactites have grown downwards, until the ends meet, and the ceaseless trickle of water fashions an unbroken crystal pillar. Some stalactites assume a spiral twist; and when this first occurs in the roof they take the form of draperies, curtains and wings—many shaped like those of angels. The guide strikes one of the wings with a small mallet, a rich musical note; another has a deep sonorous boom of a cathedral bell, another rings sharp and shrill, and now a stalactite sheet answers when touched with a gamut of notes. Your imaginative powers stir whilst you listen to such strange music in the heart of a mountain.

Walter White, *A Month in Yorkshire,* 1858

Directions to Bolton Abbey

The ruins of Bolton Abbey stand upon a beautiful curvature of the "lordly Wharfe", on a level sufficiently high to protect it from floods, and low enough for every purpose of picturesque effect. As a ruin it is perhaps equal to any in the kingdom, if its only defect, the want of a tower, be excepted; and for surrounding scenery and beauty of its site it has not an equal.

To the south is the embrochure of the valley with its rich meadow lands, its woods and homesteads; to the right is the impetuous Wharfe, flowing beneath a wood of oaks, mingled with steep shelving ground and jutting grey rocks stained with many-hued lichens, and festooned with heather and ivy; woods to the left—to the north the eye is delighted with a park-like expanse, and beyond are those aged and noble groves that hang over the rocky river, as the valley gradually narrows, and farther yet are the barren and rugged heights of Simon Seat and Barden Fell, contrasting well with the fertility and luxuriant foliage beneath.

In walking from Bolton Bridge to the Abbey, to the south east will be noticed Beamsley Beacon on the edge of Blubber Fell, from which it is said that York Minster may be seen on a favourable day. On the left of the path is a large field in which tradition says that Prince Rupert encamped amidst the rising corn on his way to Marston Moor.

The guide's house is about a quarter of a mile from the Devonshire Arms. All the gates leading into the woods are kept locked, but any person not wishing to have a guide, may, upon inserting his name in a book kept for that purpose at the guide's house, be furnished with a key on any day except Sunday.

It is almost impossible to visit all the points of view and objects of interest at Bolton in one day. Several different routes may be taken, two of which shall here be pointed out.

The one from the Holme Terrace, by the Hall, the Strid, Devonshire Seat, to the Valley of Desolation. The return being by Park

Gate Seat, and the footpath through the fields to the Devonshire Arms.

The other along the eastern bank of the Wharfe, Skiphouse-Wheel Seat, Burlington Seat, Pembroke Seat, Lady Harriet's Seat, Cavendish Seat and Hartington Seat, to the Abbey.

William Howson, *An Illustrated Guide to the Curiosities of Craven*, 1850

Two Views of Richmond

The next view I shall attempt to describe is that from the foot-road leading to Hudswell, along the top of the wood. This is quite a panoramic view of Richmond, and has been considered strikingly fine by lovers of picturesque scenery; it commands a prospect of all the country round to the north and east bounded by the Hambledon Hills. In this view, like all others described, the castle is a prominent object in the centre of the picture. The river, winding in a serpentine course amidst richly wooded banks, gives to this landscape a delightful charm.

From the top of the hill to the south, opposite the bridge, we have a good view to the castle: from this point it is seen to perfection. Mr. Turner, the celebrated landscape painter, made a drawing from this spot, to illustrate Whitaker's Richmondshire, and his choice of the station is sufficient precedent for pointing it out.

Robinson's Guide to Richmond, 1833

Hell's Cauldron—Dentdale

. . . we must descend into the valley: and here one of the most remarkable features is the river. It has all the character of a mountain torrent; huge stones, and masses of gravel everywhere demonstrating the occasional violence of the waters. But what has a most singular effect, its bed is one of solid stone, in some parts black and dark-grey marble, which is chafed and worn by the fury of the stream in flood, in such manner that it looks itself like a rushing, billowing river, petrified by enchantment. A great part of this bed during summer is dry, and therefore the more remarkable in its aspect. Here and there you may walk along it for a considerable distance; there again it descends in precipices, and amid blocks of stone of gigantic character. One of these places is known by the name of Hell's Cauldron, no doubt, in the rainy season, a most appropriate name; for the river here, overhung and dark, passes over some huge steps of the stony bed into a deep and black abyss, where the rending of the rocks and washing up of heaps of debris, shew with what fury that cauldron boils. But what are still more significant of this fury are the hollows worn into the very mass of the ledge of the rocks over which it passes, one of which is called The Pulpit, from its form, and in which you may stand. These hollows, which are scooped out with wonderful regularity, appear to be made by the churning and grinding of stones, which get in whenever the softer parts of the rocks give way to the action of the floods. Yet fearful as this Hell's Cauldron must be when the stream is swollen, we are told that a boy once slipped in, and was carried through it, and washed up on the bank below, unhurt; calling to his astounded companion—"Here am I! Where are you?"

William Howitt, *The Rural Life of England,* 1844

6. Old, Unhappy, Far-off things

The past has always had a glamour; a mixture of nostalgia, regret, and desire for lost youth give a romantic patina to past events that contrast with an inevitably prosaic present. Chivalry, heroic values, always belonged to the age before our own.

Sir Walter Scott and William Wordsworth began the fashion for sentimentalizing the past in the Yorkshire Dales. Thousands found their way to Rockeby on the Tees to savour Scott's elaborate descriptions and self-conscious medievalisms. Wordsworth's *The White Doe of Rylstone* turned a somewhat sordid story of religious persecution into a narrative poem with exactly the kind of exquisite pathos to set the tone for Dales topographers for more than a century. It became the high tide of historical Romanticism; local legends became suitable subjects for poems in the grander manner. Local squires had forebears who were knights noble and true; damsels were pure, peasants simple and loyal; and the landscape the loveliest of backcloths.

Again, contemporary Victorian society needed such a mythology. The grim new towns, the thrusting and acquisitive society needed its symbols of permanence, or purity. Whether the legends had any basis in sober fact was an irrelevance.

By the early twentieth century, the sentimentality had become a self-parody, with heavy, purple prose, limp with nostalgia, clouding out any vestiges of reality. It became a form of self-indulgence, a cliché. And it helped to produce some thoroughly bad writing.

Rockeby's Romantic Gloom

VII

The open vale is soon pass'd o'er
Rokeby, though nigh, is seen no more;
Sinking mid Greta's thickets deep,
A wild and darker course they keep,

A stern and lone, yet lovely road
As e'er the foot of Minstrel trode!
Broad shadows o'er their passage fell,
Deeper and narrower grew the dell,
It seem'd some mountain, rent and riven,
A channel for the stream had given,
So high the cliffs of limestone grey,
Huge beetling o'er the torrents way,
Yielding, along their rugged base,
A flinty footpath's ruggard space,
Where he, who winds 'twixt rock and wave,
May hear the headlong torrent rave,
And like a steed in frantic fit
That flings the froth from curb and bit
May view her chafe her head to spray
O'er every rock that bars her way,
Till foam-globes in her eddies ride,
Thick as the schemes of human pride
That down life's current drive amain,
As frail, as frothy, and as vain!

VIII

The cliffs that rear their haughty head
High o'er the river's darksome bed,
Were now all naked, wild, and grey,
Now waving all with greenwood spray;
Here trees to every crevice clung,
And o'er the dell their branches hung;
And there, all splintered and uneven,
The shive'd rocks ascend to heaven;
Oft, too, the ivy swathed their breast,
And wreathed its garland round their crest
Or from the spires bade loosely flare
Its tendrils in the middle air.
As pennons wont to wave of old
O'er the high feat of Baron bold,
When revell'd loud the feudal rout.
And the arch'd halls return'd their shout;
Such and more is Greta's roar,
And so the ivied banners gleam
Waved wildly o'er the brawling stream.

IX

Now from the stream the rocks recede
But here between no sunny mead,
No, nor the spot of pebbly sand
Oft found by such a mountain sand;
Forming such warm and dry retreat
As fancy deems the lonely seat,
Where hermit, wandering from his cell
His rosary might love to tell.
But here, 'twixt rock and river, grew
A dismal grove of sable yew,
With those sad tints were mingled seen
The blighted fir's sepulchral green
Seem'd that the trees their shadow cast
The earth that nourish'd them to blast
For never knew that swarthy grove
The verdant hue the fairies love;
Nor nodding grove, nor woodland flower,
Arose within its baleful bower:
The dank and sable earth receives
Its only carpet from the leaves,
That, from the withering branches cast,
Bestrew'd the ground with every blast.
Though now the sun was o'er the hill,
In this dark spot was twilight still,
Save that on Greta's further side
Some straggling beams through copse-wood glide
And wild and savage contrast made
That dingle's deep and funereal shade,
With the bright tints of early day,
Which, glimmering through the ivy spray,
Or on the opposing summit lay.

Sir Walter Scott, from Canto Two *Rockeby,* 1813

The Historian's Challenge

After Rilston came into possession of the Cliffords, the same ground, with part of the fell above, was inclosed for a park, of which it still retains the name, and the name only.

At this time a white doe, say the aged people of the neighbourhood, long continued to make a weekly pilgrimage from hence over the fells to Bolton, and was constantly found in the abbey churchyard during divine service, after the close of which she returned home as regularly as the rest of the congregation.

This incident awakens the fancy. Shall we say that the soul of one of the Nortons had taken its abode in that animal, and was condemned to do penance, for his transgressions against "the lord's deere" among their ashes? But for such a spirit the wild stag might have been a fitter vehicle. Was it not, then, some fair and injured female, whose name and history are forgotten? Had the milk-white doe performed her mysterious pilgrimage from Etterick Forest to the precincts of Dryburgh or Melrose, the elegant and ingenious editor of the "Border Minstrelsy" would have wrought a beautiful story.

T. D. Whitaker, *A History of Craven,* 1805

The White Doe Visits Bolton Priory

—full fifty years
That sumptuous Pile, with all its peers,
Too harshly hath been doomed to taste
The bitterness of wrong and waste:
Its courts are ravaged; but the tower
Is standing with a voice of power,
That ancient voice which wont to call
To mass or some high festival;
And in the shattered fabric's heart
Remaineth one protected part;
A Chapel, like a wild-bird's nest,
Closely embowered and trimly drest;
And thither young and old repair,
This Sabbath-day, for praise and prayer.

Fast the churchyard fills;—anon
Look again, and they are all gone;
The cluster round the porch, and the folk
Who sate in the shade of the Prior's Oak!
And scarcely have they disappeared
Ere the prelusive hymn is heard:—
With one consent the people rejoice,
Filling the church with a lofty voice!
They sing a service which they feel:
For 'tis the sunrises now of zeal;
Of a pure faith the vernal prime—
In great Eliza's golden time.

A moment ends the fervent din,
All is hushed, without and within;
For though the priest, more tranquilly
Recites the holy liturgy,
The only voice which you can hear
Is the river murmuring near.
—When soft—the dusky trees between,
And down the path through the open green,
Where is no living thing to be seen;
And through yon gateway, where is found,
Beneath the arch with ivy bound,
Free entrance to the churchyard ground—
Comes gliding in with lovely gleam,
Comes gliding in serene and slow,
Soft and silent as a dream,
A solitary Doe!
White she is as lily of June,
And beauteous as the silver moon
When out of sight the clouds are driven
And she is left alone in heaven;
Or like a ship some gentle day
In sunshine sailing far away,
A glittering ship, that hath the plain
Of ocean for her own domain.

William Wordsworth, *The White Doe of Rylstone,* 1808

With Wordsworth at Bolton Abbey

But you will turn again and again to the abbey to gaze on its walls arched, the great empty window, the crumbling walls, over which hang rich masses of ivy, and walking slowly round you will discover the points whence the ruins appear most picturesque. And within, where elder-trees grow, and the carved tombstones of the old abbots lie on the turf, you may still see where the monks sat in the sanctuary, and where they poured the holy water. And whether from within or without, you will survey with reverent admiration. A part of the nave is used as a church for the neighbourhood, and ere I left, the country folk came from all the paths around, summoned by the pealing bell. I looked in and saw richly stained windows and old tombs.

On the rise above the abbey stands a castellated lodge, embodying the ancient gatehouse, an occasional resort of the late Duke of

Devonshire, to whom the estate belonged. Of all his possessions this perhaps offered him most of beauty and tranquillity.

You may ramble at will; cross the long row of stepping stones on the opposite bank, and scramble through the wood to the top of the cliff; or roam over the meadows up and down the river, or lounge in idle enjoyment over the seats fixed under some of the trees. After strolling hither and thither, I concealed myself under the branches overhanging the stream, and sat there as in a bower, with my feet in the shallow water, the lively flashing current broad before me, and read,

> From Bolton's old monastic tower
> The bells ring loud with gladsome power . . .

And while I read, the bell was ringing, and the people were gathering together, and anon the priest

> —all tranquilly
> Recites the holy liturgy,

but no White Doe of Rylstone came gliding down to pace timidly among the tombs, and make her couch on a solitary grave.

Walter White, *A Month in Yorkshire,* 1858

In the Footsteps of the White Doe

And sure enough we found it most solitary and impracticable. The distance is six miles: not a track nor a house to be seen, except a keeper's lodge, standing in the brown heathery wilderness about a mile from Barden, with a watch-tower around it, whence he might look out far and wide for depradors of the moor game.

We had the precaution to take a young man with us as guide and as we went, ploughing up to the waist in heather, and sinking in deep moss at every step; now in danger of being swallowed up by a bog, and now put to our contrivances by some black ravine. A weary way the poor Doe must have had every Sunday from Rylstone to Bolton Priory; and well we thought, might the people deem it something supernatural. Our guide himself found it no very easy matter to steer his course aright or to pursue it when he thought it right. He directed us by way of certain crags on the distant hill-tops called the Lord's Stones, and, when we gained the highest elevation, whence we had an immense prospect, we came to a track cut through the moorland for the Duke to ride on his shooting excursions. This, the guide told us to follow and it would lead us to the Fell-gate just above Rylstone. Here, therefore, we allowed him to return but we speedily repented the permission for the track soon vanished, and before us lay only wild craggy moors with intervening bogs, which extended wider and wider as we went. The moor game, ever and anon, rose with loud cries and whirring wings; the few sheep ran off as we made our appearance and we seemed only getting further and further into a desolate region:

> Where things that owe not man's dominion dwell
> And mortal feet had ne'er or rarely been.

Knowing, however, that there was nothing for it but perishing in the extremity of waste, bring us whither it would, we hurried forward in spite of weariness and bewilderment and presently found ourselves on a savage green ridge of crags from which a wide prospect of green and champaign country burst upon us, and the village of Rylstone itself lying at the foot of the steep descent before us.

William Howitt, "A Visit to Bolton Priory"
Visits to Remarkable Places, 1839

The Boy of Egremond

"Say, what remains when Hope is fled?"
She answered, "Endless weeping."
For in the herdsman's eye she read
Who in his shroud lay sleeping.

At Embsay rang the matin-bell
The stag was roused on Barden-fell;
The mingled sounds were swelling, dying,
And down the Wharfe a heron was flying;
When near the cabin in the wood
In tartan clad and forest green,
With hand in leash and hawk in hood
The Boy of Egremond was seen.
Blithe was his song, a song of yore;
But where the rock is rent in two
And the river rushes through
His voice was heard no more!
'Twas but a step! the gulf he passed;
But that step—it was his last!
As through the mist he winged his way
(A cloud that hovers night and day)

The hound hung back, and back he drew
The Master and his merlin too.
That narrow place of noise and strife
Received their little all of life!

There now the matin-bell is rung
The "Misere!" duly sung;
And holy men in cowl and hood
Are wandering up and down the wood
But what avail they? Ruthless Lord,
Thou dids't not shudder when the sword
Here on the young its fury spent,
The helpless and the innocent.
Sit now and answer groan for groan
The child before thee is thy own.
And she who wildly wanders there,
The mother in her long despair
Shall oft remind thee, waking, sleeping,
Of those who by the Wharfe were weeping;
Of those who would not be consoled
When red with blood the river rolled.

Samuel Rogers, 1819

The Terrors of The Strid

A little higher up the stream we reach the tremendous Strid; a narrow chasm in the rocks, through which the river rushes with great fury. This chasm being incapable of receiving the winter floods, has formed on either side a broad strand of native gritsone, full of rock basins, or "pots of the lin", which bear witness to the restless impetuosity of many northern torrents. The deep and solemn roar of the waters rushing through this narrow passage is heard above and beneath, amid the silence of the surrounding woods. The river boils and foams, raging and roaring like the angry spirit of the waters, in the narrow cleft of the rock, through which the current rushes with awful rapidity.

Here it was that the boy of Egremond, ranging through the woods of Barden with his hounds and huntsmen, attempted to stride across the gulph, a dangerous step:

He sprang in glee, for what cared he
That the river was strong and the rocks were steep

But the greyhound on the leash hung back
And check'd him in his leap.

The boy is in the arms of Wharf,
And strangled by a merciless force;
For never more was young Romilee seen,
Till he rose a lifeless corpse!*

The fate of the boy of Egremond has not prevented the practice of striding from bank to bank, regardless of the consequences that await a false step. The width is only four feet five inches, but few can look down into that awful gulph without a shudder of horror.

William Grainge, *The Castles and Abbeys of Yorkshire,* 1855

ALFRED TENNYSON *toured Wensleydale and Wharfedale during the summer of 1862 in the company of F. T. Palgrave, the poet and anthologist. He later told his son, Hallam, that Middleham Castle had partly inspired his description of Yniol's Castle in "Enid", the first of his celebrated* Idylls of the King *which at that time he was in process of revising.*

Middleham Castle

At last they issued from the world of wood
And climb'd upon a fair and even ridge,
And show'd themselves against the sky, and sank.
And thither came Geriant, and underneath
Beheld the long street of a little town
In a long valley, on one side of which,
White from the mason's hand, a fortress rose;
And on one side a castle in decay,
Beyond a bridge that spann'd a dry ravine:
And out of town and valley came a noise
As of a broad brook o'er a shingly bed
Brawling, or like the clamour or the rooks
At distance, ere they settle for the night. . . .

. . . Then rode Geriant into the castle court,
His charger trampling many a prickly star
Of sprouted thistle on the broken stones.

*Wordsworth, *Force of Prayer.*

He look'd, and saw that all was ruinous.
Here stood a shatter'd archway plumed with fern;
And here had fallen a great part of a tower,
Whole, like a crag that tumbles from the cliff,
And like a crag was gay with wilding flowers:
And high above a piece of turret stair,
Worn by the feet that now were silent, wound
Bare to the sun, and monstrous ivy-stems
Clasp the gray walls with hairy-fibred arms,
And suck'd the joining of the stones, and look'd
A knot, beneath, of snakes, aloft a grove.

Alfred Tennyson, from "Enid", *Idylls of the King,* 1863

The Glory that is Departed

A more interesting relic than Jervaulx Abbey, though little more than a ground plan remains, it would be difficult to find; originally founded in 1136, and like other monastic establishments suppressed in 1536. Most thoroughly at that time the spoilers did their work, defiling the holy temple, and making "Jerusalem a heap of stones". The church is unroofed, and the convental buildings, and the walls in most places razed to the ground. As time rolled the earth accumulated, and the weeds grew in rank luxuriance, so that the once beautiful abbey is almost entirely hidden. Instead of the hymns "Jam Lucis orto sidere" or "Ales diei nuncius" welcoming the morn, no sound was heard, save the note of blackbird or thrush. It might have been truthfully said of the choir from which the loud Hosanna had once rolled and the sacrifice of prayer and praise ascended, "Ichabod, Ichabod! thy glory is departed."

. . . A charming walk conducts through green fields and pleasant pastures towards Aysgarth, leaving behind the fairy towers of Bolton Castle; and long before it is reached the noise of the waterfall strikes upon the ear, guiding the direction. There are two waterfalls, but the lower one below the bridge is much the finer, where the Yore falls over three ledges of limestone. What a charming spot on a hot afternoon! What a cool shelter is that afforded by the overhanging rocks! Amid these Arcadian scenes an idyll of Theocritus is pursued, one in which the old bard gives a graphic description of the summer melting into autumn, when the fruit is falling on the ground, and the air resonant with the hum of insect life, making what Virgil, the imitator of Theocritus, calls a "sussuras".

Rev. John Pickford, *A Week in the Yorkshire Dales,* 1869

The Legend of Semerwater

Where Semerwater now lies, says the legend, there stood some two thousand years ago (some accounts give the actual date as 45 BC) a city of imposing size, with noble buildings and great wealth. To this city there came one day in winter a poor man of venerable appearance who craved an alms at the door of every house in the place, and was driven from each with refusals and reproaches until there was left but one cottage at which he could seek his last chance of succour. Here he met with charity—the cottage folk took him in, fed, warmed and housed him, and made him welcome for the night. Next morning he rose, blessed his entertainers, and set forth on his journey towards the hills. But when he had arrived on an eminence outside the city he stretched out his arms in malediction crying:

Semerwater rise
Semerwater sink
Swallow all the town
Save this li'le house
Where they gave me meat and drink!

Whereupon the earth opened, a great flood of water appeared, and the city of hard hearted folk disappeared, never to be seen again, though it is said that an occasional glimpse of its towers and spires has been seen by curious and fearful watchers who have gazed patiently through its depths.

J. S. Fletcher, *A Picturesque History of Yorkshire*, 1900

The Ballad of Semerwater

Deep asleep, deep asleep,
Deep asleep it lies
The still lake of Semerwater
Under the still skies.

And many a fathom, many a fathom,
Many a fathom below,
In a king's tower and a queen's bower
The fishes come and go.

Once there stood by Semerwater
A mickle town and tall,
King's tower and queen's bower
And the wakeman on the wall.

Came a beggar halt and sore:
"I faint for lack of bread."
King's tower and queen's bower
Cast him forth unfed.

He knocked at the door of eller's cot,
The eller's cot in the dale,
They gave him of their oatcake,
They gave him of their ale.

He has cursed aloud that city proud,
He has cursed it in its pride;
He has cursed it into Semerwater,
Down the brant hillside;
He has cursed it into Semerwater—
There to bide.

King's tower and queen's bower,
And a mickle town and tall;
By glimmer of scale and gleam of fin,
Folk have seen them all.
King's tower and queen's bower
And weed and reed in the gloom;
And a lost city in Semerwater
Deep asleep till doom.

Sir William Watson, *Collected Poems*, 1904

EDMUND BOGG (1850–1931), *one of the most popular of all Dales topographers, was a Leeds picture-framer. He founded a society of artists, writers and musicians known as the Leeds Savage Club, and was known as "'T'owd Chief", possibly for his delight in wearing a Red Indian chieftain's headgear. The Savage Club made many excursions into the local countryside, trips which led to Bogg's highly successful* Thousand Miles in Wharfedale *which was the first of a long series of topographical accounts of the Dales which combined the usual sentimental legends with a genuine enthusiasm for the countryside, illustrated by splendidly appropriate engravings and photographs by leading local artists.*

Mary Queen of Scots at Castle Bolton

"Ruins" says one writer, "are best seen in wintry weather, when the storms are abroad, and the trees are leafless." It was so when we first stood before this massive structure of feudal days, Bolton's ancient pile. The wind sighed and moaned around the ruins, wailing and melancholy, dark patches of storm clouds casting dense shadows on the old fortress, which presented a stern, gloomy, and almost awe-inspiring look. As we stood ruminating before the medieval structure, with not a sound to disturb our reverie, save that caused by the flutter of a night-bird rustling among the ivy, or the shivering of withered leaves, bygone scenes and actors in the historic drama passed before our gaze. High up in yonder room, Mary Stuart, Scotland's Queen, spent seven lonely months, hoping for succour and pity from Elizabeth, England's Queen. From her, indeed, was neither help nor pity; instead, a long, dreary life of sorrow and imprisonment. Other figures and actors in her life's drama also pass in review—lords and ladies of high degree come and go, some curious only to see her, many out of the intense pity, compassion, and love they bore to the imprisoned Queen.

These were anxious months for Lord Scrope, a scion of that old race, ever great in senate, church and camp. Once, tradition says, the Queen escaped, and was overtaken by her captors on Leyburn Shawl. Since that time the spot has been known as "Queen's Gap". The scene changes. Yonder passes Richard Norton and his eight good sons, one of whom, Christopher, the soul of English chivalry, has already enrolled himself a devoted adherent of the fated Queen.

Thee Norton, wi' thine eight good sonnes
They doom'd to dye, alas! for ruth.

This devotion ended in disaster and ruin to his house. Fearful was the vengeance which fell on all who linked their destiny with the Queen. Figure after figure, dim and shadowy, are seen passing to the block, or ending their days in exile, far away from home and kindred. Other risings and plots to rescue only rivetted the chain of fatality more firmly round her. Thus we see her for nineteen long weary years, led from fortress to fortress, from whence neither force, guile stratagem, or the jealous soul of the English Queen could be brought to open her prison house. Hark! why the solemn toll of a muffled bell? The final scene is about to be enacted on a daughter of the Scottish regal line, once the Queen of France, then Scotland's Queen, and heiress to the English throne. Her faithful attendants are weeping bitterly. To her aged servant, Sir Anthony Melville, she used the memorable words "Weep not for me, my good Melville, but rather rejoice that an end has come to the sorrows of Mary Stuart." Centuries have passed since that day, but the dark deed perpetrated by Elizabeth Tudor has remained a blot on her illustrious reign.

Bolton Castle is one of the most complete strongholds that has escaped the ruin of war and time. It stands on the sloping moorside, a mile above the Yore, and is a most commanding and conspicuous object in the landscape for miles around. From the south the medieval fortress rises nearly as perfect as when the lordly Scropes trod its ramparts, and their banners floated from its towers. From the east the scene is most pleasing, romantic, and picturesque. The quaint little village of Bolton seems yet to cling to the fortress for protection, whilst the huge ruin soars in majesty high over all. Westward, up the river vale, one of the most beautiful landscapes melts away into the blueness of the far away hills—a subject for a Turner or Claude Lorraine.

Edmund Bogg, *Wensleydale and the Lower Vale of the Yore,* 1899

HALLIWELL SUTCLIFFE (1870–1932) *must undoubtedly be described as the high priest of the sentimental school of Dales topographers. Immensely popular he was equally successful as a writer of romantic fiction—novels with such titles as* The Gay Hazard, Pam the Fiddler *and* The White Horse. The Striding Dales, *heavy in legend and nostalgia, is still read and enjoyed with great affection throughout the former West Riding.*

At Hartlington

You take a hill or two, and a dip, and find yourself at Hartlington, where the little bridge goes over Dibble River. It is another haunted corner of the Dale—haunted by a most exquisite and melodious peace. The hollow lies so deeply sheltered that it has a climate of its own, and in February you may find stray flowers in bloom that have not dared to bud as yet outside these charmed boundaries. The wheel of the old water-mill above is humming a cheery roundelay. The stream, brown and swift, has its own song as it swings under the grey arch; and the words of the song are yours, if you have traced it from its course on the lean highlands.

Not far above, Dibble River is no more than a beck, scolding its way between dour stones and boulders. Then its banks grow steeper and more wooded, till part of its growing flood goes by a ferny way of its own to the little lake that feeds the mill-wheel. No words can explain the beauty of that lake, its lush abandonment to all that sheltered warmth can do. The trees, wide-branched and silent, gaze at themselves in a mirror starred with water-flowers. One waits, somehow, breathless and expectant, for Elaine's barge of death to steal over the hushed waters. One almost hears Lancelot and Guinevere the Queen whispering together in the woodland, and feels Merlin's spirit brooding in the sunlit air. It is as if Lyonesse and the soft West Country had sent its heart for a sojourn in our rough and forthright highlands. Yet the stream's other part, separated at the ferny way, goes down into a gorge of wildness and of tumult. Its floods have bared gaunt roots of trees, and the flotsam lies piled in heedless disarray among the cliffs. Here at the quiet bridge the divided currents mingle and are one again; and the song of Dibble Water is all made up of parting and lone adventures and gladness in reunion.

Halliwell Sutcliffe, *The Striding Dales*, 1930

7. Nature in her Glory

Our attitude to nature and to natural beauty is essentially Romantic; the absorption of the early Victorians in the grandeur and beauty of the natural world, soon became a desire to understand the mechanisms of nature.

Geology led the way, with Adam Sedgwick and John Phillips undertaking pioneer work in the Yorkshire Dales which went a long way to providing the key to the structure of the scenery.

Botanists soon followed, and it was the practice of many guidebooks to provide a list of the flora to be found in the neighbourhood.

It was surely no coincidence that the Dales, with their rich variety of natural habitats, were to produce naturalists of international standing in Reginald Farrer and the Kearton brothers.

But equally significant are the countless amateur geologists and naturalists, many of them members of the long-established local societies in and around the Dales, whose knowledge of and interest in the region's wildlife have produced a wealth of careful records and detailed information. The scientists, amateur and professional, have given the Wordsworthian view of nature an important new dimension, and if the modern word 'ecology' is over-used, it does nevertheless still imply a moral attitude, a respect for the careful balance between man and nature which we destroy at our peril.

Poet and naturalist share, albeit with a subtle difference of emphasis, a reverence for nature, a delight in its beauty and its harmony.

PROFESSOR JOHN PHILLIPS, (1800–74) *was one of the leading geologists and scientists of the nineteenth century; nephew of the great geologist William 'Strata' Smith, Phillips first became known through his work with the Yorkshire Philosophical Society. He was to become one of the founders of the British Association for the Advancement of Science, and hold chairs at Dublin, London and Oxford Universities. His great work in the north of England, including his explanation of the complex 'Yoredale' series of limestones in the Dales, was among his major achievements, and both his* Geology of Yorkshire *and* Rivers, Mountains and Sea Coast of Yorkshire *remain classics.*

But Phillips was a man of even wider talents—his interests included the cultural and the artistic; an excellent engraver himself, he was also a first-class topographer, and his Excursions in Yorkshire by the North Eastern Railway *(q.v.) occupies an important place among the early railway guide-books.*

A Geologist's Rambles

In the summer of 1832 I surveyed the vicinity of Harrogate, the whole length of Nidderdale, crossed over Great Whernside, explored the curious districts of Kettlewelldale and Greenhow hill, and added to my knowledge of other adjacent tracts. In the autumn of this year, Swaledale and Arkendale were re-examined; and I measured every visible bed on Water Crag, Lovely Seat, Bear's Head, Addleborough, and many inferior hills, beside threading several glens.

In the Spring of 1833, I again visited and measured almost every scar in Coverdale, Waldendale, Bishopdale, Simmer water, and all the head branches of Yoredale; revisited Kettlewell; crossed from Askrigg to Muker, walked over the summit of Swaledale, to Kirby Stephen; examined the curious districts of Mallerstang and Ravenstonedale; passed by Orton, and through Garsdale to Hawes. Again I ascended Addleborough, repeated observations at Askrigg, crossed the Stake, redescended Bishopdale, again crossed over Pen hill, and after clearing certain difficulties in Coverdale, once more walked to Hawes and redescended Wensleydale.

In the autumn of this year I revisited Ribblesdale, ascended Penyghent, Fountains fell and Wharnside, and measured every visible bed in those noble mountains, in two or three directions (as I had done for Ingleborough and Penyghent in 1827) and passed again through Dentdale, Ingletondale, and Kingsdale to verify former notices.

John Phillips, *The Geology of Yorkshire Part II The Mountain Limestone District,* 1836

The Discovery of the Dent Fault

Near that part of this (Pennine) range where the carboniferous mountains begin to present a decided escarpment towards the west, commences a great longitudinal fault (or perhaps a system of faults) which has been traced by Mr. Phillips from the heart of Craven to the hills of Kirkby Lonsdale and excellently described in a paper published in a former volume of our *Transactions*. I must refer to this paper that the great Craven Fault has rent asunder a part of the Carboniferous chain, and produced such a downcast on the west side, that mountain masses of limestone are tumbled into the neighbouring regions with an inverted dip; and that there a coalfield which ought to appear above the top of Ingleborough has sunk below the level of its base.

From beneath this coal field the limestone beds again rise up, and, after passing in the form of a great ark over Farlton Knot, recover their horizontal position, and are prolonged into the tabular hills mentioned above which form the south western skirt of the Cumbrian mountains. From which it appears, that the southern calcareous zone of the Cumbrian system is cut off from the central chain by the intervention of the Craven fault.

I once imagined that this great fault ranged through the neighbourhood of Kirkby Lonsdale and Farlton Knot and there terminated. It is unquestionable that the lines of dislocation do range in the direction here indicated (as is proved by the position of the limestone of Kirkby Lonsdale bridge, and the still more remarkable position of the limestone between Casterton and Barbon); but after several subsequent visits to the neighbourhood I found that the local branch of the Craven Fault ranged along the line of junction of the central chain which skirts the Cumbrian system, passing along the south flank of Casterton Low Fell up Barbondale, then across the valley of Dent, through the upper part of the valley of Sedbergh, and along the flank of Bowfell and Wildboar Fell, and the ridge between Mallerstang and Ravenstone Dale; and that along the whole of this line there are enormous and most complex dislocations. Some of these I hope to describe more at length in future communication; and for the present I only observe that a great upheaving force acting at once upon two contiguous and unconformable systems, produced a great strain and separation of parts, accompanied with fractures and dislocations, principally along the line of their junction.

In a part of the range between Mallerstang and Ravenstone Dale, the cluster of the older mountains, by deflecting to the north west, quits the central carboniferous chain; and it becomes a question of some consequence to determine the further range and nature of the great Craven fault. The ruptures produced by it are fortunately on a scale too great to be overlooked or misunderstood. It ranges through Mallerstang into the hills immediately south east of Kirkby Stephen, and those skirting the escarpment which travels towards Stainmoor, and finally stops near the foot of the mountain pass. Its progress is marked by a lofty ridge of carboniferous limestone, which has been upheaved from the very base of the whole system, contorted and shattered, and then sent headlong into the valley, where it is seen as an edge for many miles, and where its lower extremities lie buried under accumulations of alluvial matter and the horizontal conglomerates of the new red sandstone.

Adam Sedgwick, "On the General Structure of the Cumbrian Mountains", Transactions of the Geological Society of London, Vol IV (2nd Series), 1838

The Making of the Dales Landscape

Looking specially to the action of water now running in the valleys, we observe that the very channel is marked by peculiarities of the same kind, and depending on the same conditions. To instance only the most beautiful of the peculiarities of our northern rivers, the "forces" and rapids which impart so much interest to the Valley of the Yore. In accompanying many little streams which descend from the moors, several hundred feet before they reach the river, we find at almost every point where limestone beds rest upon shale, and often where sandstone beds take the similar position, a *step* in the channel, over which the water falls a few inches, a few feet, or many yards, according to circumstances. Each of these little cascades is subject to displacement. The limestone beds are slightly worn away and excavated by the sharp sands and pebbles which the stream brings downwards, but this is a feeble element of change. A more powerful effect is occasioned when the rock is *undermined* by the more rapid waste of the shale, and it consequently breaks off at one of the more numerous natural joints, and falls. Thus that operation by which Niagra has been removed, and is undergoing removal, which has furnished to Sir C. Lyell most interesting reflections, may be witnessed on hundreds of streams in Yorkshire. The scale is microscopic, indeed, but its results are of the same order, fully as instructive and not less impressive on the mind.

The mere action of the humid and variable atmospheres of England is wasting, every hour, the surfaces of what are vainly thought to be eternal hills. Even the drop of rain cannot be traced from the cloud, over the surface and through the substance of rocks to its exit in a spring, without teaching us that these rocks are continually undergoing waste, and that this waste is proportional to the nature of the rocks. Rain-drops bring down carbonic acid, and thus exert a chemical as well as mechanical action. In favourable circumstances, the actual channels which they make are preserved. On the wide and bare surfaces around Ingleborough and Penyghent, and on Hutton Roof Crags, west of Kirkby Lonsdale, these channels are innumerable, of all breadths and depths, and of length and direction depending on the slope and continuity of the masses. Where the strata are level, the little ramifications of the rain-channels run deviously, and terminate in the numerous natural joints; but where, as on Hutton Roof Crags, the strata acquire a steep arched slope, the channels take the direction of the slope, run together as valleys do, and collect into miniature dales, till some great fissure lying across their path swallows them up. Below this joint, other channels commence to be in their turn swallowed up.

The fissures here indicated are natural joints of the rock, produced by contraction during its consolidation; they are often symmetrically disposed (prevalent directions are N.N.W. and E.N.E.), and by dividing the mass of limestone present easy passages downward for water. Thus Malham Tarn delivers itself, not by a surface channel, but by subterranean passages; the river Nid is swallowed up near Lofthouse: streams which gather on the moorland fells, sink into smaller holes of the limestone below, or wind through subterranean caverns. These fissures, by giving passage to water, suffer enlargement so as to become rifts between cliffs, or channels round insulated peaks or jutting crags. Gordale, a good example of these effects, will again attract our attention.

When the fissures have one prevalent direction, the rock is split into vertical plates: a second section of joints develops prisms in these. Large joints, thus crossing at intervals, produce huge vertical masses, which, in consequence of the removal of adjoining parts, often stand out like prominent towers of a Cyclopean fortress. Kilnsey Crag is a well known example in Wharfedale.

John Phillips, *Rivers, Mountains and Sea Coast of Yorkshire*, 1853

The Green Mantle of the Dales

Throughout the north-western district, distinctions appear between the vegetable coverings of the slaty, basaltic, calcareous, shaly and gritstone tracts, and sometimes they are obvious and even striking.

Wherever the gritstone rocks rise to high ground they are thickly covered by heath, and often wrapped in deep and ancient peat; beneath a craggy summit of such grit, runs a bluish green herbage of sedges, rushes, and grass, on a slope of argillaceous shale; and very often beneath or amidst these contrasted tints are bands of beautiful short green herbage, the gift of limestone rocks. Even to the very summit of Mickle Fell, Cam Fell, and other high points, the limestone retains this superiority in character, and may thus be traced to the brows of Wharnside and Pennigent, across the thick heath which enveloped the gritstone.

The hue and quality of the herbage on the peaty tracts vary; some of the Hougill Fells have the bluish green sedgy herbage; others are heathy.

The district is only partially wooded; it is chiefly in the lower parts of the valleys, where millstone grit is divided by the rivers, at elevations less than 600 feet above the sea, the mountains and valleys are generally bare of trees.

. . . *Vicinity of limestone at Settle*—Saxifrages abound in this limestone district, and a second locality of *Dryas Octopetals* is in Arncliffe Dale. The *Ladies' Slipper* is also among the rarities of this magnificent mountain district.

Bolton Abbey—In the shales and gritstones of this part of the valley of the Wharfe, occur *Limosella Aquaticia* and *Teverium Scordium*.

Henry Baines, *The Flora of Yorkshire*, 1840

Botany in Ribblesdale

There are few persons who enjoy country walks who do not have a taste for botanical pursuits. It may therefore interest some of my readers to be told that in the neighbourhood of Thorns Gill are found many interesting plants. The water avens *(Geum rivale)* was abundant; the frog orchis *(Habenaria viridis)* and the tway-blade *(Listere oreste)* were frequent, and the generally scarce small white orchis *(Habenaris albida)* almost equally so. In one meadow there is a great quantity of dark plume thistle *(Cardus heterophyllis)* which plant is also found near Horton, in Ribblesdale, from whence it was sent at the end of last century to Sowerby, by a Mr Bingley. The wood crane's bill *(Geranium sylvaticum)* was also abundant. The great bistort or snake weed, *(Polygonum bistortis)* we saw in many places, as well as the great bell-flower *(Campanula latisfolia)*, the last of course, not yet in blossom. One of the chief ornaments of the meadows about the Ribble head, and in the earlier part of the stream, was the globe-flower *(Trollius Europeens)* its rich golden blossoms profusely decorating the fields. It is a cherished inhabitant of gardens in southern and other parts of England, but it flourishes here in all the wild luxuriance of its native north. That beautiful specimen of the primrose family, the bird's-eye primrose *(Primula farinosa)* was abundant by the sides of the stream, and around the edges of the numerous "pots" in the district, and, at the time of our visit, was just beginning to expand its rose coloured blossoms. The stalks and the under portions of this plant is covered with a powdery whiteness, (hence its name "farinosa"), and in this respect the plant resembles the *Auricula.*

William Dobson, *Rambles by the Ribble,* 1864

The Lily of the Valley

In the green coverts of the crag-crowned wood,
With tiny bells and pale,
Springs (while the wild-rose yet is in the bud)
The lily of the vale.

There it unfolds, afar from mountain-meadow,
Its modest mien and dress;
And makes within the silent, sylvan shadow
A fairy loveliness.

Not where the tulip shows its glowing splendour,
Not where the wallflower blooms;
Nor where the rose, with petals bright and tender,
Exhales its sweet perfumes—

Not to the public eye—but under cover
Of rock and branches near,
It gives its gentle charms to Nature's lover,
In its appointed sphere.

Not with the sky's deep hue is its adorning,
Nor rainbow-colours bright;
Not with the crimson flush of rising morning,
But with its own pure white.

Though oft with modest grace its bells it raises

Where seldom foot hath trod;
Yet in obedience to His laws, it praises
The power and love of God.

And we may learn a lesson from its beauty,
Shown in its lonely place—
That each, in its own lot of life and duty,
May glorify God's grace.

Henry Lea Twistleton, 1875

RICHARD KEARTON, (1862–1928), *was born in Thwaite, Swaledale; crippled in childhood through medical neglect, his chance meeting with a London publisher on the moors led to Richard, and later his brother Cherry, achieving world-wide fame as naturalists, photographers, writers and broadcasters.*

Nature Observed in the Wild Places

I love my mother's country in the heart of Fell-land with a passion that can never die. Its fresh, cool breezes, grey limestone crags, and chattering becks tumbling over mossy boulders, appeal to me with the same instinctive longing that sends a little bird over a thousand miles of sea and land to the beloved old hedgerow in which it first followed its tiny wings and learnt something of the freedom of the air.

Thither let us journey and tarry for a while amongst our feathered friends in their peaceful haunts, far, far away from the hum and turmoil of men.

From one cause or another the wild life of any given district ebbs and flows if it be watched carefully over a series of years. The peewit, or lapwing, used to be one of the commonest birds on the fells a few years ago, but the barbaric fashion of eating the bird and its eggs at the same season has reduced its numbers far below those of the curlew in the same districts. This is very regrettable from the bird-lovers' point of view, but as the lapwing is one of the farmer's most useful allies in the production of human food, there is another and far more serious aspect of the case to be considered.

The upper reaches of the River Eden are rich in bird life. Picture to yourself a few acres of more or less flat ground—an old-time deposit of the river in mighty flood. It is besprinkled with tufts of rushes and encroaching patches of bracken, with here and there a moss-gown boulder peeping out in forlorn isolation. On either hand it is flanked by steeply rising green hills studded all over with outcrops of grey limestone. Through the middle the river meanders, a mere trickle shining in the sunlight like a snail's silvery trail, wearing away when in spate first one bank then the other, making excellent breeding-places for innumerable sand martins that skim and twirl over its pools and rippling shallows all the livelong day, and you will be able to visualise the headquarters of the sandpiper and yellow wagtail in the months of May and June.

Two hundred yards further up-stream the water tumbles through a rocky gorge. Here it is so cabined and confined that it rushes in a white jet down into a rocky funnel fifteen feet deep. In dry weather this giant funnel is never quite full, because the water escapes through a hole in its lower rim and bubbles up in the deep pool below, making it look like the surface of that of a boiling kettle. Of course, in flood time a lot of the stream is spilt over the rim of the funnel, and, meeting the current rushing from below, creates a great turmoil.

Here you can always find a pair of dippers breeding in perfect safety on the upper edge of a damp, unapproachable slope of an overhung rock forming the far side of the funnel, and quite above the high-water mark of anything but an abnormal flood. If you attempted to swim to it across the pool the chances are you would not be able to scramble up its steep, slippery side, and might be sucked to destruction by the volume of water dragging for ever downwards towards hole in the lower rim.

A few yards overhead there is a small inaccessible limestone crevice in the face of the limestone cliff. In this the beautiful grey wagtail, with its canary yellow breast and long, black tail, has bred from time immemorial.

Fifty yards higher up the gorge is spanned by an old wooden footbridge in the very last stages of decreptitude. Its timbers are so deeply decayed that it would hardly be safe for two people to cross at the same time, lest it should collapse and precipitate them headlong into the unlighted depths of the narrow rock-pool beneath.

A little way below the funnel hole the river meanders over a shingle bank and tumbles into another deep pool crowded with trout of all ages and sizes. In droughty weather you can see them through the six or seven feet of limpid water all lying at rest, like a regiment of soldiers, every head pointing upstream. In these congregations the small fish are compelled to keep an ever-wary eye on the larger ones, because old trout have a disagreeable habit of turning cannibal. I have seen, nay caught, in the days of my youth, when tickling was not regarded as poaching and trout far more plentiful than in these by-law-bound times, a fish a foot and a half long with another in its mouth so large it could not be swallowed, and had to be digested piecemeal. A hungry, unsophisticated trout will rise at anything he can swallow. On one occasion I tickled a pounder from beneath the dark recesses of an overhanging bank, and discovered he had just sucked down an innocent little water shrew as he swam across a pool no wider than the surface of an ordinary-sized dining table.

Richard Kearton, *At Home with Wild Nature*, 1922

REGINALD FARRER *was born in 1880 at Ingleborough Hall, Clapham, where his interest in gardening on his father's estate created a passion for rare and unusual plants, which led to his becoming one of the world's great plant collectors and botanists. After leaving Oxford, he travelled extensively in Europe, China, Japan, Ceylon and the Himalayas, bringing many rare and exotic species back to Europe for the first time. Many of the great botanic collections, such as the Royal Botanic Gardens in Edinburgh, benefited from Farrer's collections, and at least one popular garden alpine—Farrer's Gentian —recalls its discoverer. As well as being an avid explorer, he was a capable painter, novelist and topographer, and his book* My Rock Garden *is now a much sought-after classic. He died at the tragically early age of 40 during an expedition in the mountains of Burma, catching diphtheria during an extended period of bad summer weather.*

The Bird's Eye Primrose

Primula farinosa is the "Meibuts" of North Western England, and the centre of its distribution is the mountain-masses of Ingleborough. From the days of my remotest childhood, when my anxiety was always whether I should return to the country in time to see it, *Primula farinosa* has been my best friend among English wild-flowers. Such a gallant little thing it is, and so fragrant, and so dainty, and altogether so lovable. It is a thriving species, too, increasing by leaps and bounds, until places where ten years ago there wasn't a single plant are now stained purple with it in spring. You cannot frequent this country without seeing it, for not only does it swarm on the mountains in places, but it covers the railway cuttings in the valley below, and here and there makes great patches of colour on the very highway sides, growing so stout and strong that you can scarcely believe that it is not some vigorous show Verbena, with solid heads of blossom. All through winter nothing is seen but a round, fat bud. Then, with spring, unfold the mealy little grey leaves, in themselves a joy. And then June begins, up go the white stems, and out come the semi-globular trusses of lovely pink, golden-eyed flowers, looking so sweet and friendly there is no resisting them. A curious characteristic it has, too, which shows how it still remembers the alpine and glacial period. For in the high places it hurries eagerly into bloom, as early as it can, like a true alpine, anxious to get its flowering over safely in the brief flash of summer, before the glacial winter descends again; while in the valleys and on the rich railway cuttings it makes no such hurry, but takes its own time about blossoming. So that, while the Scars are pink with it, you will not find as much as a bud in the warm lands beneath, until the hill-plants have all withered and gone to seed.

Reginald Farrer, *My Rock Garden,* 1907

To a Dipper

Thi bonny briest's as white as sna'
  It's pure, ay, lily pure;
An' puts i't'shade them bau's o' foam
  At sails away doon Eure.

Yan wonders whaur thoo's bin te skeul,
  Thoo's gey weel trained, Ah lay,
Fer Curtsey efter curtsey
  Thoo's gi'en te me teday.

Thoo cooers doon this way an' that,
  Thoo's weel-behaved, fer seur;
Yan nivver kna's just what's astir,
  It's grand to be at t'deur.

Er noo thoo sings thi gloamin' song,
  'Mang singers thoo's a swell:
Here, back o't'wau, Ah hev, thoo kn's
  A concert te misel'.

Thaur, keepen time wi' t'tinklen streeam,
  Thoo's nivver nivver flat;

Thoo's full o' tune wi'oot a doot,
  Ah'll allus stick te that.

Ah'd like te shoot "gan on mi lass",
  Thoo weel desarves a clap;
But if Ah did thoo'd pop up t'beck
  Fair scaured at sike a whap.

Thoo's weathered t'stooren, blisteren blast,
  Ah's seur Ah's varra fain;
Good-day fair Peggy, some day seun
  Ah s'mak this way again.

An' when at heeame teneet Ah lig
  Mi heead doon o' me pilla',
An' odd lang thowt, lass, be o' thee,
  A white throat on' a willa'.

John Thwaite, 1873–1941

A Place for Ravens

I sought the ravens at dawn, a time of great activity. The birds had fasted for nine hours. Search about among the boulders at the base of crags on which ravens roost and you will find small, compact pellets which the birds have ejected—neat bundles of indigestible remains of the last meals. One pellet I broke open contained beetles, sheep wool, tufts of grass and pieces of coarse grit. The hunger calls of young ravens at dawn are stilled only when ample food has been provided, when a bird's stomach is round and firm as a drum.

Ravens are faithful to a number of nesting sites, at one of which a nest is refurbished for a new season. Almost all the Pennine nests are on crags. The nests are bulky, formed of substantial twigs taken from the nearest trees, thorn or rowan. Heather is added, and the nest is usually upholstered with sheep wool.

I followed a sheep-trod along the edge of the hill. It extended on a comfortable gradient for walking, and sheep movement had kept the way clear of the coarse and draggly vegetation that elsewhere on the hillside would have wrapped itself round my ankles. The sharp cleaves of sheep, scouring the rocks, also kept the route well-defined even when I crossed a scree slope. Half an hour later I reached the line of limestone cliffs on which are the soggy remains of old raven nests and, I confidently hoped, the nest of the year.

The cliff range, which had been continuous, was now badly eroded. Promontories of light grey rock were thatched with coarse grass. Between them, gullies scoured deeply by rain and landslip. Littering the gullies were unstable screes of gritstone that had slithered from the heights—and slithered still.

Sunlight, filtered by mist, gave an illusion of warmth where warmth was absent. A cold wind blew steadily from the north-east, as it had done for days, emanating from a high pressure system centred on the North Sea. A friend who visited the raven crags with three companions during a snowbound February excused himself when the crests of snowdrifts reached as high as his waist. The others went on, gingerly climbing, and found the female raven squatting on the nest. It was the only dark patch on a hill that otherwise was sparklingly white. The raven, emboldened by the cruel weather and the necessity to keep the eggs warm, stayed on the nest and even permitted itself to be stroked.

As I began my ascent of the gully, the deep flight notes of a raven descended from a bird that regarded me gravely as it glided by. A raven is large—rather more than two feet from the tip of its black beak to the end of its graduated black tail—and in flight the wing-tips curve upwards a little. The ends of the primary feathers are distinct, like dark fingers clutching the air.

The bird's mate appeared. Both the ravens were vocal in their restlessness. They alighted, but not for long. In their effortless flights on stiffened wings, they made subtle alterations to their trim and thus harnessed the power of an air current that sang on its way up the slopes from the dale.

When I stood on the cliff-edge, the ravens glided by. One bird, banking, alighted on a boulder, hopped, then walked a pace or two. Sunlight gave its undertaker-black plumage a silver sheen. I advanced. The raven opened its wings, and the breeze carried the bird aloft, where its legs remained dangling, assisting it to maintain its balance in the turbulence.

The bird almost closed its wings, diving with something of the verve of a 'stooping' peregrine. When the wings were again opened, and the wind harnessed, the raven was swept high. Twice, in quick succession, it flicked on to its back. I have known ravens fly belly-upwards from the sheer joy of being alive, and one bird glided on its back for upwards of a quarter of a mile across a Yorkshire dale.

From my cliff-edge vantage point I beheld a raven as it swept by against a background of broad acres—the fell edge, pastures, meadows; against wall patterns, outbarns, and sparkling streams. These ravens glided, soared, somersaulted, dived with partly-closed wings or banked to reveal handsome profiles and dangling legs. Their ponderous black beaks had silver highlights, mirroring the sun's brilliance. Pointed throat feathers resembled dark ruffs.

W. R. Mitchell, *Wild Pennines*, 1976

8. The Coming of the Railways

More than any other invention known to man, railways have been the instruments of social change. Journey times shortened dramatically from a matter of days to a matter of hours. They made travel open to all, not just the rich and privileged. They carried not only people, but ideas—newspapers, journals, letters. They brought the tourists in ever larger numbers to the Yorkshire Dales, established tourism as a major industry, helped to at least delay the catastrophic decline of other local industries and kept Dales communities in touch with the teeming life and ideas of the sprawling new cities.

The first railway line to encroach on the Dales was the North Eastern from Darlington to Richmond in 1846, bringing the tourists at least to within walking distance of Swaledale's beauties. By 1849 the 'little' North Western, soon to be taken over by the mighty Midland, carried tourists from Skipton and Lancaster to the edge of the cave district around Ingleton, a route soon extended by the London North Western to Kirkby Lonsdale and Sedbergh.

Over in Wensleydale, the North Eastern reached Leyburn in 1856, and finally Hawes in 1877; by 1865 Ilkley was connected to both Leeds and Bradford by the Midland. This line was extended to Skipton to bring thousands of tourists to Bolton Abbey, and the Yorkshire Dales Railway, again soon taken over by the Midland, ran from Skipton to Grassington, and was opened in 1901. Harrogate had its route into the Dales via the North Eastern to Pateley Bridge, and the little Nidd Valley Light Railway, originally built in the construction of the Upper Nidderdale reservoirs, reached the hamlet of Lofthouse in 1907.

But most spectacular of all was the Midland Railway's great Settle and Carlisle line, opened for passengers in 1876 to carry traffic from the East Midlands to Scotland. The line, Victorian railway engineering at its most heroic, not only had a dramatic impact on the landscape—the great viaduct at Ribblehead is the largest single man-made structure in the Dales—but brought tourists quickly and easily into the very heartland of the mountain areas. For many of them it was literally an astonishing experience.

Steamers and Railroads Follow the Poets

Where would your steam boats and your railroads have been leading us, if Bishop Percy had not gathered the glorious ballads of nature and heroism that were scattered over England and Scotland . . . if the "Border Minstrelsy" had not been gathered by Scott . . . if Wordsworth had not—stricken as he confesses, by the mighty power of nature through this very medium—gone wandering over the mountains of Cumberland, filling his heart with the life of the hills, and the soul of the over-arching heavens, and the peace or passion of human existence hidden in glens and recesses where poets had ceased to look for them . . .

I say, where would the steam boats and railroads now have been leading their passengers? Why, clearly enough, to the market—to purchase cotton and printed calicos in Glasgow, Paisley and Manchester; ashes and indigo in Liverpool; teas and a thousand other things in London! They would be going, not the packhorse, but the railroad road of dull and wearisome commerce, wearing out its soul by its over-drudgery. . . .

The love of poetry and nature, of picturesque scenery and summer wandering, no sooner were generated by the means I have here stated, than lo! steamers appeared on the quays, and railroads projected their iron lines over hill and dale.

William Howitt, *Visits to Remarkable Places*, 1839

Down Wharfedale by Mailcoach

From Kettlewell Bridge there are enchanting views of the valley of the Wharfe, to Starbotton on one side, and Grass Wood and Netherside on the other, with the grey brow of Kilnsey Scar to the south. From some unaccountable reason the valley of the Wharfe, from Buckden to Conistone, is called Kettlewelldale, though the river retains its name to its source. The fall of the Wharfe from its source to Kettlewell, a distance of perhaps a little over ten miles, is at least 595 feet, a fall which is not equalled in the same length by more than two or three rivers in England.

But now we must bid "good bye" to this quaint little town, for hark! there is the blowing of the horn which signals the approach of the "Mail", and we may consider ourselves fortunate if there is room for us, for during this time of the year the passengers are always numerous. See! here it comes with its cheerful freight; its driver, who is remarkably shrewd, has already caught sight of us, and is bringing his horses to a stand; he nods to us with all the courtesy of a London cabman, and while he receives the Kettlewell letter bags we mount the omnibus and take our seats. In a few minutes we are off, and at once begin to enjoy the ride; we get a taste of old times, when stage-coaching was the swiftest mode of locomotion, and think to ourselves, "Well, I have no wish to say anything against railways, but they can give us nothing like this; how free I am here to look around me and see the country through which I pass. I can take in the beauties of the scenery, and am not tantalized with momentary glimpses of romantic places, but have time to take notes of their distinctive features; the hills, the rocks, the woods, and the streams become so fixed and painted in my memory, that I can never forget them."

Bailey J. Harker, *Rambles in Upper Wharfedale,* 1869

HARRY SPEIGHT (1855–1915) *was born in Bradford, a journalist, author and lecturer, living for most of his life in Bingley, and first publishing under the pseudonym 'Johnny Gray'. His work is noted for its careful research and wealth of detail, making it still widely sought as a reliable source of information.*

Pack-horse Bells

Before the railway extensions, twenty years ago, Hawes was one of the most inaccessible places in the kingdom, being sixteen miles distant from the nearest station. The packhorse traffic lingered in this neighbourhood long after it had ceased in other parts of England. Handloom weaving was an old local industry, and when a sufficient number of pieces were ready, they were gathered up and conveyed by teams of pack-horses over the mountains to Settle, and thence by the road to Bradford and other West Riding towns. Discharging their loads they would return laden with warp, weft, size and other articles. Occasionally they crossed by the old Cam pass—a wild rough road in misty or wet weather—but their presence was generally known by the tinkling of the bells, which could be heard at a good distance, and at the head of the pass far down Langstrothdale. When the traffic ceased, hundreds of these sonorous pack-bells were sold for old metal, and the brokers' for a time were full of them. Each bell weighed from 1lb to 2lb.

Harry Speight, *Romantic Richmondshire,* 1897

The Advantages of Railway Connection

Some time ago now it was no uncommon thing to hear in Hawes (from persons who had at least fifty summers and who were in favour of travelling with the old stage coach and paying 1s carriage on a letter) to say that it was a pity to see green fields cut up for a railway, and to argue with all the potinency of their natures that there is nothing like an old-fashioned warp after all. Since the introduction of railways into our neighbourhood, we have had the advantage never possessed by former generations. Now we have London newspapers, if we choose, delivered on the same day of issue. Now we have two deliveries of letters per day, viz at 9.30am and 6pm, an advantage which is highly appreciated by the inhabitants of Hawes. For the second delivery we are greatly, if not altogether indebted to our able postmaster, Mr E. Blythe, whose efforts to serve his fellow townsmen are untiring and unceasing. Now we have our merchandises brought to our doors at considerably less cost, and with half the delay, and what is prized by all, both rich and poor, we have coals at the station yard, at from 6½d per cwt, good household coals. Who, we ask, would like to return to the old fashioned way of carting them (coals) 16 miles or more? Then, again, what a saving is effected by private individuals wishing to visit their friends living in any of the large towns, or tradespeople who have periodically to visit the markets at Manchester, Liverpool or London; who had to suffer the inclemency of the weather for 16 or 17 miles over wild moors and unsheltered roads, paying 16s or 21s for such a ride as the old fashioned ways afforded. Now they can travel, as it is needless to say, for infinitely less money and with incomparable comfort. Such are the advantages we in Hawes are deriving from railway connections; who would like to go back to the old times; or who would be grieved at running the iron road through the beautiful green fields of Wensleydale?

Craven Herald and Pioneer, 12th October, 1878

The Toiling Artisans Can Reach the Dales

With Craven commences that romantic series of Dales which

characterize the greater part of the North of England, and include within their precincts, not only that paradise of scenery, the Lakes, but many less known though scarcely less interesting localities; and now, not only the man of leisure and wealth, but the imprisoned denizen of the crowded town, and the toiling artizan will be enabled to visit these attractive places, for the newly constructed railways, though they may encroach a little upon the retirement and pastoral character of the country, offer a facility of transit, which even the pedestrian is sometimes glad to avail himself of, and a cheapness and speed of which the poor in money or in time may reap the benefit.

William Howson, *Illustrated Guide to the District of Craven,* 1850

To the Dales in Armchair Comfort

Of all modes of travelling on wheels, there is one pre-eminent in luxurious comfort. Need we say that we refer to a journey in a Pullman Car on a Midland express? Availing ourselves of this latest product of refined civilisation, we took our places in the palace car which is attached to the Scotch express, on a bright and breezy day at the end of July. We were bound for the Craven country, and for the wild moorland mountainous region which has just been opened up for travellers and tourists by the new line from Settle to Carlisle. Seated on crimson velvet-piled armchairs, which, being fixed upon a pivot, admit of a semi-revolution, and surrounded by maps, guides and time-tables, we prepared to enjoy the varied scenery through which we were to be driven by a powerful engine at high speed, and yet with the utmost possible speed and comfort.

J. Radford Thomson, *Guide to the District of Craven and the Settle and Carlisle Railway,* 1878

The Settle and Carlisle Line

The railway from Settle to Carlisle is probably the most remarkable and interesting work of its kind in England—remarkable for the engineering difficulties that have been overcome, and interesting in the scenery through which it passes. It had long been known that if a railway were ever carried in this direction, extraordinary obstacles would have to be surmounted. Over any such path to the North "frown the huge masses of Ingleborough and Whernside, and Wild-boar and Shap Fells, and if a line were to wend its way at the feet of these, it would have to be by spanning valleys with stupendous viaducts and piercing mountain heights with enormous tunnels; miles upon miles of cuttings would have to be blasted through the rock, or literally torn through clay of the most remarkable tenacity, and embankments, each weighing perhaps 250,000 tons, would have to be piled on peaty moors, on some parts of which a horse could not walk without sinking up to his belly." Only one route was possible—along a chain of four deep valleys which in rough and massive outline stretched from south to north, the more southern rising up one of the wildest, windiest, coldest and drieriest parts of the world, and the more northern falling gently down one of the most beautiful districts in England—the Vale of the Eden. The engineer-in-chief has described the route of his line in homelier phraseology. He has said that the country may be compared to a great whale lying on its belly, with its nose at Settle and its tail at Carlisle. A steep ascent carries us up, a long incline carries us down.

Leaving the "metropolitan town" of Settle, overlooked by the lofty limestone rock of Castleber, we start upon our journey up the noble valley of the Ribble, apparently closed in the north by the mighty outlines of Whernside and Pennegent, often hid in gloomy clouds of trailing mist. Passing the works of the Craven Lime Company, we reach Stainforth, and cross the roaring Ribble. About eight miles from Settle we are at the village of Selside, near which is Hellen Pot, which Mr. J. R. Thomson declares to be "the most awful thing in all England"—a terrific chasm, 60 feet wide and more than 300 deep, down which a waterfall leaps into the gloom. Four miles from Selside we cross the turnpike which runs from Ingleton to Hawes, and now the heaviest part of the work of the railway begins. Here, a few years since, not a vestige of a habitation could be seen, and the only signs of life were the grouse, and anon a black-faced mountain sheep, half buried among the ling. We are now approaching the great hill of Blea Moor, an outlying flank of the mighty Whernside, through which, at a height of 1,100 feet above the sea, the renowned Blea Moor tunnel had to be carried. Speaking of this spot, Mr. Allport says: "I shall not forget as long as I live the difficulties that surrounded us in that undertaking. Mr. Crossley and I went on a voyage of discovery—'prospecting'. We walked miles and miles; in fact I think I may safely say we walked over a greater part of the line from Settle to Carlisle, and we found it comparatively easy sailing till we got to that terrible place, Blea Moor. We spent an afternoon there looking at it. We went miles without seeing an inhabitant, and the Blea Moor seemed effectually to bar our passage northward." We are now at Dent Head, and away to the north stretches the valley down which the Dee roars—on part of its way—over a bed of black marble, skirted by the greenest of green meadows where herds of cattle pasture, while on either side rise the moorlands, the wildest and loneliest in Yorkshire.

The Official Guide to the Midland Railway, 1880

Ribblehead Viaduct and Blea Moor Tunnel

Having referred to the prominent natural features about Ribblehead, let us say a word about the most striking work of man to be seen here. This is the immense *railway viaduct* constructed by the Midland Railway Company for the passage of trains between Settle and Carlisle. It crosses Batty Moss, and gave the contractors some trouble before solid and durable foundations could be obtained. Nearly all the piers rest on a bed of concrete six feet thick, laid upon solid rock. The length of the viaduct is 1328 feet, composed of 24 arches of an average span of 45 feet, and the height of the loftiest from the parapet to the foundations is 165 feet. It contains 34,000 cubic yards of masonry, besides 6000 feet of concrete. About a mile to the north of it (between Ribblehead and Dent) is the famous Blea Moor tunnel, one of the longest in England, being 2460 yards in length and 500 feet below the outer surface at the deepest part. The metals in the tunnel attain an altitude of 1151 feet. Blea Moor and Wold Fell being on the watershed of England, the streams of the latter descending westward, drain into the Irish Sea, and eastward into the German Ocean.

Harry Speight, *Tramps and Drives in the Craven Highlands,* 1895

Railway Boom in Sedbergh

Thirty three years ago we were half a dozen miles from a railway station. Then the opening of the Ingleton and Tebay branch of the London and North Western Railway abridged the distance to a mile; and, last of all, competing omnibuses have achieved the irreducible minimum, and gently drop all who deign to visit us at our doors. The market has improved in consequence. From an apple-cart and half a dozen admiring nondescripts, it has grown to a fairly busy throng of buyers and sellers. Among other things we abound in butter, and connoisseurs in this commodity, from populous towns like Bradford, personally or by proxy, relieve us of the golden store. The School has developed enormously, and affectionate parents look in upon us from time to time. Land in suitable situations has been set aside for building plots, and comfortable residences of modern aspect are springing up apace. Multiplied wants have quickened industry and stimulated enterprise. Gas-works, water-works, sewerage schemes, and all the resources of civilisation are upon us.

We are verily and indeed going ahead; and if the Rip Van Winkles who fell asleep half a century ago were permitted to walk this earth again, they would rub their eyes with manifest astonishment. Summer visitors have found us out, and, with increased accommodation, will be here in great numbers. Even plethoric excursion trains, after disgorging the major part of the contents at Ingleton, bring forward adventurous spirits bent on extending their conquests over the realms of space who, after a few hours' experience of our wholesome upland air, carry back to dingy streets the refreshing memory of progressiveness before us; and to the prophetic eye, that time is not far distant when the rural restfulness and picturesque scenery of the dales and hills will be more widely known and valued.

Rev. W. Thompson, *An illustrated Guide to Sedbergh, Garsdale and Dent*, 1894

9. The Railway Guide-books

Railways are mass transit. They require, and if necessary create, mass markets. It is well known how many of Britain's most popular holiday resorts owe their existence to the enterprising railway companies who built the lines, opened the stations and promoted the new fashion for seaside trips.

Country trips were another market, not quite as lucrative as the seaside resort, requiring as they did a willingness to explore the area concerned, rather than having the compact paraphernalia of piers and amusement halls provided by the seaside proprietors. The railway companies themselves produced guide-books promoting the attractions of their lines, pointing out the sights to be seen from the carriage window or what was to be seen a short distance from a wayside halt.

But other publishers and authors were keen to develop this new market, in particular to exploit the advantage of the railway in dropping the tourist off at one station where, with knapsack on his back, he could walk across moor and fell to return from a station a day's hike away. The typical tourist no longer came by carriage or on horseback; he came by train and wore boots. Railways created ramblers. The new ramblers came from a wider social class—the clerk, the better paid artisan, the seamstress. The guide-books were specifically walkers' guides, suggesting which gate to go through, which stile to use, which footpath to find.

The proximity of industrial West Riding and East Lancashire made it well worth while for the railway companies to offer special ramblers' tickets at reduced rates to a given number of stations for day trips, but period tickets to attract holidaymakers to the Dales from further afield. They took full-page advertisements in the new guide-books, alongside the adverts for tea-shops, guest-houses, country inns, and those of the owners of the new horse buses that met trains at several of the more important stations. The guide-book was part of a whole new promotion package.

But unlike most modern promotional literature, many of the

early walkers' guide-books were extremely well written, by amateurs or even professional scientists or historians who knew their Yorkshire Dales and could assume a reciprocal interest and enthusiasm in their audience. It was the beginning of a very special relationship between writers, their audience and a region with which they could share a remarkable sense of identity.

Undiscovered Swaledale

The valley above Richmond presents at the present day an aspect not wholly unlike what it wore when the Norman earl first explored its rocks and woods. Till within a few years ago, there was no proper road up the valley, the usual way to Reeth being over the bare hill by the racecourse. The road opened eleven years since is more fortunately directed, generally along the sides of the valley, which it crosses twice before arrival at Reeth. At the moment we write there is no public conveyance on this route. Perhaps the Railway Company might advantageously supply for the summer months this deficit, which is much to be lamented as shutting out one of the most beautiful tracts in the country from all but individuals with strong limbs or long purses.

Wishing our readers may have one or other of these qualifications, or that he may find this petition of mine to the able managers of the railway answered by a smart "Reeth and Swaledale Bus" at the Richmond Station, we will turn our face westward, and descend from the rock on which the town is built, only looking back now and then to notice the good effect, in a pictorial sense, of the old-looking but really modern tower, called the Temple, which stands on a pleasant hill, a little to the west of the great tower of the castle. Forward the dale begins to show its many sinuosities, promontories, and hollows most enriched by ancient wood, alternatively adhering to and returning from the stream. Beyond the mill we remark a singular round hill, crowned with trees, which stands on the centre of a semicircular sweep of the high, woody cliff.

The artist may observe in these woody escarpments two distinct beds of limestone rock, which for twenty miles up the dale appear again and again, always rising higher and higher, and always important to the geologist, as a constant mark in his sections, and to the miner as the most productive repositories of lead ore.

Arrived at the bridge, by which the road is carried to the south side of the river, we look forward on the right to a lofty hill, above which the old road runs, and on the left to a bold promontory, beneath the unseen village of Hudswell. Winding round this rugged promontory, below woods and rocks, the road opens continually new and pleasing views, in which no trace of man is visible, except where, below us, the philosophic bearer of the rod is trying to deceive the trout. These woods, in spring, are full of shrill music, softened by the cooing of doves, and occasionally startled by the scream of some jealous or clamorous vocalist. Nor is the pleasure at all lessened from a point somewhere further in the road; we look back on the oak, ash, elm and sycamore, the dark holly, the darker yew, and white-blossomed bird cherry, which diversify the broad surface of this rocky hill. Now few of my northern friends know, and how few of my southern friends have ever heard, that so fair a scene of natural beauty lies so near the proud Earl Conan's Tower. And yet we feel not half its beauty, unless, like the angler or the artist, we thread the margin of the sinuous stream, listen to its everlasting murmur, and catch the innumerable happy accidents of light and shade which escape from its rugged and shaded bank.

John Phillips, *Excursions in Yorkshire by the North Eastern Railway*, 1853

Near the Source of the Ribble

A rather out-of-the-way place this Geerstones is! There is never much traffic, and the railways have taken the most of it. There is the ghost of a fair or market held there once a month, but very few folks attend it. In winter there are very few passers; indeed the landlord said an eighteen gallon cask of ale lasted the house three months! The district is perhaps rather cold for carters to drink ale in; but the quantity is somewhat small and I thought I should not have much trouble in finding landlords nearer home who would require no visitors at all if that was to be all their store of malt liquor.

Having, on a previous occasion, travelled near the river, on its eastern bank, we now determined on going on its western side, making also a divergence to see a romantic glen, through which flows one of the feeders of the Ribble. Linn Gill is about two miles from Geerstones, and about five from Horton, and we were amply repaid by the sight of the gill for the extra walk we had, and for the sundry little inconvenience we were subject to, as, for instance, losing our way two or three times, having a few becks to cross, walls to climb over and an awkward swamp or two to navigate.

Linn Gill is a wild and romantic part of Cam Beck, a stream which flows from Cam Fell, and joins the Ribble about four miles above

Horton. There are several fine waterfalls in its course, and the recent rains had given them an unusually grand appearance. After several cascades, the course of the stream is greatly below the adjoining land, and the sides of the bed of the beck are clothed with numerous trees, whose verdure contrasted pleasantly with the limestone, which here and there cropped up. The stream had not so difficult a course to carve as that of the Gale Beck, at Thorns Gill, and there was not the variety of fantastic shapes which the limestone is capable of assuming to interest the spectator, but the scenery was altogether on a wilder and more magnificent scale. Having seen and enjoyed Linn Gill, we made our way to Ribble side, along which we walked for some distance, but its banks were bare of wood, and there was little to notice in its appearance beyond its gradual enlargement as it wended its way southwards. We then took to the road, a now almost disused highway, which leads on to the high land from Horton to the end of Cam, and so on to Newby Head, and to Wensleydale. It is now grass grown, and is seldom traversed, except by sheep and the shepherds on their way to and from the neighbouring hills, a better road from Horton to Geerstones having been found on the opposite side of the river. Its elevation however, enabled us to see the river for the greatest part of the way, and also in the valley near it. In due time we reached Horton and inspected the antique church, and again called at the neighbouring inn to enjoy the landlady's perennial meal of ham and eggs.

William Dobson, *Rambles by the Ribble,* (first series) 1864

Rambles from Ribblehead Station

After luncheon at the inn at Gearstones, you may set off to see Thorns Gill, a deep cleft in the limestone, with steep cliffs overhung with ash and rowan, through which flows the stream, Gale Beck, which is the chief confluence of the Ribble—though not that coming from Ribblehead, as it is called, close by Gearstones. The channel is remarkably tortuous, and is diversified, here with a deep, dark pool, and there with the small pot holes peculiar to the district. These pot-holes are bored by stones, which are whirled round and round by the eddying of the streams. The beck is crossed by a plank bridge, and lower down by an arch of stone.

Adjoining Thorns Gill is a cave, called Catknot Hole, which has been robbed of the stalactites that were formerly its glory.

From Gearstones or Horton the tourist should not fail to visit Lynn Gill, a wild and romantic mountain ravine, through which flows the Cam Beck, another confluence of the Ribble. On the road between Lynn Gill and Horton, near a farmhouse called Old Ing, is Brow Gill, a cavern with an imposing entrance, and near New Houses, one mile from Horton, are two chasms worth looking at, Jackdaw Hole and Sel Gill.

From Gearstones also may be made the ascent of Blea Moor, whence is a wide and glorious prospect; or the old, disused high road may be followed over Cam Fell to Hawes; or the road to Newby Head, where is a good country inn, and whence you can descend into Wensleydale.

J. Radford Thomson, *Guide to the District of Craven and the Settle and Carlisle Railway*, 1878

Ribblehead to Thorn's Ghyll

On joining the road turn to the right in the direction of Hawes. The first beauty spot to be visited is Thorn's Ghyll, and although there is a "short cut" from the station, it is better avoided unless one is familiar with the district. The great railway viaduct seen spanning the valley represents one of the many engineering triumphs in the construction of the costliest railroad track in England. When this portion of the line was being laid, no less than 2,000 navvies lived in a temporary town near the viaduct. Besides rows of wooden dwellings, the place possessed a post office, public library, and a mission house, the latter being under the auspices of the Manchester City Mission. When the work was nearing completion, and the town had almost disappeared, it is worthy of record that among the vanished institutions it was the mission hall that was missed most. A petition, signed by the remaining workers and surrounding farm inhabitants, was forwarded to the Midland Railway Company requesting that the station waiting room might be used for Sunday services. The favour was granted, and for many years fortnightly services were held at the station conducted by the vicar of Chapel-le-Dale.

About 200 yards before Gearstones (one mile) is reached, a gate upon the right opens out a grass carpeted lane which leads to Thorn's Ghyll. The stream, Gale Beck, the youthful Ribble, has here cut through great scar limestone, forming a small but picturesque ravine where vegetation grow luxuriantly, in marked contrast to the general surroundings. Upon the steep sides of each bank many species of flowering plants and shrubs add to the beauty of the scene. Among the attractive spring and early summer flowers which have found a congenial home are the bird's eye primrose and the native globe flower. The trees and shrubs include rowans, guelder rose, and bird cherry. Flood time at Thorn's Ghyll provides a grand sight, as the water rushes at a great speed through constricted channels and over curiously carved rocks.

The stream may be crossed lower down by a stone bridge, where on the opposite bank are several mammoth blocks of limestone, relics of the ice age. Some of the boulders are from twenty feet to thirty feet in circumference.

Frederick W. Riley, *Settle and the North West Yorkshire Dales*, 1923

An Excursion-party to Ingleborough Cave

On arrival at Clapham Station, and luncheon at the Flying Horse Shoe Hotel directly opposite, carriages were brought into requisition, and the party driven to the pretty village of Clapham, which lies at the foot of Ingleborough Park, the residence of the Rev. T. M. Farrer, who is Lord of the Manor and principal landowner of the district. Mr Farrer was good enough to allow the Tourists to walk through his beautiful grounds to the entrance to the cave, which runs into the bowels of the lower Ingleborough range, for a distance of more than half a mile. These grounds are delightful and add greatly to the interest of this remarkable locality. The dell or gorge by which the cave is approached, runs into the hills between Ingleton and Settle, the upper part commencing in a precipitous scar, which bars the way, the limestone cliffs on all sides closing in a dell. A small stream issues from the scar, and joins lower down that flowing from the cave, which shortly forms the grand lake in the grounds under the hill. The narrow dell, the wooded heights, the rushing stream and occasional waterfall, were full of beauty, and the walk along the terrace above the lake, to the cave, is sheltered and ornamented by the tender and graceful foliage of innumerable shrubs and trees. On reaching the entrance to the cave, the guide is first found, with candles ready lit for the tourists, in order to penetrate its dark recesses. A fairly defined road has been traced along the margin of the stream, which has frequently to be crossed, as the various cavities and chambers are reached. In some of the passages, stooping is requisite when the roof is low but they are frequently the vestibules to spacious and lofty chambers.

Ingleborough Cave is remarkable for the number and beauty of its stalactites and stalagmites some of which are quite transparent, whilst others are sonorous, and can be made to imitate a peal of bells. Amongst the most marked are the Jockey's Cap, the Elephant's Legs, the Beehive, the Fleece and the Shower Bath. There are also many others bearing resemblance to natural objects or grotesque figures of animals and birds. The Gothic arch and pillared chamber are also prominent and particular features of this interesting cave. The cave, which is the largest in Yorkshire, has been penetrated to the extent of 1,000 yards, and the stream that runs through it finds its way from the slopes of Ingleborough through a deep chasm known as Gaping Gill.

J. Brown, *Tourist Rambles in the Northern and Midland Counties,* 1885

A Warning to Ladies

I should advise all persons who pilgrimate the valley, if it is but for a day, to take with them an extra pair of shoes and stockings; for whether they visit fall or fell, they are pretty sure to get wetshod in seeking the best points of view. Besides, by wading a beck here and there, one avoids many a long and weary detour; and no harm follows being wetshod if you only change your foot-gear as soon as your march is done. The walking tourist will find it very convenient to have his light marching-kit sent by the Mail-cart that goes up and down the valley every day, and calls at the principal villages on the route.

Females pilgrimating Wensleydale, on foot, will not "merrily hent the stile-a" so long as the present preposterous form of petticoat prevails. A distinguished foreigner remarks: "It is ridiculous to call woman's the softer sect when they are hooped with steel, and it is visible to the naked eye that are a deal more sterner than men's". The stiles of Wensleydale are narrow slits in the walls, on the average from six to eight inches wide; and some I saw measured only four inches.

George Hardcastle, *Wanderings in Wensleydale,* 1864

Ask for Isabella

The Abbey of Fors took its name from the beautiful little waterfall of "fors" visible on your right just under Colby Hill. Going past Askrigg Mill, occupied by Mr. Addison, who is well "up" in the local history and in communicating his knowledge, cross a stone footbridge, and keep to the footpath till you reach nearly the top of the hill; then pass along a cart-road into the gill of Mill-Beck, and so on to the foot of *Mill Gill Fors*, a charming broken waterfall 69 feet high. Returning to the gate through which you entered, either follow the edge of the glen for a mile, where you will come to the top of *Whit-fell Gill Fors*, or, if you call at Mrs Little's at Helm, you may (if it is not Monday, her washing day), perhaps prevail upon her to allow her clever little "help" Isabella Scarr, to guide you by a rather difficult track to the foot of the fall. Seen either from above or below *Whit-fell Gill Fors* is "beautiful exceedingly" coming down in one unbroken sheet of water forty feet high.

George Hardcastle, *Wanderings in Wensleydale Yorkshire*, 1864

A Serpentine Stream of Liquid Silver Thrown Across a Brussels Carpet

As is generally the case with all sentimental tourists, I may say the morning was remarkably fine when we commenced our ramble to the Maze Holes. I trust the reader will not suppose that the first step landed us on Stag's Fell, but—as readers of newspapers say—nothing worthy of notice occurred before we reached the summit of what is known as the "Clint", and I will begin our memoranda there.

As there are said to be "sermons in stone", the adamantine cliff on which we stood invited as eloquently as possible under the circumstances to take a seat. Having toiled up the steep aclivity, at the expense of a considerable quantity of perspiration—consisting of what a physiologist would call a *sudorific*—we willingly complied with the "stony sermon" and sat ourselves down. And now, as the novel writers say, for the pen of a Trollope; but as I would say, for a pen of Wordsworth, for he alone could do justice to the grandeur of the scene. In front, but slightly to the right, lay the sunny little town of Hawes. On the slates of the houses the sunbeams were "waltzing delightfully"—to use the favourite expression of the boating miss. The brilliancy of the scintillation gave a brightness and glow to the surrounding fields and groves, which, like a scene in a love tale, may be better imagined than described. Behind these eminences which bound the valley to the south and east, we could discern flat-topped Ingleboro', with Whernside to the left of it. Nearer, at our feet, is the expanded vale of Wensley, with the meandering Yore shining like a serpentine stream of liquid silver thrown across a Brussels carpet. The villages, the few houses—but probably the reader will think I have forgotten the Maze Holes, and are going to spend the day on Stag's Fells. I will, however, assure him that we viewed the prospect with delight, and left it with regret, forming a serious but silent promise that many moons should not wax and wane before we paid another visit. . . .

J. Routh, "Ramble No 4 from Hawes Station to the Maze Holes", *Tourists' Guide and Pictorial Handbook to Wensleydale and Swaledale,* 1895

A Day Trip to Grassington

Grassington with its little picturesque railway station is soon reached. On clearing the station premises you take the uphill road on the right and then descend to the fine stone bridge over the river, said to be the oldest in Wharfedale, though we always thought that Ilkley bridge claimed that distinction. The views both up and down the river from the bridge are very pretty. The up-field path behind the seat at the end of the bridge is preferable to the road, as it brings you into Grassington at the top of the village; you can take the carriage road when you descend again to the bridge.

Grassington is a place of nooks and corners: it is the most delightfully jumbled-up out-of-the-way place it is possible to imagine. All the houses appear to be elbowing one another for front position: its irregularity constitutes its particular charm. It is a village—though the inhabitants would like you to call it a town—that is high up in the world, being 150 feet higher than the river bed, and 700 feet above sea level. You could scarcely get higher unless you lived in a balloon; and there is no need to put yourself in that perilous position while Grassington maintains its present elevated situation. It is not a beggarly-looking place either; there is an air of comfort and well-being that is very assuring to the visitor, who can obtain anything he wants, be it fish, flesh, fowl, or even "good red herring". The place is governed by a Parish Council, who are sparing no pains to make it a health resort of the highest order, as its natural position, its limestone surroundings, and the bracing nature of its atmosphere so well fit it to be. The opening of a railway station 10 miles nearer than it had ever been before, must be of incalculable benefit to the whole dale.

There are four good hotels in Grassington, besides a Temperance Hotel, a large public Boarding-House, a Mechanics' Hall with a public clock; and many private lodging-houses are open to accommodate visitors who wish to make a more extended acquaintance with the locality. These, we fancy, will have to speak in good time, for Grassington has no need to advertise.

Thomas Johnson, *A Commonsense Guide to Grassington and Skipton Shewing What May be Seen in a Day and How to See it*, 1903

No Ephemeral Tinsel Glories

Down to the past fifteen or twenty years the average holiday-seeker looked only for excitement and recreation as a set-off to the exhausting routine of a sedentary occupation in a busy centre. He was attracted by the gaiety of Morecambe: the society surges of Blackpool; or the glamour of Scarborough. He went; he saw; he dissipated—and he returned to his labours with nothing more solid than the vague memories of equally vague conquests and nebulous impressions, and no improvement of health in return for the money he had lavished to maintain a hypothetical reputation among fresh acquaintances. Now he takes a saner view of holiday proprieties. He has found that the ephemeral tinsel glories of the seaside are not to be compared to the solid advantages of inland resorts like Grassington, where one may obtain adequate accommodation, the most wholesome food, a variety of rational recreation, and revel in everything that is pleasing to eye as well as health-giving to the physical system. Hence the quieter inland resorts are becoming more generously patronised from the large centres, with the natural and gratifying result that there is a more generous distribution of holiday cash.

Waddington's Guide to Grassington and Craven Dales, 1918

Geology from a Railway Carriage

Hellifield to Carnforth

This line, part of the "Little North Western" (constructed 1850), was until the building of the Settle and Carlisle line, the main line of the Midland Coy., and their route to Scotland via Carnforth or Ingleton. It leaves the present main line 2m. south of Settle, and follows the south side of the Middle branch of the great Craven Fault, one of the few faults in England which make conspicuous surface features, owing in this case to the differences in the modes of weathering of millstone Grit and Limestone. Thus as we follow Carr Beck (tributary of the Ribble) to its head we get good views of Settle and *Giggleswick* (From Hellifield 5m.) with the background of the fault-scarp. We pass near the buildings of the Giggleswick Grammar School. The copper-covered dome of the school-chapel is a landmark on the height. The late Mr Walter Morrison, of Malham Tarn, who presented the chapel to the school, was impressed with the resemblance between the limestone country of the district and that of Jerusalem, and, the domed architecture of the Byzantine style harmonising so well with the hills of the Holy Land, he thought a dome might look equally well here. His architect, G. F. Bodley, made the experiment of wedding the dome to the English Gothic, and the result is not unsuccessful. Internally the building is rich with rare marbles, mosaics and wood-carving. The relics excavated from the Victoria Cave, Settle, are in the school-museum.

A little farther on we come into the Wenning Valley, upon a morassy bit of moorland country, typical of low-level Millstone Grit. Beyond it is a strikingly fine panorama of the Limestone hills—Moughton (1402 feet) and Ingleborough (2373 feet) revealing clearly their structure.

At *Clapham* (10¾ m.) we look south up the valley of the Keasden Beack, and see, about 5m. off, Bowland Knotts, a fine piece of rough Millstone Grit country. We are looking along the path of the ice which, coming from Ingleborough and the Hodder Basin, cutting the striae which attracted Mr. Tiddeman's attention and produced his epoch-making paper. The Knotts (not to be confused with Bowland Knotts) are separated by a series of channels cut by the overflow of lakes belonging to a stage when the ice-front had retreated from the watershed.

A branch line leaves Clapham to the north for Ingleton and Tebay via Sedbergh. It crosses on to the Ingleton Coalfield with no distinctive rocks visible, though the minehead on the left is unmistakable in its significance.

Ingleton (From Hellifield 15m.) is one of the most attractive centres for geological excursions in Yorkshire. We are here at the foot of the deep valley which separates Ingleborough from Whernside and get good views of both. We cross the river Greta by a high viaduct, which joins the L.M. & S. Rly and the L. & N.E. Rly. Mealsbank Quarry is below us on the right. Looking down stream (left) we see the river brawling over reefs of rather reddish Coal Measure rocks. We are close to one of the branches of the Craven Faults, and another branch farther up-stream brings in the Ingletonian Series.

The Morecambe and Carnforth line, which we must resume, follows westward along the Wenning, and at Upper Bentham touches the reputed edge of the Ingleton Coalfield. At *Bentham* (15m.) we reach a drift country with many elongated drift-mounds and occasional views of the Lune. At *Wennington* (18¼m.) the line, still in heavily drift-covered country, divides again, one branch following the Lune to *Lancaster* (Green Ayre sta.) (28¾m.) and *Morecambe* (32m.). The other branch runs to Carnforth (27¾m.) with connections for the Lake District and Barrow.

Percy Fry Kendall and Herbert Wroot, *Geology of Yorkshire*, 1924

10. Farming and Husbandry

Man, as much as the forces of nature, has shaped the landscape of the Yorkshire Dales. The taming of the landscape is the result of a long, slow battle with the elements, in a region where the climate is harsh, soils are thin, and hillsides are steep.

The battle began at the time of the earliest settlements in Bronze and Iron Age times, through the great period of Enclosures in the eighteenth and nineteenth centuries which brought the characteristic Dales landscape of small fields, scattered barns and long lines of drystone wall across the fell sides. The battle continues into the age of the tractor and the mechanized dairy.

The main difference in the twentieth century is that farming is no longer labour intensive; machines, and the inevitable logic of economics have replaced the farmhand, and only a fraction of those once living and working on the land now remain. But for these who remain, tenant farmers or owner-occupiers of the often amalgamated upland farms, life has not changed so dramatically as might appear. The same discipline of the seasons dominates, with the all-too-brief growing season and the production of grass crucial to the hill-farming economy; lambing, haytime, tupping occur with inevitable regularity. Walls still have to be gapped, gates hung, muck spread, pasture drained, work which, if not done, would destroy the appearance of the landscape as much as the economy of the farm. Traditional hill farming is the best guardian of the Dales landscape.

Cottage industries, once vital to maintain the fragile rural economy have changed—knitting and the making of oatcake or cheese are no longer the prerequisite of any competent farmer's wife. But traditional skills remain and flourish in every Dale, cultivated with a pride and expertise, whether on the fell side or in the kitchen.

The Great Fair on Malham Moor

. . . a prodigious large field of enclosed land, being upwards of 732

Kilnsey Crag, an engraving by John Phillips for *The Rivers, Mountains and Sea Coast of Yorkshire,* 1853

The Wensleydale Knitters from *Costumes of Yorkshire* by George Walker, 1814

The Valley of Desolation by Chiang Yee from *The Silent Traveller in the Yorkshire Dales,* 1940

acres in one pasture, a great part of which is a fine, rich soil and remarkable for making cattle both expeditiously and uncommonly fat. This GREAT CLOSE properly so called was for many years rented by Mr Birtwhistle of Skipton, the celebrated Craven Grazier, and on which you might frequently see 5,000 head of Scotch Cattle at one time. As soon as these were a little freshened, notice was dispersed among the neighbouring markets and villages, that a great FAIR would be held in this Field on a particular day, and lots being separated by guess as nearly as could such manner be done to the wants and wishes of any Purchaser, so much was fixed immediately by the eye upon that lot, of so much per head, taking them as they were accidentally intermixed upon an average. To a stranger this mode of bargaining will appear exceedingly difficult and precarious; but it is amazing with what readiness and exactitude persons accustomed to the business will ascertain the value of a very large lot, frequently of several hundreds together.

As soon as these were disposed of, a fresh Drove succeeded; and beside Sheep and Horses frequently great in numbers, Mr Birtwhistle has had Twenty Thousand head of Cattle on the field in one summer; every Herd enticed from their native soil and ushered into this fragrant Pasture, by the Pipe of an Highland Orpheus.

If the Craven Graziers will yet esteem it a benefit to the Country, Mr Birtwhistle has the merit of being the first who traversed the Hebrides and the Isles and Counties in the North of Scotland, and that at hazardous period, in 1745, beginning a Commerce, which by gradual increase ever since seems to have checked the ancient breeding the LONG HORNED Craven Cattle, which were formerly held in highest estimation. And even yet, although the price of the Scots are becoming extravagantly high, the Trade continues to wait on its highest vigour.

. . . Mr B. has had 10,000 head in cattle on the road from Scotland at one time. Vast quantities are fed in every part of Craven for the markets in the populous towns both in Yorkshire and Lancashire.

Thomas Hurtley, *A Concise Account of Some Curiosities in the environs of Malham,* 1786

Building the Drystone Walls and Burning Lime

The ride (to Malham) is truly wild and romantic; nature here sits in solitary grandeur on the hills, which are lofty, green to the top, and rise in irregular heaps on all hands, in their primeval state of pasture, without the least appearance of a plough, or habitation, for many miles. In the summer they afford good keep for cattle, great numbers of which are taken in to feed from April or May to Michaelmas, when the owners generally choose to take them away. The pasturage if a horse for that time is 14s; a cow 7s; a sheep 1s 6d. Many of these pastures, which are of great extent, have been lately divided by stone walls, of about two yards high, one yard wide at the bottom, lessening to a foot at the top. A man can make about seven yards, in length, of this in one day, and is paid from 20d to 2s. The stone brought and laid down from him, cost about 7s more.

. . . The stone of the hills around Maum, is burnt into lime, of which five pecks, each containing 16 quarts, are delivered at the kiln mouth for 7d. It takes a week in burning and when it begins to be calcined, the lowest stratum is drawn out of the mouth, and more stone and coal put in at the top.

William Bray, *Sketch of a Tour into Derbyshire and Yorkshire,* 1777
second edition 1783

Haytime

. . . The grass being strewed equally, and laid as light on the ground as possible, is suffered to remain in that condition until next day, about eleven o'clock, when the upper surface of the grass will be found dried and withered; the hay-makers then begin at the side of the field furthest from the wind, and make the grass into small rows, which, if artfully performed, will expose an entirely new surface of the grass to the influence of the sun and air: this operates with great facility. In the evening of the same day, the rows are made into small cocks ("foot cocks"); the next morning, as soon as the dew is well evaporated, the cocks are spread abroad carefully by the hand; about noon, when thought necessary, it is again made into small rows, called turnings, which, by varying the surface, expedite its complete drying; and if the weather has been perfectly fine from the cutting of the grass it is found sufficiently dry to carry it to the barn, or rick, if the quantity to be put together is not very great; but if that is the case, it is sometimes made into large cocks, but it is never allowed to remain long before it is carried, as the base of the cock would be injured by the moisture of the ground, as well as the outside influence of the weather.

In the dales, when the above method of hay-making is practised, there is scarcely an acre in tillage. Hay is the grand object of the farmer, and he bestows upon it the most sedulous attention, and has many difficulties to combat: the season commences late, the surrounding hills occasion frequent and sudden showers, and the meadows, which are all natural, abound with the *trifolium repens* . . . etc; which being more succulent than the grasses properly so called, are more difficult to harvest than the produce of meadows where the grasses greatly predominate; yet with all the difficulties, more hay is reaped in these dales with the same number of hands, than any other place I have seen.

William Fothergill of Carr End
Tukes's *General View of the Agriculture of the North Riding of Yorkshire 1800*

Undoubtedly the greatest historian of the Dales, and a figure of national importance, DR THOMAS DUNHAM WHITAKER (1759–1821) *transformed topography into serious scholarship and enquiry. As a weakly and delicate boy, he was boarded out with a Reverend Sheepshank in Grassington, and his first-hand knowledge of Dales life dates from this period, when he was a pupil at Threshfield Grammar School. He eventually became vicar of Whalley, Lancashire writing his fine* History of Whalley *before undertaking the remarkable* History of Craven *in 1805. The work remains to this day a model of careful scholarship and patient research, to which grateful scholars and topographers of succeeding generations have turned. Many of the more picturesque accounts of Craven history owe their origin to Whitaker's brilliant researches among documentary evidence.*

His transference to the industrial parish of Blackburn in 1818 proved too exhausting to the ailing scholar and his grandiose plans for a history of Yorkshire never materialized, the first volume being published with the celebrated engravings by Turner as the History of Richmondshire *in 1823.* Richmondshire *has nothing of the earlier work's insight and clarity.*

Life in Upper Wharfedale in the Eighteenth Century

Another part of the subject which yet remains in the antiquated modes of life which prevailed till within the last eighty years among the yeomanry of Wharfedale. These may be illustrated by the manners of Linton in particular. . . .

I suspect them to be of high antiquity; for though the race of independent yeomanry, the happiest, and probably the most virtuous condition of life in the kingdom, arose in Wharfedale, partly from the dispersions of the estates of the monasteries, and partly out of the vast alienations made by the Cliffords, yet, before either of those eras, the tenantry lived in so much plenty and security, the tenements descended so regularly from father to son, and the control exercised over them by their lords was of so mild a nature, that the transition from occupancy to property would not be marked by any violent change of manners of habits. But to be more particular.

There was a considerable quantity of hemp, and more anciently of line or flax, from which the place derives its name, grown within the township of Linton, which the inhabitants spun and prepared themselves. Almost every woman could spin flax from the distaff, or rock, as it was called, and card and spin wool from the fleece. There were no poor rates and no public houses. In 1740 every housekeeper in the township, excepting one, kept a cow. The estates were small, and the number of little freeholders considerable in proportion; almost all of these farmed their own property, and lived upon the produce.

At this time tea was scarcely introduced; for I remember a very sensible man, who declared that when he first saw the school-master drinking this beverage he could not conceive what refreshment he was taking.

Every landowner had a small flock of sheep, and fatted one or two hogs every winter. They all grew oats, which formed the principal article of their subsistence. The kiln, in which the grain was parched previously to its being ground, belonged to the township, and when in use was a sort of coffee-house, where the politics of the place and the day were discussed.

Their bread, and most of their puddings, were made of oatmeal; and this, mixed with milk, or water when milk was scarce, supplied them with breakfast and supper. Each owner, too, grew his own barley, and manufactured his own malt. The large steeping-trough, which belonged to the village in general, remained within my recollection. Very little fresh meat was eaten except at their annual feasts, when cattle were slaughtered and sold by persons who never exercised the trade at any other time. Indeed, under such a system of manners, there could scarcely be any tradesman; every man exercised, however imperfectly, almost every trade for himself. The quantity of money in circulation must have been inconceivably small. One great advantage of these simple habits was, that superfluous wealth and abject poverty were equally excluded. . . .

Almost everything was in common. There was a stone called the batting stone, where the women of the place beat their linen with battledores after having rinsed it in the brook; a necessary process, as it had previously been washed in a certain animal fluid, a very disgusting substitute for soap and water. Their linen was rarely smoothed with heated iron.

Their early hours rendered their consumption of candles excepting in the depths of winter, very trifling, and those were merely rushes partly peeled and dipped in coarse fat.

Cheeses were almost universally made at home; but as few kept a sufficient number of cows for this purpose, village partnerships were formed, and the milk of several farms thrown together in succession.

Few hired servants, male or female, were kept, but where this was done little distinction was kept up between the different members of the family; they invariably ate and worked together, the only effectual method to ensure diligence and prevent waste in dependents. The wages of labourers were very low, not exceeding twopence halfpenny a day with board. The facilities of learning were great. A grammar-school prepared many natives of the village for the University at no expense but part of their time. The price of a day-school was two shillings per quarter, and an excellent writing-master attended for some weeks every year at the free school for sixpence a week per scholar. Young people of both sexes availed themselves of his instruction, and the time was considered a sort of carnival.

T. D. C. Whitaker, *The History and Antiquities of the Deanery of Craven*, 1805

A Picture of Terrestrial Paradise

Arrived at Dent, after a tedious and disagreeable journey, having, in the course of it, passed through a small part of Lancashire, and travelled about eight miles in the county of Westmoreland.

We enter Dent Dale from the west, and proceeded down the Dale to the town of Dent, which is nearly in the centre. This Dale is entirely surrounded with high mountains, and has only one opening in the west, where a carriage may enter with safety. It is about 12 miles in length, and from one and a half to two miles in breadth. The whole Dale is enclosed; and viewed from the higher grounds, presents a picture of a terrestrial paradise.

At Dent we received the following information relevant to the state of the Dale. Estates are small, and chiefly in the actual possessions of the proprietors. Inclosures are small, and mostly grass. No farms above £50 a year, and none but yearly leases are granted. Sheep mostly from Scotland, but a great number of milch cows are kept, and large quantities of butter and cheese produced. The hills in the neighbourhood of the Dale, are all common, and dividing them among the different proprietors, it is supposed, would be attended with beneficial consequences. A considerable quantity of stockings wrought by women upon wires, which are disposed of at Kendal. Very few turnips cultivated, hay being the chief dependence in winter.

from the Journal of the Survey made by Rennie, Brown and Sherriff, 1793
in *A General View of Agriculture of the West Riding of Yorkshire*

Reins

A *Rein* (strip of unploughed land) is the only kind of boundary which it was practicable for the occupiers of adjoining land to make, where there were no stones and few labourers. The Danes brought the institution into these dales with them, as they did to Normandy, where I believe they are still in use. In Wharfedale, Coverdale, Wensleydale, and on the slopes of the hills east of Nidderdale, the country is covered with little step-like terraces called "raines" (pr. reeans). . . .

The sides of the limestone slopes of Wharfedale are covered with them, each being twenty or thirty yards long, and two or three yards wide, and though they almost there run horizontally, just occasionally they lie up and down. These "raines" lay on land which belonged to the village communities of the dale, and each man in the village had one. One man held a "rein" for three years, when he exchanged it for another. This system was in full working order down to the time of the grandfathers of the present generation of men now fifty years old. With the decline of agriculture and the increase of grazing farming, consequent upon the departure of manufacturing, power to enclose was applied for under the Enclosure Act, 1836. . . . Long stone walls were built, and the "raines" remained as monuments to a bygone age. This was followed by rapid depopulation of the dales. The stream of emigration set in to the great manufacturing towns of Leeds and Bradford; so that the population of the dales is not now over one third of what it was early in the century.

Joseph Lucas, *Studies in Nidderdale*, 1872

Baking Oatcake

These cakes are made of oatmeal and water or buttermilk or, what is termed blue milk—that is, milk after the cream has been skimmed off it, but very unlike the blue milk of London, to which the Water Companies' cows, the *pumps*, so mainly contribute. A regular baker of these cakes can "turn-off" thirty in an hour—a peck of oatmeal, containing twenty eight pounds, will make sixty five cakes, for the baking of which eight pence is charged, and the price of the cake is wholly dependent upon the market price of meal.

The meal is generally mixed the night before baking in the *kneading-tub*, one hand continually stirring the mixture to prevent any lumps whilst the other is employed putting in the meal. This tub, which is kept expressly for the purpose, is rarely ever cleansed with water, but merely partially scraped out with a knife.—The particles adhering to the sides ferment, and cause the next quantity of meal put into the tub to rise more speedily. . . .

On the morning of baking, the *backstone* (formerly a slate but now invariably a plate of iron let into a framework of bricks over a stove) is thoroughly cleansed—a fire is lighted at a mean temperature—near to it a table is placed and the meal ready for use. The baker, with a snow-white apron and unimpeachable hands, having ascertained the heat of the backstone, commences operations, and you cannot well conceive what a field there is for exercise of grace. —A flat piece of wood, about seventeen inches square with lines scored upon it crossways, called a *backboard*, is sprinkled with some dry meal—the hand is then moved over the surface of the board in a circular direction, leaving an area of meal in the centre, upon which a ladle-full from the kneading tub is poured. The board being lifted off the table, is shaken with both hands, and the meal obeying the rotary motion, spreads in circular form—this is transferred to a piece of thin linen, or at times cartridge paper, called the "*turning-off*" resting on a smooth board called a *spittle*, very similar to the backboard in shape, having the addition of a handle and an edge of iron; the cake is then with a strong jerk thrown laterally upon the backstone and the linen is taken up: this movement requires great dexterity, and the length of the cake proves the efficiency of the baker. After baking for a minute, the spittle is put in request in turning it—another minute completes the baking, and the cake is placed on one of the backs of the "fleeok" its shape being oval in form and half to three quarters of a yard long; it is much eaten, and considered very wholesome.

Frederic Montagu, *Gleanings in Craven*, 1838

A Dales Kitchen

My first kitchen was a stone-floored cottage in the Yorkshire dales. It had a thick rag rug on the hearth and a ceiling rack that held thin, brown oatcake. When soft and newly made, the oatcake hung in loops, which later dried out stiff and brittle. The stone slab where it was baked made a little separate hearth at one side of the fireplace. The high mantelpiece had a polished gun over it, and on it two china dogs and brass ornaments. The window, almost blocked by red geraniums in flower-pots, was set deep in the thick stone wall; and most of the light came through an open door that gave onto the moor. Fresh mountain air and the smell of cooking always filled this brightly polished kitchen. I can remember a basin of mutton broth with a long-boned chop in it. A man reached up to lift down a flap of oatcake to crumble in the broth, and I remember, too, being carried high on the farmhand's shoulder, and feeling him drop down and rise up as he picked white mushrooms out of the wet grass. Once a week the wagonette ran to Skipton to take people to market.

Dorothy Hartley, *Food in England,* 1954

Black Snails to Save the Cheese

The farmer's wife of the 17th and 18th centuries had to make her cheese under much more difficult conditions than our modern dairy-maid has to face. She had no thermometer to record the right temperature of the milk. The heat of the milk had to be judged by placing the hand in the vat or better still the elbow, or by tasting before she dare add the rennet. Even rennet was not obtained with the ease it is today. A couple of centuries ago rennet as we know it, had not been thought of. In those days when the farmer killed a young calf, the stomach was taken out, washed, salted, cured and hung on a nail in the kitchen rafters to dry. The young calf's stomach contained the properties found in our modern liquid rennet.

When the farmer's wife required rennet to coagulate the milk she would cut off a small piece of the dried stomach, boil it in a pan on the kitchen fire, and strain off the liquid to cool. This liquid would serve for the next few days' cheese making, and when it was used up she repeated the process. The dried calf's stomach was known as "keslop" but the cheesemaker of two centuries ago had no means of finding out the strength of her home made rennet. Sometimes she ran short of "keslop" and thereby short of rennet. When this happened the household had to resort to hunting the black snail in some nearby swamp. A black snail in a bowl of milk causes the same reaction as rennet and eventually cheese curd will begin to form.

All farmhouse cheeses of this period were pickled; i.e. salted in brine. This method of curing and flavouring the cheese created much more work than the present day style of dry salting the curd, although a well made, fully cured pickled cheese is still considered to be the finest flavoured Wensleydale cheese obtainable. Pickling gives a texture and flavour to the cheese which cannot be brought out by the dry salting process.

'Kit' Calvert, *The Story of Wensleydale Cheese,* 1946

The Wensleydale Knitters

Simplicity and industry characterize the manners and occupations of the various humble inhabitants of Wensley Dale. Their wants, it is true, are few; but to supply these, almost constant labour is required. In any business where the assistance of the hands is not necessary, they universally resort to knitting. Young and old, male and female, are all adepts in this art. Shepherds attending their flocks, men driving cattle, women going to market, are all thus industriously employed. A woman of the name of Slinger, who lived in Cotterdale, was accustomed regularly to walk to the market at Hawes, a distance of three miles, with the weekly knitting of herself and family packed in a bag upon her head, knitting all the way. She continued her knitting while she staid at Hawes, purchasing the little necessaries for her family, with the addition of worsted for the work of the ensuing week; all of which she placed upon her head, returning occupied with her kneedles as before. She was so expeditious and expert, that the produce of the day's labour was generally a complete pair of men's stockings.

George Walker, *The Costume of Yorkshire,* 1814

The Knitters of Dent

But perhaps the most characteristic custom of the Dales, is what is called their Sitting, or going-a-sitting. Knitting is a great practice in the dales. Men, women, and children, all knit. Formerly you might have met the waggoners knitting as they went along with their teams; but this is now rare; for the greater influx of visitors, and their wonder expressed at this and other practices, have made them rather ashamed of them, and shy of strangers observing them. But the men still knit a great deal in the houses; and the women knit incessantly. They have knitting schools, where the children are taught; and where they sing in chorus knitting songs, some of which appear as childish as the nursery songs of the last generation. Yet all of them bear some reference to their employment and mode of life; and the chorus, which maintains regularity of action and keeps up the attention, is of more importance than the words. Here is a specimen:

Bell-wether o' Barking,* cries baa, baa,
How many sheep have we lost today?
Nineteen we have lost, one have we faun'
Run Rockie†, run Rockie, run, run, run.

This is sung while they knit one round of the stocking; when the second round commences they begin again

Bell-wether o' Barking, cries baa, baa,
How many sheep have we lost today?
Eighteen we have lost, two have we faun'
Run Rockie, run Rockie, run, run, run.

and so on till they have knit twenty rounds, decreasing the numbers on the one hand, and increasing them on the other.

These songs are sung not only by the children in the schools, but also by the people at their sittings, which are social assemblies of the neighbourhood, not for eating and drinking, but merely for society. As soon as it becomes dark, and the usual business of the day is over, and the young children are put to bed, they rake or put out the fire; take their cloaks and lanterns, and set out with their knitting to the house of the neighbour, where the sitting falls in rotation, for it is a regularly circulating assembly from house to house through the particular neighbourhood. The whole troop of neighbours being collected, they sit and knit, singing knitting songs, and tell knitting-stories. Here all the old stories and traditions of the dale come up, and they often get so excited that they say "Neighbours, we'll not part tonight," that is, till after twelve o'clock. All this time their knitting goes on with unremitting speed. They sit, rocking to and fro like so many weird wizards. They burn no candle, but knit by the light of the peat fire. And this rocking motion is connected with a mode of knitting peculiar to the place, called swaving, which is difficult to describe. Ordinary knitting is performed by a variety of

*a mountain overlooking Dent.
†the shepherd's dog.

little motions, but this is a single uniform tossing motion of both hands at once, and the body accompanying it with a sort of sympathetic action. The knitting produced is just the same as by the ordinary method. They knit with crooked pins called pricks; and use a knitting-sheath consisting commonly of a hollow piece of wood, as large as the sheath of a dagger, curved to the side, and fixed in a belt called the cowband. The women of the north, in fact, often sport very curious knitting sheaths. We have seen a wisp of straw tied up pretty tightly, into which they stick their needles; and sometimes a bunch of quills of at least half-a-hundred in number. These sheaths and cowbands are often presents from their lovers to the young women. Upon the band there is a hook upon which the long end of the knitting is suspended that it may not dangle. In this manner they knit for the Kendal market, stockings, jackets, nightcaps, and a kind of cap worn by negroes, called bump-caps. These are made of very coarse worsted, and knit a yard in length, one half of which is turned into the other, before it has the appearance of a cap.

The smallness of their earnings may be inferred from the price for the knitting of one of these caps being three-pence. But all knit, and knitting is not so much their sole labour as an auxiliary gain. The woman knits when her housework is done; the man when his out-of-doors work is done, as they walk about their garden, or go from one village to another, the process is going on. We saw a stout rosy girl driving some cows to the field. Without anything on her head, in her short bedgown and wooden clogs, she went on after them with a great stick in her hand. A lot of calves which were in the field seemed determined to rush out, but the damsel laid lustily about her with her cudgel, and made them decamp. As we observed her proceedings from a house opposite, and, amused at the contest between her and the calves, said, "well done! dairymaid!" "O," said the woman of the house, "that is no dairymaid; she is the farmer's only daughter, and will have quite a fortune. She is the best knitter in the dale." That is, the young lady of fortune, earned a shilling a day.

The neighbouring dale, Garsdale, which is a narrower and more secluded one than Dent, is a great knitting dale. The old men sit there in companies around the fire, and so intent are they on their occupation and stories, that they pin cloths on their shins to prevent them being burnt; and sometimes they may be seen on a bench at the house-front, and whence they have come out to cool themselves, sitting in a row knitting with their shin-cloths on, making the oddest appearance imaginable.

William Howitt, *The Rural Life of England,* 1844

The Little World of Dentdale

About mid-way in the valley lies its hamlet, called Dent-town—a Swiss-like village, embosomed in hills, with its picturesque houses, many of which have remarkable projecting roofs and outside staircases, leading, by a little gallery, into the chambers; its low-spired church or "kirk" as it is called, and its old-fashioned endowed school, of which we shall have more to say anon.

The only road in the valley follows the course of the river, excepting where that course is meandering. Like a sedate man of business and a playful child, so proceed together the road and the little river.

The homesteads of the dale lie scattered on the hill-sides, being generally erected near those water-courses, or gills, as they are called, which, proceeding from the bogs of the hill-tops, form themselves into rivulets and have worn channels down the rocky hill-sides. They are diversified by occasional abrupt and picturesque falls, and often from their highest descent are margined by trees. Nothing can be more delightful than these clear little streams, hurrying down with living voices, each a willing tributary to the cheerful river.

As in the case in these dales, the good people of Dentdale form a little world in themselves. Each is generally the proprietor of his own section of the hill-side—that is between rivulet and rivulet—which form the natural landmarks of each demesne. Two or three fields, called "pastureheads" are generally enclosed and cultivated near the house, where oats, wheat, and potatoes are grown for family consumption; and the lower descent of the hill, down to the level of the valley, is used for grass and hay for the horses and cows; but the upper parts, called "the fell-side" are grazed by large flocks of sheep, geese, and wild ponies. Sheep, however, form the wealth of the valleys; and the sheep-washings and shearings make as blithe holidays as the harvest-homes, and the wakes and fairs, of other districts.

The greatest sociality exists among the inhabitants of this simple district, occasioning as much visiting as in more dignified and gayer society. In order that the Dee—for such is the name of the river—may interpose no barrier to the intercourse of the opposite sides of the valley, it is crossed by many little stone bridges and stepping-stones. In hot weather the dale children may be seen, on their return from school, dabbling in the water, with their shoes and stockings off, catching fish or hopping from stone to stone, playing a hundred vagaries, any of which would alarm a city mother.

Besides their small agricultural occupation, and the tending of their feathered and woolly flocks, the dales people have another employment, which engrosses a great portion of time; this is knitting. Old men and young, women and children, all knit. The aged man, blind and decrepit, sits on the stone seat at the door, mechanically pursuing this employment, which seems as natural to his hands as breathing to his lungs. The old woman, the parent of three generations, sits in the chimney-corner knitting, while she rocks, with her foot, the wooden cradle in which lies the youngest-born of the family. The intermediate generations have their knitting likewise, which they take up and lay down as their daily vocations allow. The little intercourse that the dales-people have with the rest of the world, makes them almost unconscious of the singularity of this employment. For aught they know to the contrary, the rest of England knit as much as they. Although a rumour of railroads, power-looms, and wove stockings has reached them, they still find a demand in Kendal for their goods; and, though everyone says the trade was better in their father's time, they still go on knitting, contented in the belief that, while the world stands, stockings and caps will be wanted; and consequently, that the dales people will always be knitters. Such is Dentdale, and such is its people.

Mary Howitt, "Dentdale Fifty Years Ago", 1840
from *Hope on! Hope Ever!*

PROFESSOR ADAM SEDGWICK (1785–1873) *has been described as "one of the world's greatest field-geologists". Born in Dent, son of the local vicar and schoolmaster, and educated at Sedbergh and Trinity College, Cambridge, he was Woodwardian Professor of Geology for fifty-five years. During that time his work included the elucidation of the ancient systems of Cambrian and Devonian rocks in Britain and Europe; he taught Darwin geology, was a charismatic lecturer, friend of Queen Victoria and Prince Albert, a giant of nineteenth-century science, and the benefactor and topographer of his native Dentdale. The remarkable pamphlet* Memorial by the Trustees of Cowgill (1868) *with its extended* Supplement (1870) *was written in his extreme old age and arose from an administrative muddle on behalf of the Church authorities who changed the name of the new chapel in the ancient hamlet of Cowgill.* The Memorial, *written in protest and containing a fine portrait of Dentdale and its people, accidentally came into the hands of Queen Victoria who, recalling his visits to Osborne as secretary to Prince Albert, when Albert was Chancellor to Cambridge University, and his kindness to her at the time of Albert's death, personally intervened on behalf of the people of Dentdale to secure an Act of Parliament and the restoration of the ancient name Cowgill.*

Dentdale in Decay

It was once a place of very active industry: well known as a great producer of wool, which was partly carded and manufactured on the spot for home use: but better known for what were then regarded as large imports of dressed wool and worsted, and for its exports of stockings and gloves that were knit by the inhabitants of the valley. The weekly transport of the goods, which kept this trade alive, was effected, first by trains of pack-horses, and afterwards by small carts fitted for mountain work.

Dent was then a land of rural opulence and glee. Children were God's blessed gift to a household, and happy was the man whose quiver was full of them. Each "statesman's" house had its garden and its orchard, and other good signs of domestic comfort. But alas, with rare exceptions, these goodly tokens have now past out of sight; or are to be feebly traced by some aged crab-tree, or the stump of an old plum-tree, which marks the site of the ancient family orchard.

The whole aspect of the village of Dent has been changed within my memory, and some may perhaps think that it has been changed for the better. But I regret the loss of some old trees that covered its nakedness; and most of all the two ancient trees that adorned the church-yard, and were cut down by hands which had no right to touch a twig of them. I regret the loss of the grotesque and rude, but picturesque old galleries, which once gave a character to the streets; and in some parts of them almost shut out the sight of the sky from those who travelled along the pavement. For rude as were the galleries, they once formed a highway of communication to a dense and industrious rural population which lived on flats or single floors. And the galleries that ran before the successive doors, were at all seasons places of free air; and in the summer season were places of mirth and glee, and active, happy industry. For there might be heard the buzz of the spinning wheel, and the hum and the songs of those who were carrying on the labours of the day; and the merry jests and greetings sent down to those who were passing through the streets. Some of the galleries were gone before the days of my earliest memory, and all of them were hastening to decay. Not a trace of them is now left. The progress of machinery undermined the profitable industry of Dent, which, in its best days, had no mechanical help beyond the needle, the hand-cart, or the cottage spinning-wheel. I still regret the loss within the village streets of those grotesque outward signs of a peculiar industry which was an honour to my countrymen; but which had now left hardly a remnant of its former life. I regret its signboards dangling across the streets; which though sometimes marking spots of boisterous revelry, were at the same time tokens of a rural opulence.—Most of all do I regret the noble trees which were the pride and ornament of so many of the ancient "statement's" houses throughout the valley. Nearly all the old forest trees are gone: but the valley is still very beautiful, from the continual growth of young wood which springs up, self-planted, from the gills and hedgerows.

Nearly all the landed property of the five hamlets of Dent has past out of the hands of the ancient stock of native "statesmen". Many of them, not having learnt to adapt their habits to the gradual change of times, were ruined, and sank into comparative poverty. Some migrated in search of a better market for their talents. A few old families stood the trial, and still possess the freeholds of their ancestors, with some additions of their own: and I need not tell my countrymen that there are one or two present examples of landed property in the valley which exceed any that was held by a single "statesman" in the days of its greatest prosperity. But alas, these larger proprietors are no longer among the resident yeomanry of the valley.

I well remember that, about 75 years since, several poor old men came to the Church on Sundays with coats of ancient cut, and adorned on the ample sleeves with curiously embossed metal buttons; with wigs that were once well dressed; with hats of ample brim, shewing the loops that had, in former days, drawn the brims up into a smart triple cock; and above all with manners and address which were the tokens of better days. But I must dwell no longer here upon such details. . . .

Adam Sedgwick, *Memorial by the Trustees of Cowgill Chapel,* 1868

The Condition of the Poor

There was an old custom in bygone days of dividing the common lands of every village into patches of various sizes, called in this part of Yorkshire "reins" or "reeans". It is thought that these terraces, which are seen in the vicinity of our villages, must have been levelled for this purpose, and used for the cultivation of their crops, such as flax, and lint, potatoes or oats. Each member of the community held one or more of these strips of land for three years, and it then changed hands. But it was not helpful to the improvement of the land, for naturally every holder was anxious to get as much good out of the land as he possibly could during his short tenure of it, and the Acts of Enclosure, passed in 1836 and subsequently, and the laying down of much of the arable land into pasture, all helped to diminish the work for the population, and so reduce their numbers, and send them off to help crowd the cities . . .

In the old days, intercourse even with their nearest neighbour was very exceptional; no one except the farmer moved about, and he chiefly to Skipton or Long Preston fairs on horseback. Indeed sixty years ago there was only a single "gig" in the parish—belonging to Mr Knowles of Halton Gill. They were very self-contained, they had not even an occasional visit from a butcher, a privilege much esteemed these days—and the price of mutton in 1836 was only 4d a pound! The farmers killed and salted a pig or two, and usually a large piece of "a slaughtered ox" was dried and salted, and hung up in the chimney-nook of the house. Close by were cakes and riddle-bread hanging. But the oat-cake making is dying out even in the farmhouses. As for the labourer and the farm-servant (though he usually lived in the farmhouse, and fared well) they seldom had any fresh butcher's meat; and one year, when the vicar gave a piece of mutton to a labourer at Christmas, he said "Thank you, sir: I have had none since that bit you gave me last Christmas." Porridge, tea and oatcake was their usual fare.

Ven. Archdeacon Boyd, "Fifty years in Arncliffe"
from *Littondale Past and Present,* 1893

Shepherds and their Dogs

The eyes of a sheepdog are his greatest asset. He must be able to see quickly and to be able to eye (control) the sheep. It is possible to have too much "eye", known as hard eye, which means that the dog may be excellent when concentrating on a few sheep but cannot control a large flock. Dogs that eye early are not always the best in the end. Those that start at a year are often better. Unfortunately, sometimes a dog may work splendidly for a few years and then suddenly go right off.

Yet Maddie, Mr Lancaster's ten-year-old bitch, "a great dog", had won seven trials before she was eighteen months old. "She has it in her. Put her on the fell and away she goes, she's in her

West Burton Village by Gilbert Foster from *Wensleydale and the Lower Vale of the Yore* by Edmund Bogg, 1895

ADVERTISEMENTS. v.

C. CHAPMAN,

MAIL CONTRACTOR,

Grassington, nr. Skipton.

Begs to inform the public that

THE ROYAL MAIL

Leaves Skipton at 6-0 a.m., and returns from Buckden at 3-40 p.m.

A DAILY 'BUS

Will leave Grassington for Skipton at 7 a.m., and return to Grassington from Skipton at 5 p.m.

Also a 'BUS will leave Grassington for Skipton at 8-45 a.m., and return to Grassington from Skipton at 3-0 p.m., on MONDAYS and SATURDAYS.

A SECOND CONVEYANCE,

FROM SKIPTON TO BUCKDEN,

From April to October, leaves Skipton Station at 8-40 a.m., Hole-in-the-Wall Inn 8-45 a.m., and calling at Rylstone, Cracoe, Linton, Grassington, Coniston, Kilnsey, Kettlewell, and Starbotton, leaving Grassington, per return at 6-0 p.m.

POST HORSES & CONVEYANCES

At Reasonable Charges.

Tourism in the Dales: an advertisement for Chapman's Mail Coaches from *The Buxton of Yorkshire* by Bailey J. Harker, 1890

William Wordsworth drawn by H. Edridge, 1806

John Ruskin in his twenties

Tom Twistleton, 1867

Edmund Bogg photographed in the 1920s

element." Full of sheepdog lore, he told us the most difficult manoeuvre to teach is to "learn 'em to flank, to keep their distance from sheep and to go quietly. The quieter you and dog are the better. Don't issue too many commands, and you yourself must have sheep sense." Both Tom Lancaster and Laurie Peacock always found bitches more sensitive to commands than dogs, but on the whole dogs are more popular and many people consider them to be more even in their work than bitches.

Three gifts which are born in a dog cannot be taught. The first is to be able to recognise a wanted sheep and to single it out from a flock; the second is to be able to single out his owners' sheep from those of neighbours', which is useful, but can be awkward if you want to bring in strays; the third is to be able to set sheep burying in snow drifts, although an old dog, who could set, has been known to reach young ones. To do this the dog stands rigid on scenting the sheep.

Mr Lancaster had a wonderful dog called Fan who could set sheep. In one very bad storm he lost 203 sheep, but would have lost three or four hundred but for her. "She set 'em," he said, "thirty feet down; she was as true as steel. She would walk on top of the drifts, all at once stop and *whinge* a little, and we would dig and find 'em." Dogs cannot set dead sheep, which sometimes lie on top of live ones so that some may be missed.

For two periods of seven and eleven years Mr Thomas Joy was the shepherd in charge of 1,000 sheep on Grassington Moor. "I had three good dogs—Lass, Lady and Scot. Lass was three years old before she was trained, and I never let her near the sheep for a month at first. She was always on the go *tittering* about, covering the moor twice over."

In one of the storms of the winter of 1947 George Capstick, then managing his mother's farm in Howgill, started out with the farm servant at 9 a.m. on to the hill to gather. "It takes a good man an hour to walk to the top of the fell." They were returning with the flock in mist and snow, when suddenly the mist cleared and they saw four wethers. He loosed his dog, Ken, who set off to fetch them. Then the mist closed down again. They knew if they made enough noise that Ken would know where they were. But at the Fell Gate there was no Ken, and about 5.45 p.m. they returned to the farm to milk. At night he and his mother, who sat knitting "with her knitting sheath and old bent needles", listened to the nine o'clock news. "What do you say if we go up to the Fell Gate?" he asked. Looking over her spectacles his mother replied: "Yes, it's a good idea." He and the man, taking a torch and lantern, set out. As they approached the Fell Gate they saw a sparkle. "Them's sheep's eyes," he cried, and there were the four wethers. Beside them deep in the snow, with a drift a foot high on his back, lay Ken. He could have left them and come home but he hadn't. "There's loyalty for you. I'm always thankful I went up to the Fell Gate."

If there is real understanding between you and your dog, it will pull that last bit out to help you, but in the end of course it depends on the individual dog and on its pluck. So there they are: Ben, Bob, Laddie, Lassie, Fly, Hemp, Moss, Nell, Tiger, Toss, Wiley and all the rest of them, quietly going about their masters' business on moor and fell, day after day, year in, year out.

Marie Hartley and Joan Ingilby, *Life and Tradition in the Yorkshire Dales,* 1968

11. Mills, Mines and Quarries

The Yorkshire Dales were as much a part of the Industrial Revolution as anywhere in England. The many fast-flowing rivers and vigorous mountain streams provided the head of water to drive mills which, from monastic times onwards, ground corn and oats and wove linen, wool and cotton. The centralization of manufacturing in the new centres of population, well-served by canal, railway and cheap sources of power, brought their decline.

For more than two centuries, between the beginning of the seventeenth and the later nineteenth century, lead-mining was a major source of wealth in the Dales, particularly in Swaledale and Upper Wharfedale. Its techniques, developed by the finest Derbyshire and Cornish engineers of the time, were in the forefront of industrial and technological progress, and many Dales communities grew up around the mining fields, only to suffer the catastrophic effects of decline when the veins ran thin, and cheap foreign imports destroyed the home market.

The only major extractive industry in the Dales at the present day is quarrying. No longer are the many hundreds of small stone quarries in use for building material, but a handful of massive enterprises, served by road and rail, provide limestone and roadstone for the construction industries of the North of England.

The New Cotton Mill at Aysgarth

I descended to the Bridge of Asgarth; there sending back my horses to the public house, and ordering G. to return with a guide.

During his long absence, I had to admire the delicious scenery, around this charmingly-placed bridge; whose wildness has been sadly demolish'd by a late (adametic) reparation, and the cutting down of the ivy.

But what has completed the destruction of every rural thought, has been the erection of a cotton mill on one side, whereby prospect, and quiet, are destroy'd: I now speak as a tourist (as a policeman, a citizen, or a statesman, I enter not the field); the people indeed, are employ'd; but they are all abandon'd to vice from the throng.

If men can thus start into riches; or if riches from trade are too easily procured, woe to us men of middling income, and settled revenue; and woe it has been to all the Nappa Halls and the Yeomanry of the land.

At the times when people work not in the mill, they issue out to poaching, profligacy and plunder. Sr Rd. Arkwright may have introduced much wealth into his family, and into the country; but as a tourist, I execrate his schemes, which, having crept into every pastoral vale, have destroy'd the course, the beauty of Nature; why, here now is a great flaring mill, whose back stream has drawn off half the water of the falls above the bridge.

With the bell ringing, and the clamour of the mill. all the vale is disturb'd; treason and levelling systems are the discourse; and rebellion may be near at hand.

John Byng, *A Tour to the North*, 1792
(from *The Torrington Diaries*)

The Story of Malham Mill

It stood in one of the most romantic positions for which poet or novelist could ask. Only about a third of a mile from the magnificent Malham Cove, a limestone cliff 240 ft high and about 350 yards across the chord of its splendid curve, the mill straddled as a bridge across the powerful stream which emerges at the foot of the cove after a long underground course. The stream plunges over a waterfall, at the foot of which the mill stood, almost within reach of its spray. The height of the fall and a slight dam across the stream gave plenty of head for the mill-wheel, and although only traces of the bridge foundations and of the dam and goit remain, it is not at all difficult to recreate the impressive picture the mill must have made when this gorge to the cove was better wooded than it is now.

In the opening years of the thirteenth century John Aleman gave his cornmill at Malham, with suit of 2s (10p) a year, to Fountains Abbey for the support of the poor folk who gathered at the abbey gate. In 1450 the bursar of the abbey valued it as £1, and at the Dissolution it was still one of the many mills owned and valued by the abbey. At the Dissolution it was bought with other Malham estates but continues to work as a cornmill. In 1680, when Thomas

Atkinson had been the miller for eighteen years, a dispute over the dues to be paid by tenants of Malham showed that, instead of a uniform rate for grinding corn, some tenements in the village paid one-twentieth and some one twenty-fourth, and these differences went back into past history.

Early in the eighteenth century it ceased to work as a cornmill, and in 1797 it had been converted to a cotton mill and was leased by its then owner, Brayshaw, to the three Cockshutt brothers. In 1815 it was re-leased for twenty-four years to the Cockshutts, along with John and Joseph Lister of Haworth, "cotton twist spinners", but a third part was subject to a mortgage taken by one of the brothers. The rent was £120 a year and the mill structure, the water-wheel and pit-wheel, upright shafts and naked tumbling shafts, with the miller's house, dam, goit and other appurtenances, were to be insured against fire for £2,400. The machinery in the mill was valued at £564 and there were ancient water rents of 5s (25p) and 2s 6d (12½p) per year and a lord rent of 13s 3¾d (66½p). In this lease we glimpse something of the arrangement of the mill drive. The pit-wheel would be a large-diameter gear-wheel driving through bevel wheels the vertical shaft on which the other bevel-wheels would turn the driving shaft, the tumbling shafts, on each floor of the mill. This lease, which was for twenty-four years, was renewed and for some time the mill continued to be worked by Cockshutts as a cotton mill, but ceased before 1847 when it was noted by the Ordnance Survey as a cotton mill in ruins. A few years later it was pulled down and the stone was used to build the Ploughleys Barn in Malham West Field. All that now remain are the name Old Mill Foss and slight traces of the bridge and goit.

Arthur Raistrick, *Old Yorkshire Dales,* 1967

On the Downfall and Extinction of a Mill at Malham Lately Dr. Masters' now Mr. Lister's

The days are past, the fleeting years are gone,
When Peace and Plenty crowned Malham Town,
At ev'ry house a good fat hog or ewe,
Did victim fall, men's kindnesses to shew;
All neighbours lived in unity with others,
Foreigners were treated as our brothers;
No envy, hatred, malice, rancour, spleen,
Were ever practiced and as seldom seen.
But now since Ceres from this Vale are fled,

No mill is wanted to grind corn for bread,
The wheel's askew, and all for want of work;
The rats new lodgings seek, to feed and lurk.
Canker and worms the wood and iron waste,
The bell ne'er warns the Miller to make haste
To load the hopper with a fresh supply
Of oats, or beans, cold wheat, barley or rye.
The walls, and Nature's Art assisting, will
Witness for Ages th' want of Malham Mill. . . .

Thomas Hurtley, 1781

A Calamity

Excepting what always must be excepted, the introduction of manufactories, I do not know a greater calamity which can befall a village than the discovery of a lead-mine in the neighbourhood.

T. D. Whitaker, *History of Craven,* 1805

The Grassington Moor Mines

—Our mines produce several sorts of ore,
But chiefly lead,—we have it in great store
At Patley-bridge and Green-how-hill anon,
On Craven-Moor and likewise Grassington;
There may be seen brought from the earth to light,
Great heaps of lead ore shining and bright;
By horses, wheel and ropes, and tubs for drawing,
So deep they seem quite overawing;
Then they proceed to dress the beauteous ore,
By grateing, grinding, washing o'er and o'er;
Then to the furnace which by fire is fed
Which soon refines it into solid lead;—

John Broughton, "On Craven" 1828
from *Poems: Moral, Sentimental and Satirical*

A Visit to Arkengarthdale

12th September, 1817
Left Wensley with Mr Costabadie and Mr Maude for Arkendale,

travelled over a moor entirely covered with ling to Reeth, a beautiful little town situated in Swale Dale and surrounded with mountains covered with ling, called on Mr Hall who has a fine collection of the produce of the Yorkshire Cumberland and Durham mines, did not see Mr H. but Mrs H. shewed us the collections, met there a Mr Harland a particularly handsome man who gave us a few specimens of carbonate of barytes with which the Swale Dale and Arkendale mines particularly abound, brought also a few at a shop and a few at the inn. Proceeded from Reeth to Arkendale with a letter of introduction to a Mr Tilburn who seemed at first not to know what a mineral was, tho' he was a principal clerk in the lead works, however he found us a conductor who led us towards the mouth of the level which he said was about ½ a mile further off on a very high ground which as it was near 3 o'clock was too laborious for us to attempt, we therefore returned to Mr Tilburn who gave us a few very good specimens and our guide having brought us also a few and having picked up a few from the miners living in the village of Arkendale we returned to Wensley tolerably well loaded and got there about ½ past 7. The girls and H. Costabadie had ordered dinner before I arrived and had eaten part of it. Mrs C. and Mr Maude did not arrive till we had finished and Mr C was very angry at the young ones having gone to dinner before our return as Mr C. dined that day at Leyburn Book Club.

Rev. Benjamin Newton, *Journal*

The Craven Lead-miners

Miners in general, I might almost say universally, are a most tumultuous, sturdy people, greatly impatient of control, very insolent, and much void of common industry. Those employed in the lead mines of Craven, and in many collieries, can scarcely, by any means, be kept to the performance of a regular business; upon the least disgust, they quit their service, and try another. No bribes can tempt them to any other industry after the first performance of their work, which leaves them half a day for idleness, or rioting in the alehouse.

Arthur Young, *An Account of the present state of Agriculture, Manufacturers and Population in several counties of this Kingdom*, 1770

THOMAS ARMSTRONG (1900–78) *enjoyed considerable fame as the author of massive, North-country novels of industrial life in the last century. His most celebrated books are* Crowthers of Bankdam *and* King Cotton. *Less well known is his Swaledale lead-mining novel,* Adam Brunskill, *a novel which brilliantly recreates the dale and the mines at the height of their prosperity. In this extract Adam Brunskill, newly returned to Swaledale, is investigating Mary Level . . .*

Inside a Lead-mine

As Mary Level was some distance up the gill Adam did not prolong his stay, but started off at once . . . passing Big William, the red glowing smelt hearths of the North Mill, and the range of buildings beyond; following the air-pipes which, carried on high posts, supplied air to those advanced workings in Notion Level lacking sufficient ventilation.

Near the great Peat House, with its long ladders for stacking the four thousand loads of peats it would hold, Adam paused to look about him. Everywhere was activity and, although there was nothing remarkable in men strenuously engaged, the scene was set against a background of moorland wild and bare. With the exception of Sam Kirkbride's house not another habitation, or even a barn, could be seen, either at this side of Skewdale or the other, whose upper limits only were visible.

"It's like a world apart," he reflected, his glance roving from game birds flying low to black-faced sheep chewing expressionlessly, from men shovelling and hammering to others wheeling barrows and pig-moulds. Horse teams were busy on the double tram-road, hauling the Notion Level bouse uphill to Mary Dressing Floors and rattling downhill with bing ore for storage in the Bingstead to await the smelters.

"So Mary Level ore is dressed on the spot, but Norton Level stuff is taken up there," he said to himself. "And then it's all brought back to Notion Bridge. Well, it's trailing it about, but a sight better than they manage at th'other side. It can't be economic for th'East Side Company to use three small mills an' three different dressing floors."

Hearing an increasing rumble of wheels, he diverted towards Notion Level, the swing door at the tail of which was closed. Of Skewdale levels this was one of the few so provided—but without the door groovers half or mile or so inside would have been chilled by the draught and their smoky candle flames bent horizontally whenever the wind blew from the S.S.E.

Adam was fortunate. A grey head appeared, with a mane so profuse as to bring the Pedley brothers immediately to mind. The arch-shaped door was shoved back until caught by a spring hasp when, this necessary operation was completed, Polly advanced farther into view, grey of plump body and long tail. She drew five large, bouse-laden wagons whose iron sides, outward sloping made a broad-based V.

"Well, Bill lad," he shouted, as the trammer, stooped in the queer attitude imposed by a head permanently to one side, thriftily blew out the train's single candle, "now I've seen Polly do it for myself. Yes, she's a real clever 'un."

Mazy Bill straightened like a jack-knife opening, to stare unwinkingly. This rigid stance changed suddenly, when his face puckered as though he were crying, but without tears. "Come on, Polly love," he mumbled. Then he, his beloved mare, and the creaking wagons started towards the bouse-teams.

"Aye," Adam murmured, resuming the trip up Winterings Gill, "the poor lad must be having one of his queer spells."

He stepped out again, walking in the middle of the two sets of rails laid on the narrow shelf of ground between beck and a steeply-rising, gorse overgrown bank. In due course, beyond another of the ravine's sharp bends, he sighted the vast dead heap made from worthless rock wagoned out of Mary Level.

Nearer the slime pits and buddles of Mary Dressing Floors, which occupied a broader stretch overlooking water tumbling down miniature falls, the bubbling song of the stream as it rippled over smooth sandstone pebbles and lapped against moss-covered boulders died away, lost in the clatter of dolly tubs and jigging machines, drowned by the splash from waterwheel buckets, the hiss from pipes and hose. When the roar of the drushers in the grinding mill, in its turn, fell away behind him, Adam bore to the left, along a tramroad up the gill, until he reached a low, stone building divided for its different uses: horse house, blacksmith's shop, and a "Dry" or changing place outside which an abstract from the Metalliferous Mines Regulations Act was posted.

Titus Alderson had finished his business and, their paths coinciding, they strolled towards Mary Level.

"A piece o' clay'ud do better for you than that candle-holder," the old agent said, tossing a greyish, sticky ball, but he was more approving about the decrepit hard hat Adam had been given by Blind Kit.

Within the tail of the level matches were struck. As soon as both candles were burning they entered the mine, stepping in single file upon wooden sleepers at times above but as often below ankle deep pools, the slit of daylight gradually fading away. The wavering flames revealed sides damp and glistening, a level walled and arched in parts, cut through solid rock occasionally and supported elsewhere by timbering of great strength. Here and there the passageway widened into a chamber, with turn-rail and space enough for a horse to face about; at intervals refuge niches were hewn into the side.

The three main chambers were visited, two of which were winning mineral, the third an attempt to attain an area where profitable ore was supposed to be.

At Mary Level Forehead, ten fathoms beyond the sump in which a pump, worked by the immense spear-rod in Glory Shaft, clank-clanged monotonously, Adam saw an onrush of water through the rock face. As he knew already, the boundary common to the two mining companies ran almost equidistant between this forehead and the forehead of the East Side Company's Martha Level. The two levels were designedly driven at the same depth and would have been connected had not the old Skewdale Company failed. To Adam it seemed feasible that the water might quite easily have seeped from the neighbouring company's side, in which case the remedy was obvious.

"No, lad," Titus Alderson shook his head, "it's been tested for just that, wi' oil, an' nobbut the merest trace came through. These underground streams i' limestone are oft mysteries."

In cross-cuts off the main horse level, and in drifts off the cross-cuts, Adam heard picks at work, the thud of sledge hammers meeting the heads of borers, and here and there, twinkling yellow, were the lights of candles—candles, as many as eight of them close together, a smoky bright zone in which the same number of partners toiled in sweet air; elsewhere, the atmosphere foul, a pair of dimly-burning candles lit the labours of three or four slightly lethargic, heavily breathing men. In most cases the bases of the candles were embedded in a small piece of clay, which, pressed against rock or timer, held securely to form a convenient wall bracket. But some of the groovers, usually the older ones, preferred a lantern—as less susceptible to draughts, though the cylindrical canister and the shield, especially when of horn, cut off or absorbed a great deal of light.

Thomas Armstrong, *Adam Brunskill,* 1952

A Tourist Trip to the Mines

No visitor to Grassington ought to omit a visit to the mines which are about two or three miles from the town. They commenced working them before the time of James the First, and it was stated at a public meeting held in Skipton, in connection with the Skipton and Wharfedale Railway, that even lately they produced a profit of ten thousand pounds per annum. It is very interesting to strangers to enter them, though perhaps the descent may frighten them a little. The bottom of some of the shafts are reached by ladders, and others by ropes. When you are safely down you will be led by one of the miners into the different "levels", holding in your hand a candle in a piece of clay, to keep your hand from melting the tallow by its warmth. At the first it will prove curious work for you, sometimes to be "climbing up ladders then rambling over rocks, then wading through water, then marching through mud, then creeping through holes; at times clambering up a narrow bore, hobbling along a narrow passage, squeezing through a tortuous crevice; then going on all fours, bear fashion, crawling, scrambling, struggling" along the subterranean recesses, from which the precious ore has been dug. But to see the rich veins of lead "glinting and sparkling like jewels in the rock", and the "little caverns of spar"—"glittering grottos of well-defined crystal"—that "sparkle like fairy halls", or "miniature palaces of pearl, spangled with more than oriental splendour", will give pleasure that will more than reward you for your toil.

Bailey J. Harker, *Rambles in Upper Wharfedale,* 1869

The Last Days of the Grassington Moor Lead-mines

The mines in question, during their most prosperous days, employed between one and two hundred men and boys, who lived in the towns of Grassington and Hebden, about two miles away from the works. They worked in periods, or shifts, of eight hours—the first commencing at six a.m. and running till two p.m.; those coming on at two would work till ten; and when demand was good, and the mine was worked "all round", another set of men and boys worked through the night till six o'clock next morning. While staying a few weeks in this unfrequented but delightful district, the writer was introduced to an old but very intelligent man, who has worked for half a century under the Dukes of Devonshire, and knows the whole process of mining, from blasting the rock to smelting the ore. The information now given was elicited from him in an afternoon's visit to the now deserted workings. One thing we will note in passing. My guide was on the shady side of 70, as before observed; but his step was firm, his back was straight, and his eye was clear. Moreover, his father, who had followed the same calling, was still alive, though upwards of 90 years of age; so we may conclude that hard work and exposure on the moors breeds a hardy race. These miners appear to have been a steady class of men, for the most part chapel-goers, and of sober and careful habits; though out of the small wages which they earned (an average of 17s per week) it was almost impossible for them to save money. Indeed, it has often been said that the shopkeepers of Grassington were the real workers of the mines, as they gave credit to the men, who, when they were successful in their "takes" paid their debts.

On the last Saturday in each month the mining agent, from the window of the office, put up the various "takes", such as driving the galleries in search of the veins, sinking the shafts, or getting the ore and rubbish to the surface, which work was usually done by fathom (six feet), the price varying according to the difficulties met with. Sometimes the workings ran through ground so soft that the sides required propping with wood every foot of the way; sometimes rock of the hardest millstone grit had to be blasted with powder or gun cotton, and the work proceeded slowly. The nature of the ground was, however, pretty well known to both the agent and the men, who were not very particular in the price at which they took the work, as they knew that if they made too good a monthly bargain, the price would be pulled down next letting; or if, on the other hand, they had taken it too dear, they would next time be allowed to have it correspondingly cheap; i.e. they would demand more and get more for their work.

There was, however, this disadvantage for the owner, that if the men found out they had easier work than they expected, they were tempted to spin out their time in order to deceive the agent. All candles, powder, and gun-cotton were charged to the men, and the tools were weighed out to them at the commencement of the month —so much iron, so much steel—these latter being credited to them when returned at the end of the month, so that they were only made responsible for the wear and tear. Thus a check was kept upon them, and it became their interest to prevent waste.

The depth of the shafts and workings varied from 40 to 80 fathoms (i.e. 240 ft to 480 ft). The veins of lead ore are, unlike the beds of coal, found to lie perpendicular, or with a slight inclination towards the north, and can be followed as deep as it is profitable to work, the thickness varying from a few inches to several yards, though the thickness of the veins was no criterion of their richness, many of the smaller and thinner veins being more profitable and purer than the thicker ones. When ore is found and brought to the surface, it has to go through quite a succession of washings, grindings and screenings, before it is finally sorted into heaps according to its various qualities and fit for sending to the smelting mills. It must be borne in mind that pure lead is never found, it has some mixture of rock, mostly millstone grit, and all this must be separated from the ore. One of the latest of many items spent by the present Duke was for the fitting up of a crushing mill to separate the rock from the ore. This is done by immense and ponderous wheels capable of crushing the hardest rock, and the motive-power is water, which turns a noble wheel of 36 ft diameter, or 108 ft circumference. When the earthy and stony particles by which the ore is surrounded have been crushed and washed away, the last process is the smelting, by which the metal is melted in furnaces, run off into pans, and taken by immense iron ladles whilst in the liquid state and run into moulds holding about 1 cwt. The lead cools sufficiently in about five to seven minutes to be turned out in bars called "pigs", which are weighed, and each one marked as it weighs over or under the cwt., and piled with others in stacks ready for sale or removal.

The smoke from the furnace of this smelting mill has to traverse a 'flue a mile long before it eventually emerges from the chimney on the top of the hill. Formerly the hill-side, for hundreds of acres round, was destitute of verdure, as every green thing was killed by the poisonous vapours. No sheep or cattle could be safely pastured on the adjoining hill-sides, as the wind frequently carried the smoke long distances and affected everything on which it fell. But a few years ago a clever Welsh mining agent of the Duke's suggested this alteration in the flue, by which, instead of escaping immediately from the furnace to the chimney, the smoke is made to traverse a long distance, and by means of several condensers, fixed at various points, it is rendered comparatively harmless, and made to deposit its leaden fumes in such quantities that it soon repaid the first outlay, and has since been thousands of pounds to the credit of the workings. Two or three sweepings per year of this immense flue resulted in the recovery of many tons of the purest lead, which would otherwise have been worse than wasted. The hill-side is green again, and sheep and cattle may now be safely pastured in the neighbourhood of the chimney. The mining operations were continued about three years ago, but as there was a quantity of ore on hand the smelting house was kept going about another twelve months, so that this might all be used up. There is still about 50 or 60 tons of pig lead stacked in the yard, the proceeds of a consignment of ore from the Buckton Mining Company, the last work these furnaces have done, and it was rather melancholy to see already the evidences of decay and ruin where for so long a period an industry had given employment to so many families. The Duke of Devonshire has upwards of 1,000 tons of pig lead stacked at Gargrave station; and it will give some idea of the depreciation in value and the unprofitable character of lead-mining when it is known that the price is now about £10 per ton, whereas upwards of £20 per ton was the market price ten years ago. This is partly owing to foreign competition by which lead, more easily and consequently cheaper, got than our own, is poured into the market, and partly because lead is not now nearly so much in demand as formerly, other compound metals having largely superseded it.

The hill-sides in the neighbourhood of the smelting mill are dotted over with the remains of the workings, looking in the distance like large mole-hills, but not a soul now goes near them except from curiosity. The ladders by which the various levels were reached, the iron trucks, rails, tools, and various gears have all been brought to the surface, and are heaped together in a rusty pile of old iron, too far from a railway to make the carriage worth any price being offered. The barrows are under cover, and the remains of the last fire raked out from the furnace; the great water-wheel and crushing mill are left properly oiled, the wire rope in good order round the drum, but it is too evident that the works will not be resumed. The Duke is said to have carried on the mines for the last ten years at a positive loss. If this is so, however, there is a handsome set-off against it, as my informant assured me that some twenty-five years ago he could not having been making less than twenty thousand pounds per annum out of them. The history of these mines is an illustration of the well-known mutability of all earthly things. New industries spring up, old ones decay, and populations naturally congregate where work is plentiful. As for the good people of Grassington they are firmly convinced that nothing but railway communication can revive the spirit of the place. There is one thing it certainly would do; it would open up to the tourist and holiday-maker one of the finest dales in Yorkshire, and bring into public notice one of the most charming summer resorts for the lovers of nature, and in some degree relieve the pressure which is felt in the month of August on all Yorkshire coast towns.

Joseph Lucas, from *The Leeds Mercury Weekly Supplement*, 1885

Emigration

Edward Broderick writes in his diary for October 16th, 1830: "Now the mines are exhausted, the price of lead is low and miners are forced to obtain a living in other countries which they cannot get here. The independence of spirit is gone."

So the young men began to go. Some of them, like Joseph Daykin, went to the Durham coalmines, where they earned more money (and, nearer the coast, the dislike amounting to hatred of some of the natives, because they were prepared to work for less pay). More went over the Pennines, into the cotton towns of Lancashire. Steam power and the "spinning jenny" had transformed the manufacturing process, and now mill-owners needed a vast supply of "hands". The factory life in Lancashire, rather than the distance in miles, made it seem like foreign parts. There were sad partings as young folk left Gunnerside to find work over the Pennines. Tom Reynoldson, going to Nelson, hoping to find a job in the cotton mills, with his brothers James and David, got as far as Satron, looked back into the village, and wept. . . .

Others left this country for the U.S.A. They were men already used to long hours of discomfort, and they could turn their hand to almost any country craft. Their wives were tough and self reliant, and prepared to bring large families into the same frame of mind as themselves; that with God's help, and in His good time, they would make the desert blossom.

The Atlantic Ocean was spoken of as "The Gert Dub". Emigrants had to make the best of their journey to Liverpool on horseback, carrying as well as their possessions, sacks of home-made oatcakes to last the journey. . . .

Edward Broderick related how they sold up at Gunnerside in April 1833. "All kept their spirits well up considering they sold nearly all except their bedding . . . I got up at 2 o'clock and after attending to a cow which we had calving, I came back and found William busy packing the boxes and preparing to load the carts. He possessed wonderful resolution . . . they set off soon after 5 o'clock."

These few were the pioneers who made life easier for their successors in the next two generations. After the 'forties, mining began to pick up again, and between 1850 and 1870 there was some prosperity in Gunnerside; in 1862 they had a collection for "distressed cotton operatives in Lancashire"—no doubt some of them natives of Gunnerside.

Then, after 1870, when the end was in sight as far as lead-mining was concerned, the emigrations began again. Between 1871 and 1881, 92,250 people left the English countryside, half into towns and half overseas.

Margaret Batty, *Gunnerside Chapel and Gunnerside Folk,* 1962

Life at the Burtersett Quarries

The quarries were owned by Richard Metcalfe (Dicky Bocketer) and Tom Metcalfe, and these two quarry owners employed about 50 workers each. Also there were at least another two strangers to the district, prospecting along the hillside in the hope of finding a suitable seam of good slate and flagstones. These quarries were worked as "levels" running deep into the hillside, and the stone was dragged out by horse and bogie on a narrow gauge railway line.

Both quarry owners had two large waggons (four wheels) drawn by two horses to each waggon, which carried about 5 to 6 tons of dressed stone on each load, to Hawes Station, and was expected to deliver four load one and three load the next.

On the three load day the waggoner delivered three loads and loaded the fourth, bringing it to Burtersett, where it was left overnight loaded, so between them these four waggoners would deliver to the station approximately 80 tons of stone in various shapes and sizes each day.

This was when business was good, but it fluctuated enormously. Markets rose and fell in a depression, the quarrymen dressed stones in anticipation of better days, and the owners hoped for a break for the better. (Often they had to lay off men.)

By the time I was born (1903), "Dicky Bocketer" had twice been in financial difficulty, and "Tom Mecca" once, but they were still at the head of the businesses.

Dicky had built nine cottages in two rows on the east side of the main street and Tom Mecca on the west side, facing each other. These were all occupied by quarrymen, and all other cottages were tenanted by quarrymen, but as about 100 men were employed many had to travel from Gayle, Hawes, Sedbusk and even Hardrow. In those days the railway bridge spanned the river, and Sedbusk workmen crossed over the bridge to get to and from work.

The top wage for a skilled worker either underground or on "The Hill" was 18/- (90p) per week for a six day week starting at 7.30 until 4pm—half an hour break for dinner. Many received 16/- (80p). "Sally Will Dick", a simple, honest workman, walked a distance of 3½ miles to and from Hardrow every day, a distance of 3½ miles single journey, and never had more than 16/- per week in his working life. Chipping wheelers started at 6/- a week and graduated to be craftsmen.

My Grandfather came from Gayle with his bride into one of the quarry owners' houses in the 1870s, worked for 18/- until age made him slower and his wage was reduced to 16/-, then he finally was turned off, to eke out a pittance working for the District Council, breaking stones at 1/10d (9p) per cubic yard, from Burtersett Lane bottom to the quarry gate (through Burtersett village) for £3 per annum.

T. C. 'Kit' Calvert, *Burtersett Seventy Years Ago,* 1974

The Stone Men

On guard in dusk's violet dome
  a young and cut-throat moon
  reflects the south-west sun
that floodlights, though gone early home,
  our mountain's ermine fin.

Over the valley—Dis,
  quarry and limeworks—wars
  with explosive on ancient moors.
Thence, like a travelling house,
  glides the low light-hollowed bus.

It pauses to take me in
  to its mobile sitting room:
  I pay for my journey and turn
expecting the usual din
  of the widows riding to town.

Instead, in silent pairs,
  like statues carved in stone,
  grey with lime, in the gloom,
on the bus's double chairs
  sit quarrymen, going home.

The sculptor's cast of thought
  was the social realist school:
  his patiently chipping tool
drew snapbags, peaked caps, short
  thick donkey-jackets, and all

these death-mask-plaster faces
  with stonedust powdered hair
  and darkness-seeing stare
of men who've spent their forces
  in Earth-subduing war.

For Earth wears all men out—
  even the mountain-movers
  and their globe-lifting levers;
so widows laugh about
  the prowess of dead lovers

while snow creeps down the hill,
  and buses, through cut drifts
  shuttle the changing shifts,
and new children, to school,
  down valleys quarry-cliffed.

Anna Adams, 1977

12. The Yorkshire Dalesman

It is impossible to separate the landscape of a Yorkshire Dale from the history and the character of its inhabitants. The people have left their mark upon the landscape as surely as the landscape has left its mark on them. The rugged beauty of the Yorkshire Dale has its equivalent in the clipped, vivid language of the local dialect, still very much alive in the older and the farming communities, a direct descendant of the Anglo-Norse settlers of a thousand years ago.

Few people have written more eloquently about the character of the Dalesman than the late Ella Pontefract, the gifted writer and local historian whose early death was a great loss to the Dales. Her splendid little essay, in the first issue of *The Dalesman* magazine, written more than forty years ago, admirably summarizes the essence of the Dales personality. It is fitting that such a piece should appear in the very first issue of *The Dalesman*, a periodical that has done more than anything else to establish a special Dales identity, and to do much to create an awareness of Dales culture, in all its manifestations.

It may well be, that the greatest single contribution to our literature that the Dales have made is through the character of the people, whether satirized through the caustic wit of J. H. Dixon, or perceived through the perceptive eye of that small handful of true dialect poets—men of the calibre of Tommy Blackah, Tom Twistelton and John Thwaite who, if lacking the genius of Burns and MacDiarmid to turn their native dialect into a major literature, have demonstrated what the potential might have been.

If social and economic change were finally to destroy this culture, we should have destroyed our inheritance as surely as if we had bull-dozed away the scenery.

The Character of the Dalesman

Celts, Angles, Danes and Norsemen have gone to make up the

Pennine Dale character, which varies in the upper dales according to which predominated, but the country itself has done much of the moulding of it. The narrow cultivated valleys with grazing on the fells support the people chiefly as small sheep farmers who are independent and self-reliant because, whether they are yeoman or tenant farmers, they are their own masters. The farm man is generally a neighbour's son who will presently take a farm of his own. The fells also gave lead to mine, and the becks provided power for corn mills and later small woollen mills, bringing industries which developed alertness and enterprise.

We think of four lead miners, three of whom died within the last three years, who between them drew for us a picture of lead mining in the dales. One described long journeys over the moors in snow, rain, and sunshine, and how as they neared home they could smell the bacon cooking; another told of the network of levels and the molten lead in the smelt mills; another of accidents when roofs of mines had fallen in; another of the thrill of finding and following a vein; and all of them spoke with love of the "grooves" and joy in the work.

Joy in work reminds us of the dale mason, proud of his skill, his eyes lighting up as he discusses plans, testing his achievement by those of his predecessors, who built the stone walls thick to keep out the weather, and in their simplicity produced buildings which harmonised with their surroundings.

This gallery of dalesfolk are most of them old. Not that individuality is lacking amongst the young. Up and down dale young and energetic men are raising the level of dale farming, liming and draining neglected land, concentrating on pedigree stock, encouraging the Young Farmers' Club. But the old have a life time's memory behind them; they have known people whose names are worn now on the churchyard stones, and who lived in an era which has sunk into history. They belong in a time when the fells shut the dales in from the outside world and in a great measure from each other. They are reflections of their dale.

Of necessity the people intermarried, and each valley became, what to a smaller extent it is still, like a large family. As families are given to quarrels, so there have been bitter feuds in the dales. They are interested in each other as members of a family. We are sitting now in a farmhouse kitchen whose window looks on to the road. Conversation stops as we hear footsteps approaching, and we gaze out to see who it is, and if there is any doubt we settle between ourselves who it is likely to be.

The influence of the old grammar schools is apparent in the men whose parents scraped the few shillings to send them for a year or two to be taught by the vicar. Here is one, a farmer, offering with simple courtesy the hospitality which comes naturally to dales folk; or returning from shepherding the fells, eager to tell of the curlews and plovers' nests he has seen.

Industries have left their mark, but the true dalesmen are connected with farms. Even when they retire the old life holds them, and they keep a few hens, and are not content for long between walls. Pictures of them crowd up—two old men standing in a pasture discussing the points of a cow; a farmer prodding the tups at a show; a young man fishing for trout after a storm; a farmer's son mending a dry stone wall; a shepherd with his dog turning sheep and lambs onto the high fells; a group of farmers milking cows in a cow pasture; an old man and woman round a farmhouse fire promising a neighbour "a good sheep body".

It is such people, the men and women of the dales, who bring the towns and villages, the hamlets and farms, to life.

Ella Pontefract, "Dales Folk", 1939
article in *The Dalesman*, No 1, Vol 1

By-names

As you watch, the ease and placidity of the village lay hold of you. You take the place to your heart, but you must not imagine that it has done the same to you. Gayle is a difficult place to get inside, unless your family belongs. This suspicion of strangers, characteristic of all the remote parts of the Yorkshire dales, probably has its roots far back in the days of invasions and raids. It seemed to reach its height in Gayle. Here the "foreigner" was not necessarily from far away, but anyone who had not been born and brought up in the village. They even resented one of their men bringing a wife from another part. It would take this wife most of her married life, always behaving tactfully, to be accepted as one of them. As a result the people have intermarried, and so many have the same name that nicknames are used, and often their real names are forgotten. A stranger once came into Gayle and asked for Mr John Dinsdale, but but nobody could tell who he was or where he lived. Then his nickname, Brassy Jack, was mentioned, and everybody knew.

The habit of using by-names has probably descended from the Viking settlers, who are known to have been fond of them. Sometimes a man is called by his trade, as John o' t' Post (pronounced "Posst"), Butcher Tom, Cobber Dickey; or some characteristic is taken, as Brassy Doad, Kit Moss; or the name of their farm is added as Geordie Horrabank. The name of Peacock is often turned into "Puke". And there is the usual dale habit of calling a man after his father or mother, as Kit Tom, Bella Jimmy, Betty Ned. Other names are Jappa, Shappa, Romma, Nelse, Rannock. Rannock is sometimes applied to Swaledale men.

Ella Pontefract, *Wensleydale,* 1936

The Yorkshire Horse-dealers

Bane ta Claapam town-gate live an oud Yorkshire tike,
Who i' dealin i' horseflesh hed n'er met his like;
'Twor his pride that i'aw the hard bargains he'd bit,
He'd bit a girt monny, nut nivver bin bit.

This oud Tommy Towers (bi that naam he wor knaan),
Hed an oud carrion tit that wor sheer skin an' baan;
Ta hev killed jim for t'curs wad hev bin quite as well,
But 'twor Tommy opinion he'd dee on himsel!

Well! yan Abey Muggins, a neighbourin cheat
Thowt ta diddle oud Tommy was be a girt treat;
He'd a horse, too, 'twor was than oud Tommy's, ye see,
For t'neet afore that he'd thowt proper ta dee!

Thinks Abey, t'oud codger'll nivver smoak t'trick,
I'll swop wi'him my poor deead horse for his wick,
An' if Tommy I nobbut can happen ta trap,
'Twill be a fine feather i' Aberram cap!

Soa to Tommy he goas, an' the question he pops:
"Betwin thy horse and mine, prithee, Tommy, what swops?
What wilt gi' me ta boot? for mine's t'better horse still!"
"Nout," says Tommy, "I'll swop ivven hands, an' ye will."

Abey preeached a land time about summat ta boot,
Insistin' that his war the liveliest brute;
But Tommy stuck fast where he first had begun,
Til Abey shook hands, and sed, "Well, Tommy, done!"

"O! Tommy," sed Abey, "I'ze sorry for thee,
I thowt thou'd a hadden mair white i'thy ee;

Good luck wi' thy bargain, for my horse is deead."
"Hey!" says Tommy, "my lad, soa is min, an' it's fleead!"

Soa Tommy got t'better of t'bargain, a vast,
An' cam off wi' a Yorkshireman's triumph at last;
For thof 'twixt deead horses there's not mitch to choose
Yet Tommy war richer by t'hide an' fower shooes.

Traditional, mid-nineteenth century

The Knockers

It is a common belief in Craven (or perhaps we should say it *was*) that mushrooms are *made* by the fairies. Shakespeare, who was well versed in folk-lore, speaks of "demi puppets, & c., whose pastime is to make midnight mushrooms".

We have also in Craven a race of dwarfs called "Knockers", who inhabit or haunt the mines (particularly those of Grassington moor), and are said to work at night. They seem to be the same as the gnomes, *lutins*, and *puchs* (Pucks), who, in Scandinavia, by their knockings, show where metals may be found. The shepherds who reside in the mining districts say that these *fairies* also protect the farm houses and the flocks. From this circumstance some authors would connect them with the *lares* or household gods of classic mythology. But as our celtic fairy-lore is totally independent of the popular superstition of Greece and Rome (which ignore our Fairyism), we put aside all idea of such a connection, and seek for origin elsewhere.

Our fairies are addicted to smoking, and their old pipes, called by the peasant *Fairy-pipes*, are often turned up by the farmer's men. These pipes are small in bowl, and of clumsy formation. They are found in large quantities, not only in Craven and the north of England, but also in Scotland and Ireland. The Scotch call them *Puch* or *puck* pipes, and the Irish know them as Dane pipes. Pipes of a similar form, but made of *iron*, have recently been found in Switzerland.

The belief in fairies is not extinct with us; but it is by no means so prevalent as it once was. They, however, still make an occasional appearance to drunkards, fiddlers, besom-makers, and ignorant old wives. It is on the testimony of such that we have generally to rely now-a-days!

J. H. Dixon, *Chronicles and Stories of the Craven Dales*, 1881

THE REVEREND WILLIAM CARR, (1763–1843), *vicar of Bolton Priory was a man of prolific energy and varied talents. He laid out the winding pathways and romantic views through the Chatsworth Estate woodlands, at Bolton Priory and the Strid, and in Grass Woods; he bred the celebrated gigantic 'Craven Heifer'; he introduced Wordsworth to Whitaker and the White Doe legend; and perhaps his crowning achievement was to produce the first ever glossary of the Craven Dialect. The following extract from one of the "Dialogues" accompanying the glossary was intended to demonstrate the language in use.*

The Dialect of Craven

Bridget. What, Giles, thou's gitten back then, fray Girston.

Giles. Eigh, but I'll uphodto, I'd a saar day on't, wi teughin eftert' beeos, they scutter'd about seea, I wor quite fash'd an doon for, afoar I gat haam, at dosk.

Brid. What thou raad, didto nut?

Giles. Raad! eigh, I raad o' shanks-galloway.

Brid. I marvel at thou sud gang o' ten taas, as I sa yower yaud i'th' garth, i'th' mornin.

Giles. Is yower Joan at haam? I's come to tell him at he mun gang to William Palay's, at Skirethorns, 'bout fail, Monday come a sennight, to lot some Scots.

Brid. He's gain toth' peeot moor, bud thou may lite on't, I'll mind to tell him at neet, when he comes haam.

Giles. Girt like Is'l meet him, as I'se gangin theear mysel.

Brid. Come, man, thou's i' na girt hurry, squat thysel down a bit i'th' langsettle, byth' hud-end, an I'll fotch the a whishin; for I lang to knaw sadly what aw them lads and lasses wor cutterin an talkin aboute, at I gat a cliff on gangin up yower croft yuster neet.

Giles. Didto nivver hear at there wor a Methody meetin at Jack Smith's. There wor a weight on 'em to hear t' uncuth preacher, as fine a man as ivver E clapt my een on, at wor he, he bangs aw, quite an clear, at I ivver heeard tell on.

Brid. Now I like 'em awt' better for that; for I ken 'em aw seea weel, at my heart nivver fails to gang wi' 'em whent' parson prays. Nows an thens I've been at yower meetings, an hev heeard what ye call tempory prayer. But, thou minds, while I wor hearkenen wi' aw my might, toth' preacher's prayer, I could not join wi' him a bit; for while I wor tryin to catch his words an liggin an splicin 'em togither, to mack sense on 'em, they mainly scapped me, and did not warm an enleeten my heart hauf seea mitch as our prayers does.

Giles. Methodies say, how yower prayers er tiresome, 'cause they nivver change.

Brid. Prethenow, what does't preacher pray for?

Rev. William Carr, *The Dialect of Craven*, 1828

TOMMY BLACKAH (1828–95) *was a lead miner on Greenhow Hill. He published* Songs and Poems *in 1867 and also edited* T'Nidderdale Olminac, *published in Pateley Bridge.*

Pateley Reeaces

Attention all, baith great an' small,
An' dooan't screw up yer feeaces;
While I rehearse, i' simple verse
A coont o' Pateley Reeaces.

Fra all ower t' moors, they com by scoores,
Girt skelpin' lads an' lasses;
An' cats an' dogs, an' coos an Hogs,
An' hosses, mules, an' asses.

Oade foaks wer thar, fra near an' far,
At cuddant fairly hopple;
An' laughin' brats, as wild as cats,
Owe heeads an' heels did topple.

The Darley lads, arrived i' squads,
Wi' smiles all ower ther feeaces,
An' Hartwith youths, wi'screw'd up mooths,
In wonder watch'd the reeaces.

Fra Menwith Hill and Folly Gill,
Thorntyat, an Deacre Paster,
Fra Thrushcross Green, an t'Heets wer seen
Croods comun' thick an' faster.

'Tween Bardin Brigg and Threshfield Rig
Oade Wharfedeale gat a thinnin'
An' Gerston plods laid heavy odds
On Creeaven Lass fer winnin'

Sich lots wer seen o' Hebdin Green
Ready seean on i' t' mornin',
While Aptrick chaps, i' carts an' traps,
Wer off ta Patela spernin.

All Greenho' Hill, past Coadsteeanes kill,
Com taltherin' an' singin'
Harcastle coves, like sheep i' droves,
Oade Palmer Simp wer bringin'.

Baith short an' tall, past Gowthit Hall,
T'up-deealers kept on steerin'
For ne'er before, roon Middlesmoor,
Had ther been sich a clearin'.

All kinds and sorts o' games an' sports
Had t'Patela chaps pervided,
An' weel did t'few, ther business do,
At ower 'em persided.

'Twad tak a swell munth ta tell
All t'ins an' oots o' t'reeaces,
Hoo far the' ran, which hosses wan,
An' which wer back'd for pleeaces.

Oade Billy Broon lost hauf-a-croon
Wi' Taty-Hawker backin'
For Green Crag flew, ower t'hurdles true,
An' want t' match like a stockin'.

An' Creeaven Lass won lots o'brass,
Besides delightin' t'Brockils,
An' Eva danc'd, an rear'd an' pranc'd;
As gif she stood o' cockles.

But t' donkey reeace wer t'star o' t' pleeace,
For oade an' young observers;
'Twad meeade a nun fra t' convent run
An' ne'er again bi nervous.

Tom Hemp fra t'Stean cried oot, "Weel deean,"
An' t' wife began o' chaffin';
Whal Kirby Jack stack up his back,
An' nearly brast wi' laughin'.

Sly Wilsill Bin, fra een ta chin,
    Wer plaister'd up wi' toffy,
An' lang-leg'd Jane, he'd browt fra t'Plain
    Full bent on winnin' t' coffee.

Young prony slirts, I' drabbl'd skirts,
    Like painted peeacocks stritches;
While girt chignons like milkin'-cans
    On ther top-garrits perches.

Fat Sal fra t'Knott scarce gat ta t'spot,
    Afore she lost her bustle,
Which sad mishap quite spoil's her shap
    An' meeade her itch an' hustle.

Like pug-nooas'd Nell, fra Kettlewell,
    Com in her Dolly Vardin,
All frill'd an' starch'd sha prrodly march'd
    Wi' squintin' Jooa fra Bardin.

Ther cuffs an' falls, tunics an' shawls,
    An' fancy pollaneeses,
All sham displays, ower tatter'd stays,
    An' hard-worn ragged chemises.

Ther mushroom fops, fra fields an' shops,
    Fine cigarettes wer sookin'
An' lots o' youth wi' beardless mooths,
    All kinds o' pipes wer smookin'.

An' when at last the sports were past,
    All heeamward turn'd ther feeaces;
Ta ne'er relent at e'er the' spent
    A day wi' Patela' Reeaces.

Thomas Blackah, (1828–95)

TOM TWISTLETON (1845–1917), *son of a farmer of Winskill, near Settle, was arguably the most talented poet to use the Craven dialect. His early work, contained in the little 1867 collection* Splinters Struck off Winskill Rock, *is as near as the Yorkshire Dales came to having a Robert Burns. In his best work the language is crisp and vigorous, with the wit and compression of dialect speech achieving a genuine mock-epic comic effect.*

'Owd Johnny Meets a Ghost

He trudged along wi' au his might,
Sa confident an' fearless,
Though weel he knew t'owd wife would flyte,
An' t' neet was cowd an' cheerless:
Dark, heavy clouds across o't' sky,
Urged on be t'wind, were rolling;
A hullat, fra a tree hard by,
Wi' wild an' dismal howling,
    Screeam'd loud that neet.

But when he com to t'fir-tree wood—
At t' farther side o' t' common,
War t' carrier, in a pool o' blood,
Yance fand a murder'd woman,—
His courage au began to dee;
He slacken'd in his walking;
He scaarce durst look around, lest he
Sud see her spirit stalking
    Abroad that neet.

For oft, 'twas said, in t'deead o't'neet,
Near t'spot whar t'carrier fand her,
Au drest i' white, a ghastly seet,
Her ghost was seen to wander.
Two chaps, returning fra a spree,
Wi' mony a drucken caper,
Yance sah her walk beneath a tree,
An' vanish like a vapour
    Fra view that neet.

The wind did waft amang the trees,
Wi' moaning deep an' hollow,
Then deed into a gentle breeze,
The heavier gusts wad follow;
An' in a nook, i't'edge o' t' wood,
As he looked round wi' terror,
He sah a seet 'at fraaze his blood,

An' filled his soul wi' horror
        An' awe that neet.

Aghast he stood, wi' fear hauf deead,
His hair began to bristle,
And stand streight up upon his heead,
Like burrs upon a thistle;
For, fra that corner two girt een,
Wide oppen, breet, an' glaring,
Whose colour shaan a bluish green,
War through the darkness staring
        On him that neet!

Cowd drops upon his forheead stood,
His knees did knock together;
Hed ye bin thear, I'm sure ye mud
Ha' fell'd him wi' a feather.
To stir fra t'spot he nivver tried;
His brain, on fire, was reeling;
His senses au war stupefied,
An paralyzed each feeling,
        Wi' fear that neet.

It mud be t'ghost, he couldn't tell,
That stood i' t' nook to watch him;
Or else it was t' "owd lad" hissel
Hed come up here to catch him;
Saa on his knees he down did fo,
He pray' loud as a Ranter,
Till t'ghost sprung out fra under t'wo,
An' started off o' t'canter
        Down t'rooad that neet.

Then au at yance, wi'leetsome spring
On to his feet he started;
He laughed for joy, wal t'woods did ring,
His fears hed au departed:
An' when his noise the ghost did hear,
It faster went and faster,
For it was nought but t'potter's mear,
That hed bin turn'd ta paster
        Down t'looan that neet.

Tom Twistleton, "Owd Johnny an' t' Ghost"
from *Splinters Struck off Winskill Rock,* 1867

Tony of Todcrofts

We met a man of most gaunt and miserable appearance. A young man not more than thirty years of age. He had all the aspect of a penurious fellow. Dirty, unshaven, with soiled clothes and unwashed linen. He was coming along the lane with a rude tumbrel. This man was as thorough a miser as ever existed. He lived totally alone. He suffered no woman to come about his house. If his clothes were ever washed they were done by himself, but he never bought an ounce of soap. He had brought a small property, a house and some adjoining crofts, where he lived. From this place he was called Tony of Todcrofts. This man was never known to part with money except to the tax-gatherer. If he wanted a board put on his cart, or a nail to keep it together, he bargained with the wheelwright or the blacksmith to pay them in peat. He baked his own oatcake, and paid the miller in peat for grinding his oats. He drank milk from his own cow, and made his own clogs, cut from his own alder. He continued to purchase little, and what he did purchase he still paid for in peat. On the fells he cut peat all summer, making days of uncommon length; and in the autumn he drew it down with a sledge, and on one occasion, having no horse, he carried the sledge, every time he re-ascended the hills, on his back.

William Howitt, *The Rural Life of England,* 1844

C. J. CUTCLIFFE-HYNE (1868–1944), *most widely remembered for the popular* Captain Kettle *novels, lived in the Yorkshire Dales for many years.* Ben Watson, *published in 1926, captures the essence of the landscape and rural community with characteristic vividness. In this extract we meet Ben's future wife, the spirited Polly Tennant:*

The Female Poacher

Miss Tennant had out-of-doors tastes, and indulged them freely. She walked a good deal, she fished a bit when there was a spate, she helped Mr Christopher Cray with his hay (which was a near cut to Kitty's elusive heart), and now and again she tickled trout.

I have always found this last-named occupation a wet and messy job myself, and up to the day I caught Polly Tennant at it, imagined that the distaff side of the Dale left it severely alone. It requires a good deal of art: it is unremunerative for labour expended—at least, I have found it so; and, incidentally, of course, it is the rankest poaching. I don't know precisely what the penalties are, and, of course, what you get depends very much on the Bench; but I can imagine a chairman who was a keen trout preserver putting its penalties on a par with those for bigamy.

Polly said it was only the poaching touch that made it worth doing. According to Polly Tennant, if tickling trout was legalised, it would be as insipid as eating an egg without pepper and salt. That is as may be. Anyway, I saw her, one quiet Sunday afternoon, lift three that must have weighed a pound between them, from behind three consecutive boulders up Calf Ghyll, and noted that she was an artist at the job. She pulled down her sleeve after this, stowed the spoil in her hand-basket, and covered it (if you please) with a piece of knitting through which was stabbed its demure needles.

We met on the way down to the village. "I didn't know there were such good trout so high up that beck," I pointed out.

"You've been watching!"

"Not at all. Only I happened to see. And after all, if you come to think of it, I'm supposed to preserve all that water. Not that I wish to spoil your sport in the least, Polly. I only mention the circumstance to extenuate my existence. Carry on, by all means. It's a much more healthy occupation than painting in water-colours or writing a handbook on Epictetus, which seem the only other two intellectual pursuits of the village. Won't they make that knitting smell?"

"Doesn't matter if they do. It's used to trout. And, anyway, it's Mrs Kitty's. I—"—Polly grinned—"I can't knit, or mend my clothes, or cook, or do any of the ordinary things I ought to do, and I'm no good at dairying, or hen-farming, or gardening or—or beekeeping. And I can't go out as a secretary because I can't spell. I'm the most useless and ignorant of all the Tennants. That's why I've had to fall back on school-teaching. There's only one thing I'm fit for, and that's being a gamekeeper, and, worse luck, nobody wants a woman keeper."

C. J. Cutcliffe-Hyne, *Ben Watson,* 1926

JAMES HENRY DIXON (1803–76) *is perhaps the most neglected of all Dales writers. Born in London, he spent his boyhood in Skipton, attended Ermystead's Grammar School, and lived for a time in Grassington. Wit, poet and scholar, he was a leading member of the Percy Society, and his anthology of traditional verse* Ancient Poems, Ballads and Songs *(1846) is still considered an important piece of scholarship. His* Chronicles and Stories of the Craven Dales, *first published in serial form between 1853 and 1857 is an undoubted minor masterpiece. A book impossible to define, it combines topography, folklore, local history, literary history and satire, developing into a brilliant satire of country life and country manners, poking affectionate yet malicious fun at his friends and acquaintances. In this extract one Horatio Trenoodle, a local squire, decides to call on his neighbour, the boorish Jerry Plankley. . .*

A Gentleman of Craven

Jerry Plankley was the owner of Bogley Swamp Hall, a venerable mansion, situated about a quarter of a mile from the limekiln, about the same distance from the village of Bogley, and somewhere about three or four miles from "The Flatts" and "High Laithes". Mr Plankley was known as "The Laird o' Bogley", a title bestowed because he was the Lord of the Manor, and, as such, supreme possessor of four thousand acres of rather sterile moorland, with all the valuable rights and appurtenances thereunto belonging and appertaining. To maintain these important privileges, he held an annual court Baron (or, as Mr Thomas Pickles called it, "a barren court"), at which the vassals, after making their suits and services, were regaled with a gigantic bowl of "oatmeal poddish", out of which each tenant helped himself, by the assistance of a wooden spoon, that was passed from hand to hand and from mouth to mouth, with a most remarkable velocity.

Mr Plankley had another title, and although it was one that the Herald's College had no hand in conferring, it was one whereby he was known in the grazing circles; for who is there in Craven that has not heard of "LORD HES-NOWT-IS-NOWT"? For this strange *soubriquet*, Mr Plankley had nobody to thank but himself. He was an almost uneducated man, for his parents, believing that "ignorance was bliss" and that it was "folly to be wise", had bestowed on their son and heir all the "happiness" and "wisdom" that could result from a practical carrying out of that oft-quoted poetical axiom. Jerry, in consequence of such a bringing up, was a man of few ideas, and they were all centred on the possession of a huge landed estate.

When Trenoodle stayed his steps, he looked over a stone wall as if he were taking a survey of the adjoining pasture, but in reality, he was observing the contour and doings of the Laird of Bogley. Mr Plankley was dressed in a fustian "cwoat", a "red wescut", and corduroy extensions; his rough, uncombed head being ornamented by a cracked, crowned beaver, which it would be a sad breach of

Christian charity to suppose was his Sunday hat. The Laird sat on a curbstone at the very entrance to a kiln, and was amusing himself by throwing, to four huge pointer dogs, some large balls, which looked like "taws" that had arrived at years of maturity! Trenoodle, as our readers are cognizant, was of an inquisitive turn of mind. He had witnessed the performance of "The wonderful dogs", and he was also well read in "Hoyle's games", but he could not comprehend the nature of the sport that was being enacted—for the Captain had not the least idea that the quadrupedal party were enjoying their *table-d'-hote*, and that the round masses were balls of oatmeal, with which Mr Plankley had filled his pockets, previous to walking out with his sporting companions. It was only on making an approach to the kiln, that Trenoodle was able to ascertain the nature and intent of the game, which he did from the accompanying remarks of "That's for thee, Bess!" Tek thee that Basto!" & c. each soliloquy being attended by a chuck into a wide opened mouth.

"Good afternoon!" said the Captain, "you've some fine dogs, sir!"

"Bow! wow! wow!" responded Basto, Bess, Don and Lady, a response which, whether intended for a compliment or not, was somewhat unpleasantly silenced by sundry whacks from a huge knob stick, wielded by the leg-of-mutton fists of their lord and master.

Mr Plankley stared at the Captain, and set him down for a gentleman farmer—one of a class he abominated as much as he did a miner or a millowner. He then remarked "I'se givin' t' dogs thir dinner—I've just hed mi awn."

J. H. Dixon, *Chronicles and Stories of the Craven Dales,* 1881

13. Two Notorious Schools

By a curious irony, on the fringes of the Yorkshire Dales, were situated two of the most notorious schools in history, Bowes Academy, the model for Dickens' Dotheboys Hall, and Cowan Bridge, where the Brontë children suffered.

The thinly disguised rage of *Nicholas Nickelby* effectively put paid to some of the worst outrages of the Yorkshire schools. Charlotte Brontë used her own traumatic experiences in *Jane Eyre,* and her biographer, Mrs Gaskell, writing too close to the relatives of those who perpetrated the horrors at Cowan Bridge to give full rein to her anger, could none the less give a clear idea of the cruelty and ignorance that shortened the all-too-brief lives of the most gifted family known to English letters.

Nicholas Arrives at Dotheboys Hall

"Is it much farther to Dotheboys Hall, sir?" asked Nicholas.

"About three mile from here," replied Squeers. "But you needn't call it a Hall down here."

Nicholas coughed, as if he would like to know why.

"The fact is, it ain't a Hall," observed Squeers drily.

"Oh, indeed!" said Nicholas, whom this piece of intelligence much astonished.

"No," replied Squeers. "We call it a Hall up in London, because it sounds better, but they don't know it by that name in these parts. A man may call his house an island if he likes; there's no act of Parliament against that, I believe?"

"I believe not, sir," rejoined Nicholas.

Squeers eyed his companion slily at the conclusion of this little dialogue, and finding that he had grown thoughtful and appeared in nowise disposed to volunteer any observations, contended himself with lashing the pony until they reached their journey's end.

"Jump out," said Squeers. "Hallo there! come and put this horse up. Be quick, will you!"

While the schoolmaster was uttering these and other impatient cries, Nicholas had time to observe that the school was a long cold-looking house, one story high, with a few straggling outbuildings behind, and a barn and stable adjoining. After the lapse of a minute or two, the noise of somebody unlocking the yard-gate was heard, and presently a tall lean boy, with a lantern in his hand, issued forth.

"Is that you, Smike?" cried Squeers.

"Yes, sir," replied the boy.

"Then why the devil didn't you come before?"

"Please, sir, I fell asleep over the fire," answered Smike, with humility.

"Fire! what fire? Where's there a fire?" demanded the school-master, sharply.

"Only in the kitchen, sir," replied the boy. "Missus said as I was sitting up, I might go in there for a warm."

"Your Missus is a fool," retorted Squeers. "You'd have been a deuced deal more wakeful in the cold, I'll engage."

By this time Mr Squeers had dismounted; and after ordering the boy to see to the pony, and to take care that he hadn't any more corn that night, he told Nicholas to wait at the front door a minute while he went round and let him in.

A host of unpleasant misgivings, which had been crowding upon Nicholas during the whole journey, thronged into his mind with redoubled force when he was left alone. His great distance from home and the impossibility of reaching it, except on foot, should he feel ever so anxious to return, presented itself to him in most alarming colours; and as he looked up at the dreary house and dark windows, and upon the wild country around, covered with snow, he felt a depression of heart and spirit which he had never experienced before.

"Now then!" cried Squeers, poking his head out at the front door. "Where are you, Nickleby?"

"Here, sir," replied Nicholas.

"Come in, then," said Squeers, "the wind blows in at this door fit to knock a man off his legs."

Nicholas sighed, and hurried in.

Charles Dickens, *Nicholas Nickleby,* 1839

The End of Dotheboys Hall

The artist and his wife were enjoying a happy holiday. They had come down into Yorkshire with a fortnight's excursion ticket, and a scheme for visiting as many of the abbeys and as much picturesque scenery as possible within the allotted time. Sometimes they walked eight or ten miles, or travelled a stage in a country car, content to rough it, so that their wishes should be gratified. They had walked across from Stainmoor the day before, and told me that in passing through Bowes they had seen the original of Dotheboys Hall, now doorless, windowless, and dilapidated. Nicholas Nickleby's exposure was too much for it, and it ceased to be a den of hopeless childhood—a place to which heartless fathers and mothers condemned their children because it was cheap.

What a contrast! Wackford Squeers and the Thracian cohort. Bowes under the name of Lavatrae, was once a station on the great Roman Road from Lincoln to Carlisle. Ere long it will be a station on the railway that is to connect Stockton with Liverpool.

Walter White, *A Month In Yorkshire,* 1858

A School for Clergymen's Daughters

Cowan Bridge is a cluster of some six or seven cottages, gathered together at both ends of a bridge, over which the high road from Leeds to Kendal crosses a little stream, called the Leck. This high road is nearly disused now; but formerly, when the buyers from the West Riding manufacturing districts had frequent occasion to go up into the North to purchase the wool of the Westmorland and Cumberland farmers, it was doubtless much travelled; and perhaps the hamlet of Cowan's Bridge had a more prosperous look than it bears at present.

It is prettily situated; just where the Leck-fells swoop into the plain; and by the course of the beck alder-trees and willows and hazel bushes grow. The current of the stream is interrupted by broken pieces of grey rock; and the waters flow over a bed of large round white pebbles, which a flood heaves up and moves on either side out of its impetuous way till in some parts they almost form a wall. By the side of the little, shallow, sparkling, vigorous Leck, run long pasture fields, of the fine short grass common in high land; for though Cowan Bridge is situated on a plain, it is a plain from which there is many a fall and long descent before you and the Leck reach the valley of the Lune. I can hardly understand how the school there came to be so unhealthy, the air all around about was so sweet and thyme-scented, when I visited it last summer. But at this day, every one knows that the site of a building intended for numbers should be chosen with far greater care than that of a private house, from the tendency to illness, both infectious and otherwise, produced by the congregation of people in close proximity.

The house is still remaining that formed part of that occupied by the school. It is a long, low bow-windowed cottage, now divided into two dwellings. It stands facing the Leck, between which and it intervenes a space, about seventy yards deep that was once the school garden. Running from this building, at right angles with what now remains of the school house, there was formerly a bobbin-mill connected with the stream, where wooden reels were made out of the alders which grow profusely in such ground as that surrounding Cowan Bridge. Mr Wilson adapted this mill to his purpose; there were schoolrooms on the lower floor, and dormitories on the upper. The present cottage was occupied by the teachers' rooms, the dining-room and kitchens, and some smaller bed-rooms. On going into this building, I found one part, that nearest to the high road, converted into a poor kind of public house, then to let, and having all the squalid appearance of a deserted place, which rendered it difficult to judge what it would look like when neatly kept up, the broken panes replaced in the windows, and the rough-cast (now cracked and discoloured) made white and whole. The other end forms a cottage with the low ceilings and stone floors of a hundred years ago; the windows do not open freely and widely; and the passage up-stairs, leading into the bed-rooms, is narrow and tortuous; altogether smells would linger about the house, and damp cling to it. But sanitary matters were little understood thirty years ago; and it was a great thing to get a roomy building close to the high road and not too far from the habitation of Mr Wilson, the originator of the educational scheme. There was much need of such an institution; numbers of ill-paid clergymen hailed the prospect with joy, and eagerly put down the names of their children as pupils when the establishment should be ready to receive them. Mr Wilson was, no doubt, pleased by the impatience with which the realisation of his idea was anticipated, and opened the school with less than a hundred pounds in hand, and, as far as I can make out, from seventy to eighty pupils.

Mr Wilson felt, most probably, that the responsibility of the whole plan rested upon him. The payment made by the parents was barely enough for food and lodging; the subscriptions did not flow very freely into an untried scheme; and great economy was necessary in all the domestic arrangements. He determined to enforce this by frequent personal inspection; and his love of authority seems to have led to a great deal of unnecessary and irritating meddling with little matters. Yet, although there was economy in providing for the household, there does not appear to have been any parsimony. The meat, flour, milk etc., were contracted for, but were of very fair quality; and the dietary, which has been shown to me in manuscript, was neither bad nor unwholesome; nor, on the whole, was in wanting in variety. Oatmeal porridge for breakfast; a piece of oat-cake for those who required luncheon; baked and boiled beef, and mutton, potato-pie, and plain homely puddings of different kinds for dinner. At five o'clock bread and milk for the younger ones; and one piece of bread (this was the only time at which food was limited) for the elder pupils, who sat up till a later meal of the same description. Mr Wilson himself ordered in the food, and was anxious that it should be of good quality. But the cook, who had much of his confidence, and against whom for a long time no one durst utter a complaint, was careless, dirty and wasteful. To some children oatmeal porridge is distasteful, and consequently unwholesome, even when properly made; at Cowan Bridge School it was too often sent up, not merely burnt, but with offensive fragments of other substances discoverable in it. The beef, that should have been carefully salted before it was dressed, had often become tainted from neglect; and girls, who were schoolfellows with the Brontës during the reign of the cook of whom I am speaking, tell me that the house seemed to be pervaded, morning, noon and night, by the odour of rancid fat that steamed out of the oven in which much of their food was prepared.

Elizabeth Gaskell, *The Life of Charlotte Brontë*, 1857

Spring at Lowood

I discovered, too, that a great pleasure, an enjoyment which the horizon only bounded, lay all outside the high and spike-guarded walls of our garden: this pleasure consisted in prospect of noble summits girdling a great hill-hollow, rich in verdure and shadow; in a bright beck, full of dark stones and sparkling edges. How differently had this scene looked when I viewed it laid out beneath the iron sky of winter, stiffened in frost, shrouded with snow!—when mists as chill as death wandered to the impulse of east winds along those purple peaks, and rolled down "ing" and holm till they blended with the frozen fog of the beck! That beck itself was then a torrent, turbid and curbless; it tore asunder the wood, and sent a raving sound through the air, often thickened with wild rain or whirling sleet; and for the forest on its banks, *that* showed only ranks of skeletons.

April advanced to May: a bright, serene May it was; days of blue sky, placid sunshine, and soft western or southern gales filled up its duration. And now vegetation matured with vigour; Lowood shook loose its tresses; it became all green, all flowers; its great elm, ash and oak skeletons were restored to majestic life; woodland plants sprang up profusely in its recesses; unnumbered varieties of moss filled its hollows, and it made a strange ground-sunshine out of the wealth of its wild primrose plants: I have seen their pale gold gleam in overshadowed spots like scatterings of the sweetest lustre. All this I enjoyed often and fully, free, unwatched, and almost alone: for this unwonted liberty and pleasure there was a cause, to which it now becomes my task to avert.

Have I not described a pleasant site for a dwelling, when I speak of it as bosomed in hill and wood, and rising from the verge of a stream? Assuredly, pleasant enough: but whether healthy or not is another question.

That forest-dell, where Lowood lay, was the cradle of fog and fog-bred pestilence; which, quickening with the quickening spring, crept into the Orphan Asylum, breathed typhus through its crowded schoolroom and dormitory, and, ere May arrived, transformed the seminary into a hospital.

Semi-starvation and neglected colds had predisposed most of the pupils to receive infection: forty-five out of the eighty girls lay ill at one time.

Charlotte Brontë, *Jane Eyre,* 1847

14. An Escape from the City

The Yorkshire Dales in the twentieth century cannot be understood in isolation from the great industrial areas of which they form the hinterland. Their lines of communication, their services, their very economy are inextricably linked with the vast urban sprawl just over those seemingly limitless horizons.

Viewed in the other direction, inhabitants of the Pennine cities look to the Dales as their lung, their escape—somewhere to go walking at weekends, to take the family for a drive, a region with which they have a special sense of identity.

This explains the extraordinary relationship many West Riding people have with the Yorkshire Dales, the same dales which lie just beyond the hills they see from their factories, offices, shops, homes, schools. Nor is this identification limited to adjacent conurbations, including Teesside and South Lancashire. From all over Britain, and increasingly from Europe, the special qualities of the countryside, generate this response, a response which both reflects the vast quantity of books and articles about the region, and to some extent, as we have seen, is a product of it.

Since the 1930s, improved means of transport, excursion trains, buses, coaches, and above all in recent decades the private car, have allowed all but the most impoverished to reach the Yorkshire Dales, to walk, to go angling, potholing, sailing, canoeing. The rush of trippers has become a torrent, and no longer confined to the proximity of railway stations, this torrent at peak holiday times may appear to overwhelm the area.

Though farmers suffer nuisance and damage, such damage can be exaggerated, and who would willingly close the door to the fundamental human and spiritual needs the region can provide for urban dwellers; even though their view of the countryside may be naïvely romantic, who dare argue that their experience is not an enriching one?

The final argument is economic. Tourism is a major source of employment in the Yorkshire Dales, and compared with many other regions in Britain, the area is a prosperous one. Tourism is our biggest single earner of foreign currency; beauty, properly managed, has a high economic value. The production of guide-books, travel books and topography is, in a real sense, part of that economic activity. And some of this may include some surprisingly good literature.

The Escape to the Dales

However poor you are in Bradford, you need never be walled in, bricked up, as around a million folk must be in London. Those great bare heights, with a purity of sky above and behind them, are always there, waiting for you. And not very far beyond them, the authentic dale country begins. There is no better country in England. There is everything a man can possibly want in these dales, from trout streams to high wild moorland walks, from deep woods to upland miles of heather and ling. I know of no other countryside that offers you such entrancing variety. So if you can use your legs and have a day now and then to yourself, you need never be unhappy long in Bradford. The hills and moors are there for you. Nor do they wait in vain. The Bradford folk have always gone streaming out to the moors. In the old days, when I was a boy there, this enthusiasm for the neighbouring country had bred a race of mighty pedestrians. Everybody went on enormous walks. I have known men who thought nothing of tramping between thirty and forty miles every Sunday. In those days the farmhouses would give you a sevenpenny tea, and there was always more on the table than you could eat. Everybody was knowledgeable about the Dales and their walks, and would spend hours discussing the minutest details of them. You caught the fever when you were quite young, and it never left you. However small and dark your office or warehouse was, somewhere inside your head the high moors were glowing, the curlews were crying, and there blew a wind as soft as if it came straight from the middle of the Atlantic. This is why we did not care very much if our city had no charm, for it was simply a place to go and work in, until it was time to set out for Wharfedale or Wensleydale again. We were all, at heart, Wordsworthians to a man. We have to make an effort to appreciate a poet like Shelley, with his rather gassy enthusiasm and his bright Italian colouring; but we have Wordsworth in our very legs.

J. B. Priestley, *English Journey*, 1933

The Hiking Craze

For years men have been tramping the hills and dales in increasing numbers and nobody took the least notice of them; but during the past year the noble legion of walkers became so formidable that obviously something had to be done about it.

And then, in some mysterious fashion, the old Saxon word "hiking" arrived on the American boat—and legs came into their own again! Perfectly respectable men who had never committed a crime in their lives, or done anything more sensational than climb Ingleboro', found their photographs confronting them in the newspapers on Monday morning in their old weather-beaten walking-kit; more remarkable still, they found themselves as hikers in hiking bent! Useless for them to protest that they were no such thing, or that they had been tramping in the same kit long before the war. The mysterious power that shapes our ends and snaps us unawares decided that they were exponents of a new craze. Jokes began to be made about them. They were even said to be "'iking" in every limb, which was clearly libellous. But very soon their novelty passed and the female hiker was discovered. At first she was recognisable as a genuine girl-walker in sensible skirt or shorts; but when this type palled, we were entertained to groups of reclining bathing belles who had obviously never walked further than the beach before. These, however, were "hikers" (or so it appeared) enjoying a temporary relaxation from the rigours of the Road. Even motorists picnicking by the roadside were photographed in all their glory and shown to belong to the true hiking breed.

Old hard-bitten ramblers laughed at the excellent jest and went on tramping and climbing as they had done before, until the temper of the reporters changed and they found themselves praised and photographed in one column as hikers and pilloried in the next for faults they had never committed: such as leaving litter and empty bottles on public commons, outraging decency, playing ukuleles and gramophones in peaceful glades, and generally behaving like hogs.

Is it surprising that the walker at last turned? In the West Riding, among the walking clubs and federations, the word "hike" is anathema, and press photographers are politely refused a special sitting.

Nevertheless, having said so much against it, let me admit that there is *something* to be said for the odious word "hike". It *has* drawn attention to the rapidly growing army of walkers, and the consequent publicity has helped to swell the ranks still more. Not all the recruits will last the pace; some are obviously attracted more by the possibilities for garish costume rather than from any real love for the road. Weird tribal head-dresses and brilliant blazers have appeared, and some of the ladies have cast convention to the winds and are returning to nature in too big a hurry. Many of these have not learnt the rudiments of the art and craft of tramping. They wander in pathetic clusters along arterial roads, singing sentimental songs, and looking tired to death before the day is half spent. Even so, I would not be thought for a moment to sneer at them. On the contrary I welcome them with open arms. Many of them, no doubt, will soon tire of the road and find solace or sensation in gliding or football instead, for the modern girl is nothing if not versatile. But a large number of them will get over their growing pains and develop into real ramblers and trampers in time. And there are thousands of others—girls and youths—who have taken to walking in earnest during the last two years, as the new clubs and journals show; and every week-end more and more are finding "their feet" and revelling in their new freedom.

A. J. Brown, *Moorland Tramping in West Yorkshire,* 1931

A Walking Tour in Wensleydale and Swaledale

The day was fine and warm by this time, and so we decided to make Redmire by going over Whitaside Moor, ESE of the village, and there were three roads open to us; the main road, the river road, and a road some distance up the southern fell. The last was the one we chose, so we recrossed the river to Hag Wood and climbed the hill into sunshine again. The wood and the hedges were at their richest in colour, and the road is most charming and makes a good terrace over Swaledale. It leads round steeply to Crackpot, from which we hoped to cross to Whitaside. At Crackpot on the west side of the road, there is a cottage, and opposite to it, a sloping garden, mostly full of blackcurrant bushes. The harsh scent of them was strong. Below them is the hollow in Summer Lodge Beck, and above the beck, very steeply placed, is a copse of strong trees. We were hanging over the wall of the blackcurrant patch, wondering how to go without trespassing too obviously, when the gardener himself came up; a pleasant bearded man, who first pretended in good Yorkshire speech to think we had a car with us, and only after some minutes of indirect teasing would accept the view we were really walking. Then it became simple, for he himself had used the track which the miners in Apedale used when the mines were working. He showed us a gate at the far end of the blackcurrants, down to the water; whence we made a zig-zag to the right and left, to climb up through the trees. Under them the grass was long and thin. When we ascended beyond their tops we looked back and saw that he was still watching us and waved us onwards, half-left from the bank of trees, towards a road between fields, parallel with the trees. This we crossed, seeing a way by gates and a barn, to a second parallel road on the moor-edge.

The moor in front is broken and irregular. We went left, north-east, till we were level with a farm set in trees, Birks End, apparently, and then struck up the moor, south-east, by the gully of a stream and past one set of old working. There are two old workings, but those on the right appear not to be at the point marked as Whitaside Mine. The higher levels of the moor are a blank plateau, covered with peat-hags, whose channels, when we crossed them, were very wet. Sometimes these black pools, in their peat-black walls, are flushed red by the reflection from the western sky making them ever so much more sinister and melancholy than they need be, but the second degree escaped us, as we were travelling with the sun over our right shoulders. The wetness of the channels by which the hags were surrounded made travelling slow, and although it is not more than a mile from Whitaside Mine to Apedale Head, it took us about half an hour to clear the hags. Then we could see the tree-tops rising from Bolton Gill. After the hags there was another mile of tangled heather, very dusty and tough, and this brought us to Apedale Mine. Here the verdure changes altogether; for the whole of this valley is one vast rabbit warren, densely populated, and the turf is well cropped, so that it has the appearance of a garden landscape tended by a fantastic gardener who preferred rabbits to human beings. It must be a splendid place for rabbits, with many sorts of occasional hazard upon the grass, gorse and heather and stones, old shafts and heaps of spoil, half grown over. Walking was easy along this valley which drops to the south-east by a series of shallow curves, leaving the sky beautifully exposed. The rough road on the east of Bolton Gill continues to make a fine outlook, and is only tedious for the last mile or so into Redmire, which is as pleasant a village as there is in the dales. This walk is about 22 miles.

. . . I had no doubts about Redmire, so we returned to get directions from the Bolton Arms, which sent us to Mrs Robinson who took us in. Her cottage stands with others on an arc of grass which looks along the green southward. It was a dim summer evening, and the cottage doors stood open. The lamps were not lit, and the womenfolk sat at the doorways and stitched in the end of the day's light, looking for their men coming home from the fields. As a scene it had some affinity with the spirit of De Coster's *Tyl Eulenspiegel* and was more beautiful for that reminder.

We were hungry, of course, and were occupied with the degree of tiredness which is one of the pleasures of walking. There is a definite thrill of satisfaction when cold water, after such a day, breaks over the skin, and I would not say that eating is a very much keener pleasure, though it is more necessary, perhaps. After the first cold splashes, it is another satisfaction to make up a good lather and reverse the stresses and strains which boots and shoes and stockings have made. Even the soap seems more memorable in the country than in the town. One might imagine a fanciful connoisseur collecting memories of soaps in their rustic hues and scents, as other more ordinary travellers collect memories of inns, churches, flowers or landscape. When the satisfaction of water comes to the ebb the insatiable walker again begins to think of food. It was at this happy moment Mrs Robinson chose to knock loudly on the door and call us to supper, which was eggs and bacon in large quantities, and three sorts of cake, one of them a sponge-cake of a delicious sort which I have only found in Yorkshire.

. . . We ate in the kitchen, under a big oil-lamp which shed its light so discreetly that the steady glow of the fire was not diminished, and by the fire Mrs. Robinson sat, chatting to us. A soft-voiced wireless had been playing the Mastersingers when we sat down, and now Mrs Robinson turned it off, saying firmly that the thing ought not to play all the time. Soon after we made our last sally of the day; to the Bolton Arms with thanks, and then slept in complete absence of mind until breakfast-time, when the ration of bacon and tomatoes seemed even larger. Getting up here I noticed, as walkers must often do, how much colder the morning feels when one has done a longer walk the day before. The bill for our two suppers, bed and breakfast, was 11s 6d.

Donald Boyd, *On Foot Through Yorkshire,* 1932

Darrowby

It was hot in the rickety little bus and I was on the wrong side where the July sun beat on the windows. I shifted uncomfortably inside my best suit and eased a finger inside the constricting white collar. It was a foolish outfit for this weather. . . .

The driver crashed his gears again as he went into another steep bend. We had been climbing steadily now for the last fifteen miles or so, moving closer to the distant blue swell of the Pennines. I had never been in Yorkshire before but the name had always raised a picture of a county as stodgy and unromantic as its pudding: I was prepared for solid worth, dullness and a total lack of charm. But as the bus groaned its way higher I began to wonder. The formless heights were resolving into high grassy hills and wide valleys. In the valley bottoms, rivers twisted among the trees and solid grey-stone farmhouses lay among islands of cultivated land which pushes bright green promontories up the hillsides into the dark tide of heather which lapped from the summits.

I had seen the fences and hedges give way to dry stone walls which bordered the roads, enclosed the fields and climbed endlessly over the surrounding fells. The walls were everywhere, countless miles of them, tracing their patterns high on the green upland. . . .

I realised the bus was clattering along a narrow street which opened on to a square where we stopped. Above the window of an unpretentious grocer shop I read "Darrowby Co-operative Society". We had arrived.

I got out and stood beside my battered suitcase, looking about me. There was something unusual and I couldn't put my finger on it at first. Then I realised what it was—the silence. The other passengers had dispersed, the driver had switched off his engine and there was not a sound or movement anywhere. The only visible sign of life in the centre of the square was a group of old men sitting round the clock tower in the centre of the square but they might have been carved from stone.

Darrowby didn't get much space in the guide books but when it was mentioned it was described as a grey little town on the river Darrow with a cobbled market place and little of interest except its two ancient bridges. But when you looked at it, its setting was beautiful on the pebbly river where the houses clustered thickly and straggled unevenly along the lower slopes of Herne Fell. Everywhere in Darrowby, in the streets, through the windows of the houses you could see the Fell rearing its calm, green bulk more than two thousand feet above the huddled roofs.

There was a clarity in the air, a sense of space and airiness that made me feel I had shed something on the plain, twenty miles behind me. The confinement of the city, the grime, the smoke—already they seemed to be falling away from me.

James Herriot, *If Only They Could Talk*, 1970

Sunday Afternoon in Malham

Nowadays visitors have replaced sheep as a source of Malham's prosperity. They come to this dale from many parts of the West Riding at weekends and on public holidays. The green at Malham on a hot Sunday afternoon in summer resembles a seaside beach, with fancy-dressed visitors, picnic parties, impromptu dances to the ever-present transistor, family games of cricket, sun-bathers, some earnest elderly walkers who disdain hiking regalia and many pseudo-potholers who carry enough equipment to descend a hundred potholes but who rarely move from the green. As a background to all this, instead of the fisherman's nets of seaside resorts there is a fringe of bicycles, scooters, up-to-the-minute motor cycles and ancient cars, for modern youth must be mobile and these weekend visitations are, save for the few elderly earnest walkers, mainly youthful—and noisy. By evening the crowds begin to move away, for they have to return to Leeds, Bradford, Keighley, York. The noise dies down and apart from the late roar of a group of motor cycles or a late-dawdling car changing gear on one of the hilly roads home, somewhere around midnight peace descends upon the dale, the caterers "side away" the last plates and dishes, local residents come to their doors for a reassurance that peace has returned to the dale and probably shake their heads over the day's litter deposits. Somewhere an owl hoots in the stillness. In a moment the ancient dale slips back a thousand years almost unchanged.

Harry J. Scott, *Portrait of Yorkshire,* 1965

15. A View of Paradise

The experiences of the twentieth century have, if anything, intensified the notion of the Yorkshire Dales as a kind of sanctuary of traditional values in a world of constant change. Although the image of a perfect, hallowed harmony between man and nature may, upon a profounder examination be a misleading one: hill farming may be declining, weekend commuters and second-home owners replacing the older communities and rural facilities dwindling away. But for all that the spell remains a potent one.

For many of us it is a metaphor of a simpler existence, a world of older loyalties, of certainties. In our modern world of cynicism, neuroticism and destruction, we need such images if we are to survive at all. Earlier centuries would have described this as a form of pastoralism—a Romantic view of the countryside which goes back as far as Virgil.

Many contemporary writers have drawn creative sustenance from this awareness, something to contrast against the corrosive meaninglessness of much of modern life.

But it has a reality. We need standards of permanence, of beauty, against which to measure ourselves. It goes beyond mere escapism, towards an awareness of something beyond ourselves. It has an aesthetic dimension; some people might call it a religious awareness. Perhaps it is less within the Yorkshire Dales than within ourselves. But without it men are mere dust and ashes.

There Must Be Dales in Paradise

. . . There *must* be dales in Paradise
   Which you and I will find,
   And smile (since God is kind)
At all the foreign peoples there
Enchanted by our blessed air!

There must be dales in Paradise
  With noble tops atween:
  Swart fells uprearing to the skies
  And stretching to the green—
And ower t'tops we two shall go,
Knee-deep in ling or broom or snow!

There must be inns in Paradise
  Where nappy ale is sold,
  And beef and pickels—even Pies
  Such as we've known of old!
And we will find a parlour there
  And call for pints for all to share!

A. J. Brown, from *Four Boon Fellows*, 1928

WILLIAM RILEY (1866–1961) *was an extremely successful Yorkshire novelist of the sentimental school, the most successful of many imitators of the Brontës; his novel,* Windyridge *is still read with enthusiasm. Like Halliwell Sutcliffe, Riley produced novels which were a peculiar mixture of fiction and topography.* Jerry and Ben *is set in Grassington and Hebden, in a setting so accurately described that the farmhouse in Hebden Gill still bears the name "Jerry and Ben's"; actual photographs were used to illustrate the text. Mamie, the heroine of the story, has just inherited a cottage in 'Scargill' (Hebden) and, with her companions Peg and Betty is off to inspect it . . .*

Jerry and Ben's

From the moment they had set foot on the platform of the little mountain terminus at Girston, the spirits of all three had been exhilarated; and when Jim Halliday, at Peg's request, had pulled up his bus (a one horse waggonette by the way) on the bridge that spanned the waters of brown Wharfe, only a few hundred yards below the station, their delight had found expression in superlatives.

"Didn't I tell you?" exclaimed Peg. "You can bracket me with the Queen of Sheba. I expected much and the half was not told me. Let all crochety and pit-shaft pessimists be covered with confusion. I predicted expanse, and here it is!"

"Yes, yes you get it *here*," said Betty suggestively.

The country was richly wooded beyond the bridge and pleasantly patterned—a wide amphitheatre of green and gold, almost encircled by hills that were belted with limestone, and in the distance the faint outline of mountains. "You get it here, but our cottage is two miles away."

"Just below the mines, miss," said Jim, who was listening without concealment, and had grasped the meaning of the reference to pit-shafts. Hill-folk have the gift of humour if not laughter.

"Rubbish!" said Peg, and Jim smiled.

The two miles of dusty, hill high road were accomplished in twenty minutes, and, alighting at the inn, the three friends were informed by Jim that the cottage was a "tidy step" up the valley that ran at right angles with the high road, and that if they cared to walk he would follow a little later with his luggage.

The new path, when it left the houses, had still its attractions. A roaring stream tumbled over a stony channel, and the green-boarded cart-track ran parallel with it and led apparently into the heart of the hills. The ground on the right rose sharply, affording herbage, but what seemed fearfully insecure foothold, for a number of mountain sheep. There was a wider view on the left, with meadows where the hay harvesters were busy, but there too the hills closed in as the road ascended.

"It strikes me," remarked Mamie, "that the expanse you saw in your dreams Peg—"

Peg laid her hand on her friend's arm.

"*Et tu Brute*?" she pleaded. "'Nuff said."

The road grew steeper, angular; but its attraction neutralised the discomfort of the ascent. When they reached the top they saw the cottage at the farther end of an avenue of majestic trees, with Jerry's farm, its only neighbour, across the way. High hills crowded it, but though expanse was lacking, the picture was wonderfully attractive. Mamie's heart beat quickly in spite of her outward appearance of composure. This was her legacy—this low, whitewashed building that stood close to the road from which it was separated by a low paling. A few creepers struggled up the front of the house, but it was the ivy-covered south gable from which the cottage had evidently derived its name. The gable abbuted on the garden which was of the useful order—brown earth and its produce, never a blade of grass—but with greens enough in the paddock that sloped to the musical stream.

"Thank goodness," said Betty, "there's an upper storey. I should hate to wake in the night with the uneasy feeling that someone was peeping in at the window."

They found the door unbolted, and no one was within the house, so they were able to bound with unrestricted interest and excitement. Betty was the calmest of the three, but even her eyes has a glow in them, and Peg's positively sparkled. As for Mamie, her usually pale cheeks were pink, and she had a sensation of lumpiness in the throat, for this had been Fanny's cottage, and now was hers—the gift of her friend in return for kindliness.

"Was black oak included in your visions?" Betty asked, and Peg shook her head. "The Queen of Sheba isn't in it," she replied.

W. R. Riley, *Jerry and Ben,* 1920

The Punch and Judy Man at Bolton Abbey

It is not my function in life to pay shillings at turnstiles, buy picture postcards, and study ancient monuments, but seeing the skeleton arches of Bolton Abbey about fifty yards away it was but natural to be curious, and to get a little nearer to them. And, heavens be praised, there was no turnstile, only a ragged, broken hole in the grey old wall, and stepping through I was on the crest of a hill, looking down a sort of sloping park, the green lawns falling away to the river, which ran between the cliffs and hanging woods; the grey ruins of the Abbey were in the midst of the greenery, drawing up the wild nature to an exquisite point of order, art and dignity.

What splendid artists these old monks and their builders were; the Abbey, the lawns, the river and woods combine into a perfect work of art, expressing an immense conception of human life, of human need and capacity for perfect loveliness and nature. One almost wants the old stones to leap into their places again, to change one's braces and trousers for kirtle and cowl, to be a monk, working in this retreat of the gods at the illuminating of manuscripts, and chanting Latin hymns in the company of the ever-murmuring river. Surely, these men of seven hundred years ago knew something of the art of life—you are tempted to think they knew everything—aspiring, as they did, to live a holy life in an atmosphere of natural beauty and exquisite aestheticism. But there is the Abbey—a reed broken by the wind—and we can hardly travel that road again.

Some subtle power still emanates from this saintly settlement and once through "The Hole in the Wall" I forgot all about Punch and Judy showing, and walked on by the river in a mood far removed from modern life. The path wanders from the broad river meads into the woods, now by the flowing stream, now high above it. The valley narrows and you are shut in with the trees and the voice of the waters, of the dark flood roaring over the rocks, a headlong torrent charging through the woods in swirling currents and whitening foam and spray. One sinks deeper into the seclusion, walking alone on untrodden paths, until you come to an old summer house, and find dates of eighty years ago carved in the woodwork, and are struck by the thought that myriads of pilgrims must have walked these sylvan ways.

I came to some level grass by the river, and sat down among the rocks, and was ridiculously pleased with the bits of flowers, the clover, the golden ranunculus and the blue harebells that coquetted among the ferns and tall grasses. The swirling water was but a foot away, the brimming edge of a broad curve in the river, sweeping round under a craggy cliff, dashing itself against the boulders, and leaping on irresistibly, in a dozen flashing currents, down to the deep and narrow Strid. I chewed my lunch, and stared at the river until, intoxicated by its perpetual energy, something moved within me, and I began to join in its roaring song:

While Wharfe goes singing through the trees,
And runs its ways by meadows green,
Here without taxes, tips or fees,
English beauty may yet be seen.

This was not strictly true, because, about a mile from the Abbey, a bandit emerges from a cottage and demands money, and I was actually the proud possessor of a purple ticket. But to proceed:

By Bolton's tranquil arches grey,
By darkening wood and field between:
If England's roads have had their day,
English river may yet be seen.

In varying pool and sudden race,
Now passionate and now serene,
Where motors cannot "go the pace"
English rivers may yet be seen.

Though cities darken other dales,
And gasp beneath the sooty screen,
Here, without shops of Bargain Sales,
English beauty may yet be seen.

Where the wilding river pours along
This dale beneath the Pennines green,
There, more than in this flagrant song,
English beauty may yet be seen.

The path, and the purple ticket carry you through the woods out to the open fell-sides, and after crossing the river you plunge into the woods again, returning on the opposite bank to find that the bandit is now supplying teas, and you sit in the garden with the wild chaffinches hopping about the table, believing yourself to be in paradise at last.

Walter Wilkinson, *Puppets in Yorkshire,* 1931

By Kisdon Beck

—Lately, in that dale of all Yorkshire's the loveliest,
Where, off its fell-side helter-skelter, Kisdon Beck
Jumps into Swale with a boyish shouting,
Sprawled out on grass, I dozed for a second—

W. H. Auden, "Stream" from *Bucolics,* 1953

JOHN DOWER (1900–47) *was a gifted architect and planner, deeply involved with amenity and outdoor movements, including YHA and the Council for the Preservation of Rural England. Invalided out of the Royal Engineers at the start of the Second World War, Dower was given the enormous task of preparing a report on the establishment of a system of National Parks in England and Wales. His historic report to Parliament—now known as the Dower Report—led directly through the Hobhouse Committee to the passing of the great National Parks and Access to the Countryside Act of 1949.*

Dower wrote his report while living, an invalid, in the village of Kirkby Malham. Amongst a number of articles written for The Dalesman *at the time—including an important series on the restructuring of the rural economy of the Dales—is this delightful account of his invalid existence.*

From a Bedroom Window in the Dales in Wartime

Fate has so willed it that I—a Londoner for almost the whole of my adult life, though by birth and upbringing a Yorkshire Dalesman—should now, for the last few months and probably for some time to come, be living for the first time where I have always wanted to live, in a small Dales village. At the same time fate has added the limitation that, as a temporary invalid, I have so far spent nearly all my time confined to one room.

It is emphatically "a room with a view". All day long I can look from my open window on a charming and typical piece of Dales scenery; a little group of cottages and barns, stone-walled and stone-slated, my neighbours' kitchen gardens and paddocks and meadows with their grey-stone walls, the closely wooded bank that hangs over the village beck, and glimpses of the valley road, both where it passes my own front lawn and where it bridges the beck at the other end of the village.

To be confined to a single view-point is for me a new experience, but not by any means the monotonous one that I might, had I foreseen it, have expected it to be. True the setting is constant, but the scene is ever changing. Each day from dawn to dusk, has its own unique progression of light and shade and colour—its own moving pattern of hurrying or lingering clouds, of rustling in the swaying trees, of gloomy and glistening rain, or of calm sunshine lazily spanning from misty morn to misty eve. Behind these daily and hourly permutations, the passing scene brings more tangible changes. Slowly the massed greens of summer have given way to the russets of autumn, and now, all too quickly, gusts of wind and rain have stripped the leaves and revealed woodland winter's naked tracery.

"When every prospect pleases" sang the poet, "and only man is vile." My single prospect is infinitely pleasing, but men, women and children, far from being vile, bring the best pleasures as they pass the scene: the birds and beasts add their quota of delight. In the crowded city the misanthrope may fairly find material for his gloomy creed, but not in a secluded farming village.

Though secluded, we are not, even in wartime, by any means cut off from the outside word. The special beauties of our dale-head are widely known, and a considerable stream of visitors still goes through on the valley road. We residents can have no regret that petrol restrictions have much reduced the number who come only to gaze for a moment from the closed windows of their cars. But we welcome the cheerful, pink-kneed cyclists, solo and tandem (though they don't seem, as they race along to give themselves much chance to appreciate the landscape); and still we welcome the stout-booted, rucksacked walkers, old and young—some in their 'teens, as I was when I first followed this trail twenty-five years ago—the smiling pilgrims of our hills and valleys. But far more interesting than any visitors are the home-folk, my neighbours, the farmers from up and down the dale, the tradesmen on their van-rounds, whose comings and goings punctuate my watchful day. There were few of them that I knew by sight and scarcely any that I knew by name those few months ago, but now—though an occasional "Good morning" or "fine evening" as one of them passes below my window, is about the sum of our talking intercourse—they seem as familiar as old acquaintances, as well-known as neighbours of many years' standing. Their names and something of their histories I have learnt from my family or of from the friends who come in to see me; their stout Yorkshire characters they have shown me all unknowingly as they worked and walked and gossiped beneath my eye.

They are rarely hurried—it is a blessing of country life that makes it hurry unnecessary—but most of them, I fancy, make a pretty full day of it themselves, and certainly for me. The red and white bus spins along its half-dozen times a day, performing its punctual service just as cheerfully whether carrying a full week-end or market-day load, or riding lightly or empty for the rest of the week. The children clatter by in their clogs "crawling like snails" (though not I think "unwillingly") "to school" and travelling expectantly home again to their dinners or their teas. The milk-cows in twos and threes clump patiently from field to byre and byre to field; and from time to time there comes the patter of a flock of sheep with their attendant dogs and shepherd—drove after drove of them, in surprising numbers when there is a mart day at the next village.

Monday is the generally accepted washing day when the lines of clothes hang out in the back gardens, and the busy village housewives pegging them up or taking them down, bring a pleasant change and animation to the right-hand of my picture. But on other days of the week there have not been many rainless daylight hours when some work has not been in progress in one or more of the gardens; broad if elderly backs are doggedly bent to weeding, to digging potatoes, to chopping down the wood-pile into logs and kindling for the winter's fires, and to many other useful earthy tasks. The chief feature of my picture's left-hand half, the nearest paddock, is at least equally animated, for it houses a very mixed assortment of farm animals, which seem to require pretty frequent and noisy attention from a couple of farm lads and at least a couple of dogs. Just now there are brown and white hens and a squealing litter of eight little pigs, but several elderly rams have recently departed, and before them were successions of calves and bullocks and sheep and lambs, and a most interesting and athletic goat, whose sport was walking along wall-tops, and whose preferred diet was gooseberry bushes. From the next field came the merry quacking of ducks and the whinnying of horses or the bellow of a young bull.

I had almost left out the most constant of my companions, the wild birds. All day they hop and perch and flight before my window—a noisy pack of house-sparrows, starlings chattering on the telephone wires, circling swallows (now long departed on their southward journey) pied wagtails, sleek blackbirds, loud-voiced thrushes, perky chaffinches, two handsome magpies, a shy jenny-wren, half a dozen blue tits ever busy in the apple-trees and in the crannies of the walls, and, dearest of all, a pair of sweet singing, devoted robins—who could not be content in such good company.

John Dower, *The Dalesman* Vol 2 No 9, December 1940

In the Valley of Desolation

I did not want to rush upon the waterfalls, so I took a footpath going up the side of the hill in order to catch a glimpse of them first from there. The hill was bare of trees but covered with long thick grass. Coming down again, to where the slope shelved steeply down to the valley, I met two or three fine old oaks with beautiful twisted trunks, looking as if they had come straight out of some old Sung painting. A few of the branches were dead but the lower ones were covered with green leaves. The sight of old and young growing together pleased me and I made one or two rough sketches. Through the gaps between the trunks and the spaces between the branches I had glimpses of the waterfalls. The spring sun poured down on the hills with their white and green and brown, making them look warm and drowsy. Near at hand the mass of deep green oak leaves showed against the dark hollow background of the valley which stretched away grim and mysterious before me. The scene suggested adventure and inspiration for verses, and not by any means a sense of desolation. Climbing again a little I saw one of the falls streaming down like a sheet of thick silvery-white paper. The thought of it having rolled down like that for centuries made me marvel at Nature's persistence and imperturbability.

At length I began to take my way down the valley, following a narrow path which led me zig-zagging along the hillside. The sound of the falls grew louder and nearer. The woods on either side of the valley, with the hills rising behind them, seemed like the two arms of Nature spread out to enfold me. Sitting on a small rock in front of the waterfalls I felt caressed, as content and peaceful as a child in its mother's arms. Drawing a long breath I relaxed my body and smiled happily to myself. Everything was still except the cool refreshing waterfalls. There was no movement among the trees, rocks, and hills, and I felt that I must be still too. Yet the great moving mass of water seemed to fit naturally into the scene, for the more I watched it the more I had the impression that it was not moving at all. The water in the basin at the foot whirled and eddied and then flowed out into the seemingly endless valley, with the dark woods rising on either side of its silver path. I could see no living thing except one or two birds flitting among the branches of near-by trees.

Chiang Yee, *The Silent Traveller in the Yorkshire Dales,* 1940

Swaledale's Tide of Colour

When the sun shines no spot is more welcoming, no paths more inviting than those by the river banks across flower-filled meadows, through green and shadowy woods in deep gorges, rounding the slopes of lovely hills like Kisdon. Even the confirmed motorist who stays in Muker becomes enthralled and discovers there is more in this 'countrygoing lark' than just passing up and down dales in cars.

A spring morning, sun chasing across fell and dale, breezes tossing green boughs and scattering blossom in showers white and pink: this is a day for Kisdon, for mounting its rounded shoulders, birds blown screaming across our path, mountain pansies and purple orchises in our way, and as we stop to look around every upward yard raises up more heavenly ridges and ranges, each changing from blue to gold as sungleams and cloud shadows race over them. Or when the dale floor paths please me best, across the flower-filled June or early July meadows before the hay cutter mows down swathes of dark-headed burnet, creamy pignut, meadowsweet and campions, pale pink bistort and dark crimson clover heads, and drifts of blue and purple, deep cerise and red cranesbill. Only Tyrolean slopes are more thickly set with flowers then those above Swale in midsummer, or in late spring when the low pastures are awash with bluebells, the tide of colour flowing into the hazel copses and invading the very sides of Kisdon and Swinnergill.

Jessica Lofthouse, *A Countrygoer in the Dales,* 1964

Spring Journey

Brag, sweet tenor bull,
descant on Rawthey's madrigal,
each pebble its part
for the fells' late spring.

Dance tiptoe, bull,
black against may.
Ridiculous and lovely
chase hurdling shadows
morning into noon.
May on the bull's hide
and through the dale
furrows fill with may,
paving the slowworm's way.

A mason times his mallet
to a lark's twitter
listening while the marble rests,
lays his rule
at a letter's edge
fingertips checking
till the stone spells a name,
naming none,
a man abolished.
Painful lark, labouring to rise!
The solemn mallet says:
In the grave's slot
he lies. We rot.

Decay thrusts the blade
wheat stands in excrement
trembling. Rawthey trembles.
Tongue stumbles, ears err
for fear of spring.
Rub the stone with sand,
wet sandstone rending
roughness away. Fingers
ache on the rubbing stone.
The mason says: Rocks
happen by chance.
No one here bolts the door,
love is so sore.

Stone smooth as skin
cold as the dead they load
on a low lorry by night.
The moon sits on the fell
but it will rain.

Under sacks on the stone
two children lie,
hear the horse stale,
the mason whistle,
harness mutter to the shaft
felloe to axle squeak,
rut thud the rim
crushed grit.

Stocking to stocking, jersey to jersey,
head to hard arm,
they kiss under rain,
bruised by their marble bed.
In Garsdale, dawn;
at Hawes, tea from the can.
Rain stops, sacks
steam in the sun, they sit up.
Copper-wire moustache,
sea-reflecting eyes
and Baltic plainsong speech
declare: By such rocks
men killed Bloodaxe.

Fierce blood throbs in his tongue,
lean words.
Skulls cropped for steel caps
huddle around Stainmore.
Their becks ring on limestone,
whisper to peat.
The clogged cart pushes the horse downhill.
In such soft air
They trudge and sing,
laying the tune frankly on the air.
All sounds fall still,
fellside bleat,
hide-and-seek-peewit.

Basil Bunting, from *Briggflatts,* 1965

Over Fountains Fell

From Malham you climb up two thousand feet into curlew country, on the very roof of the Pennines. The little road shrinks to a path, the path to a track and as the last visible farmhouse disappears far behind, the sense of space tremendous and the view for ever. I went up Fountains Fell, to where Great Whernside, Littondale, and Langstroth appeared as dark clefts in the undulations of the hills. The men who put names to the peculiarities of those places knew what they were about. There is Green Hackeber and Gauber, Gatekirk, Ellerbeck, Blackshiver, Quaking Pot, and some deep holes called Boggarts Roaring. They look gigantic.

No less striking than the landscapes are the sky vistas. Like so much of nature the air in high places is an inexhaustible source of beauty. A cloud pattern seen once can be reckoned unique; it may not be repeated again for thousands of years. Instead of the lowering blankets of stratus that hung over the Hebden and Howarth moors, here above was cirrus so feathery it might have been chalked on the backcloth of the sky. Among the cirrus, wind, water vapour, and sunlight combine to form splinters of rainbow known as glints, which usually betoken rain. That afternoon those glints hung suspended like bits of opal until the celestial scenery-shifters shifted them somewhere else.

John Hillaby, *Journey Through Britain,* 1968

Landscape With a Little Sunlight

(after Sibelius: Symphony no 4)

I watch brightened skeins of cloud slowly break
to hazy sun; bracken turns brown and the Ure's
stream is silvered—but chill damp air murks
mountains across the wide valley to vagueness.

Light changes. The fell's edge cuts clear
across the grey sky, its high crag
like a jutting, exposed bone of grit
flung at the remorseless scour of the weather.

The wound in the cloud closes, an East wind
softly enters my clothes, reforms ice on streams,
hints at unendurable night; the far farms
soon to raise faint beacons; freedom's end.

And still the erosion, rivulets scar flesh
and mind; light's brief cry like anguish.

Colin Speakman, 1969

16. A Paradise under threat

The idea of conservation is not a new phenomenon. As early as the turn of the nineteenth century, Dr Whitaker could regret the loss of native woodland in Wharfedale, and Ruskin's passionate outcry in the 1870s against human pollution has a familiar ring. Man has merely increased his capacity to destroy the thing he loves.

The designation of the Yorkshire Dales as a National Park in 1954 has been widely misunderstood. Neither a 'park' in the urban sense, nor 'national' in any sense but that of a national heritage, its very name has brought confusion. Its inhabitants frequently assume that the august measures of the Town and Country Planning Acts operate exclusively in their area, or that visitors are enticed to come because of the name. Visitors look for urban-style facilities and the freedom to trespass where they wish. Perhaps 'rural conservation area' or 'national heritage area', though not as neat, might have explained the situation better. Nationally financed but locally controlled, some people consider that British National Parks perhaps suffer from the worst of both worlds. Though the mechanisms of local and national government have their shortcomings, nevertheless they have some important achievements to their credit. The worst horrors of exploitation and despoliation are avoided, and there is a growing awareness, among the general public, and among both public and private agencies, of the need to conserve this heritage. There is, too, a growing involvement in positive measures of management and conservation which may help maintain a rural infrastructure that otherwise would be doomed.

Whether, in an era of declining resources, such modest momentum can be maintained is another story. Political decisions are often dictated by considerations of short-term expediency; conservation requires long-term foresight, and is concerned with moral, aesthetic as well as economic values.

Writers, of the present as in the past, can only warn.

The Destruction of the Woodlands

The last portion of Wharfedale is a tract of fifteen miles from Kettlewell to the source of the river. The Wharfe, though now an inconsiderable stream, repays the skill of the angler by the finest trout, and waters (often unseasonably) some of the richest meadows in Craven.

The sides of the hills on either hand are hung with meagre bushes, just surviving to prolong the memory of much valuable wood, which the avarice of the proprietors has gradually destroyed, to their own merited inconvenience, as well as the loss of posterity.

This work of havoc is, comparatively, of recent date. A respectable correspondent, born in Langstrothdale, remembers many of the brows and upland pastures to have been clothed with the ash, the mountain-ash, the asp, holly, hawthorn, and hazel, native and ornamental coverings, of which they are now wholly disrobed: nay he has heard an aged person declare, that in his younger days there was a continued forest from Deepdale to Oughtershaw.

What renders this improvidence the more extraordinary is that a great part of the district remains in the hands of the proprietors; for in the early part of the 17th century Longstrother, which had, from time immemorial, been a forest dependent on the Percy Fee, was parcelled out by the Earls of Cumberland, mostly, as it should seem, to the occupiers of the farms, who, having held them at low rents, were almost universally able to purchase. The descendants of these purchasers, a plain and hardy race of yeomanry, still continue to own their own estates, rich in the primitive wealth of flocks and herds, but careless alike of present ornament and of remote advantage.

T. D. Whitaker, *History of Craven,* 1805

Desecration of a Famous View

Bolton Bridge
24th January 1875

I have been driving by the old road from Coniston here through Kirkby Lonsdale, and have seen more ghastly signs of modern temper than I yet had believed possible.

The valley of the Lune at Kirkby is one of the loveliest scenes in England—therefore in the world. Whatever moorland, hill and sweet view and English forest foliage can be seen at their best is gathered there; and chiefly seen from the steep bank which falls to the stream side from the upper part of the town itself. There, a path leads from the churchyard out of which Turner made his drawing of the valley, along the brow of the woodland bank, to open downs beyond; a little bye footpath on the right descending steeply through the woods to a spring among the rocks of the shore. I do not know in all my own country, still less in France or Italy, a place more naturally divine, or a more priceless possession of true "Holy Land".

Well, the population of Kirkby cannot, it appears, in consequence of their recent civilisation, any more walk, on summer afternoons, along the brows of this bank, without a fence. I first fancied this was because they were usually unable to take care of themselves at that period of the day: but saw presently I must be mistaken in that conjecture, because the fence they have put up requires far more sober minds for safe dealing with than ever the bank did; being of thin, strong, and finely sharpened skewers, on which if a drunken man rolled heavily, he would assuredly be impaled at the armpit. They have carried this lovely decoration down on both sides of the woodpath to the spring, with warning notices on ticket—"This path leads only to the ladies' well—all trespassers will be prosecuted" and the iron rails leave so narrow footing that I myself scarcely ventured to go down—the morning being frosty, and the path slippery—lest I should fall on the spikes. The wall at the bottom was choked up and defaced with iron all round so as to look like the "pound" of old days for strayed cattle: they had been felling the trees too; and the old wood had protested against the fence in its own way, with its last root and branch—for the falling trunks had crashed through the iron gating in all directions, and left it in already rusty and unseemly rags, like the last refuse of a railroad accident, beaten down among dead leaves.

Just at the dividing of the two paths, the improving mob (I include in my general term "mob" lords, squires, clergy, parish beadles, and all other states and conditions of men concerned in the proceedings described) of Kirkby had got two seats for themselves—to admire the prospect from, forsooth. And these seats were to artistry of Minerva mere propitious—in the style of Kensington. So they are supported on iron legs, representing each, as far as any rational conjecture can extend, the Devil's tail, with a goose's head stuck in the wrong end of it. Thus: and what is more—two of the geese-heads are without eyes (I stopped down under the seat and rubbed the frost off them to make sure), and the whole symbol is perfect, therefore—as typical of English populace, fashionable and other, which seats itself to admire prospects in the present day.

Now, not a hundred paces from these seats there is a fine old church, with Norman doors, and lancet east windows, and so on; and this, of course, has been duly patched, botched, planted and primmed up, and is kept as tidy as a new pin. For your English clergyman keeps his own stage properties, nowadays, as carefully as a poor actress her silk stockings. Well, all that, of course, is very fine; but, actually, the people go through the churchyard to the path on the hill-brow, making the new iron railing an excuse to pitch their dust-heaps, and whatever worse they have to get rid of, crockery and the rest—down *over the fence* among the primroses and violets to the river—and whole blessed shore underneath, rough sandstone rock through the deep water off into eddies among shingle, is one waste of filth, town drainage, broken saucepans, tannin, and mill refuse.

The same morning I had to water my horse at the little village of Clapham, between Kirkby and Settle. There is another exquisite rocky brook there; and an old bridge over it. I went down to the brook-side to see the old bridge; and found myself instantly, of course, stopped by a dunghill, and that of the vilest human sort; while, just on the other side of the road, not twenty yards off, were the new schools, with their orthodox Gothic belfry—all spick and span—and the children playing fashionably at hoop, round them, in a narrow paved yard—like debtor children in the Fleet, in imitation of the manners and customs of the West End. High over all, the Squire's house, resplendent on the hill-side, within sight of belfry and brook.

I got on here, to Bolton Bridge, the same day; and walked to the Abbey in the evening, to look again at Turner's subject at the Wharfe shore. If there is one spot in England where human creatures pass or live, which one would expect to find, in *spite* of their foul existence, still clean, it is Bolton Park. But to my final and utter amazement, I had not taken two steps by the waterside at the loveliest bend in the river below the stepping stones, before I found myself again among the broken crockery, cinders, cockle-shells and tinkers' refuse;—a large old gridiron forming the principal point of effect and interest among the pebbles. The filth must be regularly carried past the Abbey, and across the Park, to the place.

But doubtless, in Bolton Priory, amiable school teachers tell their little Agneses the story of the white doe:—and duly make them sing in psalm tune "As the hart panteth after the waterbanks." Very certainly, nevertheless, the young ladies of Luneside and Wharfedale do not pant in the heat after their waterbanks, and this is the saddest part of the business to me.

John Ruskin, *Fors Clavigera* (Letter 52), 1875

OUIDA, *the pseudonym of the popular novelist Marie Louise de La Ramée (1839–1908), was stirred to produce this brilliant polemic in support of the Aysgarth Defence Association, a group of local land-owners and conservationists, anxious to preserve the unspoiled beauties from the depradations of the railway engineers who proposed a railway line from Skipton to Aysgarth, meeting the existing North Eastern Railway line in the vicinity of Aysgarth Falls. Its significance lies not in its effect on the railway project (which was, in any event, financially unsound) but as perhaps the earliest demonstration of a national movement for the conservation of the Yorkshire Dales.*

Havoc, Dirt and Smoke at Aysgarth Falls

The Editor
The Times
Sir,

The opponents of the projected extension of the Skipton and North Eastern Junction Railway to Aysgarth Force have written to me to ask for my public assistance in these columns. I should be happy indeed could I hope that any words of mine would have the power to stem the tide of ruin from contractors' heedless greed, which in devastating the whole world, and from which England, by reason of her small proportion and crowded soil, suffers the most hideously.

The opponents of this railway extension can prove that it has not the slightest excuse of any utility, as the farmers in this portion of the Yorkshire Dales are all of them already within a few miles of market towns for their cattle and produce, while the reckless brutality which would thus destroy one of Turner's best loved scenes cannot be too severely censored. I say "destroy" because not only would the contemplated railway works, which cross Aysgarth Falls in a high brick bridge raised on skew arches, annihilate all the beauty of these secluded waterfalls for ever, but the erection of the bridge and function of a junction would inevitably be accompanied by all the havoc, dirt and smoke, and general ruin of green and trees, of streams and atmosphere, which are the attendant Furies of every engineering works. A little while ago, contractors, who have neither eye nor ear, neither sentiment nor sense, for anything save the immediate opportunity of putting money in their own pockets, actually brought forward a scheme to make a railway through Dovedale, to poison the classic stream beloved of Izaak Walton, and to carry the vileness of steam, stench and soot into that lovely world of transparent waters, waving reeds, aquatic plants and wood-clothed cliffs, which still remains serene and fair as in the days of the gentle Father of Anglers. Of this more anon, if ever the iniquitous plan should be mooted again; as yet Dovedale has been saved. What is immediately menaced now, and what will be doomed unless the House of Commons will consent to save it, is Turner's Aysgarth of the High Force. A committee of Yorkshire gentlemen is already formed, and all who love nature and the memory of that great painter of it are entreated to send in their names to Mr John Henry Metcalf, Leyburn, Wenslydale, a Yorkshireman, who, as dalesman born and bred, is foremost in his efforts to save his noble country from this defilement and degradation. The falls of the Yore at Aysgarth united to the heather-clad fells and the flowing pastures and golden gorse and blossoming thyme around them, are foremost among which a nation should be most grateful for and should most completely protect. If the junction intended to be made there is made, 'Arry and his bestial associations will speedily replace the innocent loveliness which no hand of man's can ever again restore.

A railway may be said to be, at its best, a questionable advantage; it beggars as many as it benefits, it enlarges the take of a town at the cost of half-a-dozen others, whilst any utility it may offer is dearly purchased by the pollution of the air and the noxious gases it creates. If science has any of the wisdom it pretends to possess, so ugly, noisy, clumsy and dangerous a method of locomotion as railways offer will, before 50 years have passed, be superseded by some other invention. Meanwhile, why deface the country, spoil the air, and vulgarize solitudes that are the parents of all high thoughts, in the sole interest of railway contractors? The extraordinary apathy of English people before the wholesale destruction of the natural beauty of their country is in strange contrast with their affected wakening to the necessity for artistic beauty within their homes. The contrast would be ludicrous were it not so melancholy.

I remain Sir, obediently yours

OUIDA

Friday February 1st, 1884

The Destruction of the Lady's Slipper Orchid

In the Arncliffe valley the history of the Lady's Slipper has been even darker. The Arncliffe valley is a very narrow mountain glen, with steep fells rising through woods on either side towards the great moorlands overhead. It runs due north out of Skipton, and ends, a blind alley, under the eastern slope of Penyghent far above and out of sight. Here, in these mountain copses, ever since the time of Withering, the Cypripedium has been known. And one old vicar kept a careful watch over it, and went every day to pluck the flowers and so keep the plant safe, for without the flower you might if uninstructed, take the plant for a Lily of the Valley. Then one year he fell ill. The plant was allowed to blossom; was discovered uprooted without mercy, and there was an end of him. And worse was to follow: for a professor from the north—I will not unfold whether it were Edinburgh, or Glasgow or Aberdeen, or none of these, that produced this monster of men—put a price on the head of Cypripedium, and offered the inhabitants so much for every rooted plant they sent him. The valley accordingly was swept bare, and, until the patient plant was rediscovered last year, there was nothing left to tell of the glen's ancient glory except one clump of the Cypripedium which, to keep it holy, had been removed to the vicarage garden, there to maintain, in a mournful but secure isolation, the bygone traditions of Arncliffe. . . .

Accursed for evermore, into the lowest of the Eight Hot Hells, be all reckless uprooters of rarities, from professors downwards. . . .

Reginald Farrer, *My Rock Garden,* 1905

Grass Wood Belongs to Future Generations

It is now nearly thirty years since the first attempt was made to close the public footpaths in Grass Wood. The wood is the property of the Duke of Devonshire, subject to certain rights of way. The ancient right of way of footpaths to Conistone etc, was not challenged previous to 1898, when by order of the Duke's agent, the footpaths were closed a day in December, and it has been the custom to close them once a year.

To express the sentiments of Mr S. J. Eyre Hartley, "I believe it is our duty to the public to assist in the preservation of their rights to the enjoyment of the beauty spots adjacent to our populous centres in these and the comings days of stress and strain," especially now the main roads are almost appropriated by motorists. I regard the annual attempt to close the paths as an infringement of the ancient rights of the public, especially the residents of Grassington; and I have never ceased to urge the members of the Parish Council to maintain the pedestrians' right of way. In spite of my efforts, either through indifference or some other cause, the Council have failed to take the matter in hand.

Prior to the early Enclosure Acts, the wood belonged to the town. About 200 years ago the authorities of the Government instructed the township to make a high road through it, but the latter, on a plea of poverty, failed to comply.

The Duke of Devonshire (Lord of the Manor) then living, legitimately took advantage of the Enclosure Acts, constructed the road, and enclosed the area subject to certain rights and privileges of the public.

The wooded area, including Bastow Wood, the property of the Trustees of the Linton Hospital, is full of archaeological and historic interest, and is a veritable paradise for wild life. It is carpeted with a variety of wild flowers of all hues, and there are many interesting native wild birds, butterflies, etc. As seen from elevated positions the scenery of the lovely valley of the Wharfe, flanked on each side by majestic limestone and gritstone hills, is unsurpassed in beauty. It is the duty of the public to do all in their power to preserve the wild plants and animals in the district and to prevent vandalism whatever form it takes. On no account should wild plants be taken up by the roots, and even the flowers of rare and local plants should be spared, so as to avoid the risk of extermination.

It should be our aim to pass intact to the next generation all our treasures of wild life. We must remember that the lady's slipper orchid once grew in Grass Wood, and had it not been for thoughtless people it would be growing there now.

The courtesy of the Dukes of Devonshire is proverbial, and they have ungrudgingly in the past given facilities to the public to enjoy the beauties of the wood, provided they abstained from doing wilful damage. It is only the recent action of closing the wood, that grieves the inhabitants of Grassington, and the visitors. May we look forward to the time when the area will be acquired as a sanctuary for wild life?

John Crowther, *Silva Gars,* 1930

The Yorkshire Dales as a National Park

The whole mass of moor and dale country that makes up the Central Pennines has a strong claim to National Park status, but it covers, between the Stainmore Gap in the north and the Craven Gap in the south, some 1,400 square miles—far too large an area to be included in a single Park. We therefore propose as the Yorkshire Dales National Park what seems to us the finest stretch of this country: an area of 635 square miles of continuous and outstanding beauty and interest, comprising Swaledale, Wensleydale, Wharfedale and Upper Ribblesdale, with the headwaters of the Aire in Malhamdale and the valleys of the Greta and Wenning in the Ingleborough District.

Though the whole of this area is characteristically Pennine country, it embraces a wide variety of landscape. Each of its three main geological formations contributes its own typical forms of moor and dale, and its own characteristic vegetation and colouring. The Great Scar Limestone gives the dramatic cliffs and gorges of Malham Cove, Gordale Scar, Kilnsey Crag and Attermire, the bare rock pavements of numerous "clints" and "grikes", the sweet green turf of the upland pastures and the white field-walls which enclose them; and beneath its surface is a widely famed underworld of potholes and caves, such as Gaping Gill, Alum Pot and Stump Cross Caverns. The overlying Yoredale series of alternating limestones, sandstones and shales has its most striking effect in the terraced slopes of Upper Wharfedale and Wensleydale; here the moorlands are clothed with coarser and browner grasses and the dry-stone walls are of varying shades of grey. The Millstone Grit which lies above again, gives a wholly different character to the easterly parts of the area; here the rock which breaks out in many crags and "edges" and is the material for the field walls, weathers to a dark, sometimes almost black, colour; the moorland slopes are clothed with heather and bracken; large peathags and bogs lie on the flatter hilltops and fill the hollows of the moors, contributing, by the whiteness of the cotton grass and the greens and browns of moss and rush, a further variety to the rich colouring of the landscape.

The region is one of wide, sweeping moorlands. Their great scale has an impression of its own, and there are many summits of 2,000 feet and over, of which the most famous are the crag-girt mountains of Ingleborough, Pen-y-ghent and Whernside. But the outstanding attraction is rather that of the peculiarly lovely valleys than of the moortops. There is much good farmland in all the dales and a long tradition of pastoral farming, with famous breeds of sheep and a high reputation for dairy cattle. The rich pastures of Wensleydale produce a cheese which rivals Stilton. The frequent lynchets of pre-Saxon times are witness to the antiquity of cultivation, but it is from the farming of the last three centuries that the typical pattern of to-day is derived—the dry-stone walls which bound the innumerable fields of the valley bottoms and lower slopes, and the frequent punctuation of solid, stone-built field barns. The valley sides are too broken for this pattern to become monotonous. Moreover, beautiful woodlands are a feature of all the dales—notably those of the Ingleton Glens, the Grass Woods near Grassington, the valley woods between Reeth and Richmond in Swaledale. Wensleydale too owes its beauty as much to its wealth of trees and small scattered woodlands, as to any other feature. Not least of the delights of the valleys is that of the rivers themselves, with their ever-varying succession of pools and rapids, their numerous waterfalls and their clear, sparkling waters.

The natural beauty of this area is worthily matched by its traditional architecture of local stone with stone-slate roofs. From castle to barn, from Middle Ages to the mid-nineteenth century, this fine building has developed in harmony with its landscape setting. Discordant buildings of more recent years are comparatively few and most of the villages and hamlets remain essentially unspoilt; many of them, notably Clapham, Linton, Burnsall, Appletreewick, Bainbridge, West Burton and East Witton, are outstandingly beautiful in their disposition and architectural character. Many buildings of special historic and architectural interest are found in the main valleys—the Abbeys of Jervaulx and Bolton; Bolton and Middleham Castles and Barden Towers; bridges at Barden, Linton, Arncliffe, Stainforth and Aysgarth; the school at Burnsall and numerous halls and manor-houses of the 16th and 17th centuries, such as Friar's Head at Eshton and Nappa Hall at Askrigg.

The wild life and geological interest is generally high, and outstanding in the Great Scar Limestone stretch between Malham and Ingleton; and there is plenty to interest the archaeologist in prehistoric and Roman remains.

Report of the National Parks Committee
under the Chairmanship of Sir Arthur Hobhouse, 1947

DR ARTHUR RAISTRICK *is the greatest living scholar of the Yorkshire Dales. One of the country's leading industrial archaeologists, he has combined scholarship in many related fields—geology, archaeology, architecture, cultural history—with a lifetime of teaching and writing. His deep involvement with the adult education and outdoor movements led to his involvement at a national level, with the work of Dower and Hobhouse and the setting up of National Parks. He served for many years on the Yorkshire Dales National Park Committee as one of the committee's most respected and influential appointed members.*

The Future of the Dales

The beauty and interest of the dales country, with its well-established way of life and its vast reserves of little-altered wild life, have been recognised by the designation of the Yorkshire Dales National Park, the creation of the Teesdale and Moorhouse National Nature Reserves and of many other parts as Nature Reserves of more local character as areas of Special Scientific Interest. . . .

This designation of special areas is not without its acute problems. Within many of the dales—in particular, Ribblesdale, Wharfedale, lower Wensleydale, Teesdale, and Weardale—there is a thriving and developing quarry industry on a very large scale of working. Economically this is a most valuable and natural development and brings much needed employment into the area. Can the Planning Authorities control this with all its attendant problems of dust and noise, and, most of all, with its great demand for heavy traffic along the country roads, so that its desirable progress does not injure the equally desirable natural beauty? This is not an insoluble problem but it is not one capable of rapid or easy solution. An acceptable compromise, if it is to endure, demands great skill and equally great understanding and forbearance on both sides.

The attraction of the area and the rapid increase in mobility of the population is bringing thousands of cars into the winding, narrow roads as well as along the main roads of all the dales. Quiet places are now becoming noisy and crowded at the weekends. Pressure is increasing for wider roads, which would only intensify and tempt more traffic. Noisy sports like motor and motor-cycle trials (essentially races), water ski-ing and boating on some of the reservoirs, are being demanded more and more, and together with the ever-increasing number of caravans with applications for permanent commercial sites are threatening those very attractions which people come to enjoy. Are our demands going to destroy the very things we most admire? The basic problems arise from the deployment of increasing numbers of an urban population into remote rural areas. There must be a long transitional period, with an inevitable clash of outlook and habits, before the urban-minded adjust themselves to the life of the country. It is certain that all the powers of education, planning, and control must be focussed on the preservation of the countryside from urbanization. To maintain both sanity and health this increasing urbanization must be balanced by areas of rural life and natural beauty. We can create "new towns", and are doing so, but we cannot create new dales and mountains with their natural beauty and solitude. We must treasure those we have for the deeper spiritual refreshment they can afford to the town-weary majority. The rural farming community must be helped to live comfortably on the land, but not by its commercialization and destruction. The majority of those who farm in the dales have a deep-rooted love of them which would prefer to keep their beauty and quiet, but if farming is allowed to decline then they will be bound to seek profit by other means.

Tourism is an industry that will develop in the dales, but only if their characteristics can be maintained. By education the visitor must be taught not to destroy the thing he loves; he must be helped to understand and respect the life and routine of the farmer and to respect the land.

At the footpath survey tribunals held during the last few years too many landowners and farmers have secured the closure of short footpaths. The retention of many of these paths, cleared of obstructions and clearly marked, would tempt the person trying to escape from the noise and danger of traffic, would reduced the trespass on farmland, and would keep more gates safely closed. But this demands a responsive understanding between town and country that at present is all too rare. The Countryside Act, the training which children are getting through "field study" activities, and the growing numbers of young folk in outdoor organizations give promise of improvement. The demand for patience and acceptance of some measure of control, however, cannot be avoided.

Some planners see in the near future the need to control the volume of traffic into and through the National Parks and other areas of increasing tourist attraction. The new motorways are bringing populations of fifteen to twenty millions within an hour's run of the dales and the Lake District. Are these lovely areas to be opened to more and ever more cars, without limit, until they become one vast car park with crowded, jammed traffic on every road on to which a car can force its way? Or are we as a nation going to accept a measure of planning and control as the price of keeping our greatest treasures? This choice has not yet been put to trial nor explained to the nation with sufficient force and clarity; it is still left too much to the voice of a rather quiet minority. It is a choice that cannot be avoided if we are to keep for the enjoyment of future generations such areas, and there are many, as the dales. . . .

Arthur Raistrick, *The Pennine Dales*, 1968

Requiem for the Dalesman

What is vitally necessary is for County Councils and planning authorities to take a much wider view of the social and economic factors involved, and not look only at the landscape. If all development . . . is to be prevented, then some sort of National Parks subsidy should be paid, of at least £400 per year per farm involved, in compensation. But it should be clear from this brief review that to keep these dales as museum pieces is the one certain way of killing them stone dead. Unless dales farms are allowed to cash in on tourism in some way, or realise capital from buildings now agriculturally useless, other strong economic forces already at work will lead to the dales becoming sterilised areas of holiday cottages, afforestation and game preserves.

Indeed the dales and the dalesmen as they were are already doomed. Perhaps the process was inevitable. We have had the Wild Life societies preaching conservation—"people need pandas." It seems to me that we needed the old type Yorkshire dalesman a great deal more. But he is disappearing fast. Few will be left in another ten years. All that reservoir of wit, character and folk-lore will have gone, the blunt independent small farmers, full of dry humour, heroic in mould and poetic in speech, hard-working but deeply contented, part of the scenery and of history. Even farming is a rat-race now, and only the most economically efficient will survive. Some will be dales people, and they will remember their fathers, but they will not be like them.

Bill Cowley, *Farming in Yorkshire,* 1972

Index